Negotiability in the Federal Sector

Henry H. Robinson

New York State
School of
Industrial and
Labor Relations,
Cornell University,
and American
Arbitration
Association

© Copyright 1981 by Cornell University

Cover design by Lauren Kasman

ISBN: 0-87546-080-1 (cloth), 0-87546-081-X (paper)
Library of Congress Number: 80-28672

Library of Congress Cataloging in Publication Data

Robinson, Henry H   1948-
   Negotiability in the Federal sector.

   Includes indexes.
   1. Collective labor agreements—Government
employees—United States.   2. Negotiation.
I. Title
KF5365.R6   344.73′0189041353   80-28672
ISBN 0-87546-080-1
ISBN 0-87546-081-X (pbk.)

To Jenny, who put up with me while writing this and who showed love and understanding,

and

To Kurt Hanslowe, who helped me gain admission to study industrial and labor relations after the deadline had long passed.

Contents

Foreword

The issue of what should be considered negotiable between unions representing federal employees and federal agencies and departments came up during the task force discussions that led to Executive Order 10,988 of 1962. This was the original order calling for labor-management cooperation and a limited form of collective bargaining in the federal goverment. Secretary of Labor Arthur Goldberg had been named chairman of the task force by President John F. Kennedy. In one of the early task force discussions Goldberg commented that he did not think there was any necessity to specify in detail areas of negotiability in the federal government. Reflecting on his experience as general counsel for the Steelworkers, Goldberg noted that the original contract between the Steel Workers Organizing Committee and U.S. Steel had been typewritten double-space and still had covered only one side of one piece of paper. He contrasted this original agreement with the Steelworkers' 1960 contract, by then printed in two volumes of small print. Secretary Goldberg concluded that general experience in private industry had been that the scope of subjects considered appropriate for negotiation evolved gradually. He anticipated that the same evolution would take place in the federal government.

The letter from Secretary of Labor Goldberg to President Kennedy transmitting the task force report, dated November 30, 1961, reiterated some of this same lack of specificity regarding what was to be considered negotiable in the federal goverment: "We are not proposing the establishment of uniform government-wide practices. The great variations among the many agencies of the government require that each be enabled to devise its own particular practices, in cooperation with its own employees."

Executive Order 10,988 itself contained two sections generally referred to as the "management prerogatives" clause of the executive order. The first was section 6(b), which listed certain "areas of discretion and policy" to which "the obligation to meet, confer, and to try to negotiate agreements with unions granted exclusive recognition shall not be construed to extend." The second was section 7, which

vii

listed certain other areas in which management officials retained the right to perform their assigned function, "in accordance with applicable laws and regulations." Controversy over the intent of these two sections arose almost immediately after the promulgation of the order. Federal unions argued that the wording of both sections expressed a clear intent that agencies should exercise individual discretion whether to invoke their privilege of declining to negotiate on matters falling within the scope of either section or to waive that privilege. From the point of view of the Civil Service Commission, however, as reflected in the guidelines it promulgated soon after the order became effective, these two sections of the order set up an absolute negotiability bar. In its view, agency management was prohibited from bargaining on any matter that could be identified as falling within the purview of either section.

These differences were sharply delineated very soon after Executive Order 10,988 was promulgated. As a result, commentators quickly concluded that collective bargaining in the federal service would essentially come to little or naught. For example, as early as May of 1964, B. V. H. Schneider concluded that probably no more than 20 percent of the subject matter areas contained in the average private sector collective bargaining agreement could be negotiated over in federal bargaining relationships. Echoing this point of view, during the meeting of the Industrial Relations Research Association in the spring of 1966, representatives of federal unions and federal management and I agreed that federal collective bargaining by that time probably encompassed no more than a quarter of the subject matter areas commonly considered mandatory or permissive subjects for bargaining in the private sector. We unanimously concluded at that time that the chief hope for change in federal employment relationships lay not so much in collective bargaining per se but in the potentialities inherent in grievance procedures culminating in binding neutral arbitration.

The present volume is the first systematic analysis of federal negotiatiability issues and is particularly enlightening in terms of those gloomy prognoses of the early and middle 1960s. It summarizes all collective bargaining proposals that have been declared to be negotiable or nonnegotiable in the federal sector and the reasons why. It covers all negotiability opinions rendered by the Federal Labor Relations Council and its successor, the recently created Federal Labor Relations Authority. The authority, established under Title

VII of the Civil Service Reform Act of 1978, is the neutral body that now has the task, among others, of deciding controverted negotiability issues in the federal service.

Nothing of similar comprehensiveness has before been attempted. The scope of federal labor relations and negotiations is expanding, but systematic study of it has been neglected. More issues regarding the appropriateness of negotiations on performance standards and other areas related to worker productivity have been filed before the new authority in the last year than were filed before the council in the previous decade. One cannot predict with any certainty the outcome of these current issues, but there is no doubt that the authority will soon be issuing many significant negotiability precedents. As a consequence, it is the hope of the American Arbitration Association and the New York State School of Industrial and Labor Relations at Cornell University to keep this volume current by periodic updating. Some of the author's ideas have already been confirmed, others reversed, by recent authority decisions. Hence this book and its intended updatings should be an essential reference tool for all concerned with federal bargaining.

It is no secret that negotiability controversies have been one of the major stumbling blocks to effective collective bargaining in the federal sector. The present volume itself reflects some of this controversy. It represents the personal views of one of the participants in the process. In some respects, it is a partisan book, and from time to time the reader may find himself or herself in disagreement with the author's forecasts or reasoning. But negotiability in the federal sector is a highly debated subject, and this provocative book addresses many of the issues under discussion. It is with this in mind that the AAA and the ILR School present this work.

This study assumes that the Federal Labor Relations Authority may from time to time apply reasoning similar to that used by its predecessor agency, the Federal Labor Relations Council, when it considers contemporary negotiability issues. The author cites cases where the authority has already done so. On the other hand, there are those who believe that subjects declared nonnegotiable under earlier executive orders will always be reexamined de novo by the authority when it decides negotiability issues brought before it. They believe that the authority will take a fresh look at these issues, particularly those concerning management rights, and that this was the intent of Congress when it enacted Title VII of the Civil Service Reform Act.

My own view on this issue is that both the author and those who might criticize his point of view are correct. The Federal Labor Relations Authority has already looked back at earlier council decisions and has quoted them approvingly. On the other hand, the authority has also begun to establish new precedents. For example, the authority and its general counsel have recently, and for the first time, cited with approval private sector bargaining precedents of the National Labor Relations Board. It thus seems fair to conclude that private sector precedents will inexorably creep into negotiability determinations in the federal sector, just as they have in the public sector in several states. In short, the new Federal Labor Relations Authority is finally looking ahead toward the very evolution and growth of negotiability issues and the scope of bargaining anticipated by Secretary of Labor Arthur Goldberg twenty years ago.

Charles M. Rehmus
July 1980

A Note on the Citations

When citing a case decision of the Federal Labor Relations Council, only the decision's docket number is provided in the footnote. This method has been chosen to avoid the complications in citations caused by changes in the council's mode of publishing decisions. The docket number is the basic information that is required to locate a copy of the decision. As a convenience, at the end of the book the reader will find an appendix relating the docket number to both the report and the bound volume in which the decision was published. The first column lists in numerical order the docket number of every negotiability decision rendered by the Federal Labor Relations Council. In the second column is the report number in which the decision may be found, and in the third column is the bound volume and page citation for the case.—H. H. R.

1.
A Short History of Current Legislation

In January 1962 President John F. Kennedy issued Executive Order 10,988, setting forth policies governing the respective rights and obligations of federal employees, employee organizations, and agency management in pursuing the objective of effective employee-management cooperation in the executive branch of the federal service. While Executive Order 10,988 produced substantial accomplishments, shortcomings also emerged. One of these was an overly constricted scope of bargaining, and a presidential study committee called for "an enlarged scope of negotiation and better rules of insuring that it is not arbitrarily or erroneously limited by management representatives."[1] On October 29, 1969, President Richard Nixon issued Executive Order 11,491, which became effective on January 1, 1970, the same day on which Executive Order 10,988 was revoked.[2] Executive Order 11,491 extended the scope of negotiation and clarified it by providing for negotiation of appropriate arrangements for employees adversely affected by the impact of realignment of work forces or technological change. Also, it established the Federal Labor Relations Council (FLRC),[3] consisting of the chairman of the Civil Service Commission (CSC), the secretary of labor, and the dirctor of the Office of Management and Budget.[4] One of the council's duties was to issue rulings on petitions requesting negotiability determinations.[5]

---

1. "Study Committee Report and Recommendations, August 1969, which led to the Issuance of Executive Order 11,491," in *Labor-Management Relations in the Federal Service* (Washington, D.C.: GPO, 1975), p. 65.
2. Executive Order 11,491 § 26.
3. Executive Order 11,491 § 4(a).
4. The chairperson of the CSC was already vested with the inherently conflicting duties of advising agency management on how to act in personnel matters and reviewing agency management's personnel actions. Encumbering the director of the CSC with the additional FLRC review of agency management's acts in personnel matters served to add inherent conflict within the various duties of the director of the CSC.
5. Executive Order 11,491 § 4(c)(2).

Commencing in 1970 the Federal Labor Relations Council launched a review of Executive Order 11,491.[6] This review led to issuance on August 26, 1971, of Executive Order 11,616, amending Executive Order 11,491. Executive Order 11,616 primarily ushered in changes in the provisions of Executive Order 11,491 concerning the negotiated grievance procedure, the unfair labor practice procedure, availability of official time to union negotiators, and dues withholding. On December 17, 1971, Executive Order 11,491 was amended a second time, this time by Executive Order 11,636, which established a separate program for employees of the Foreign Service.

On February 6, 1975, President Gerald Ford issued Executive Order 11,838, which once again amended Executive Order 11,491 and affected negotiability law in two respects. First, before issuance of Executive Order 11,838, bargaining proposals conflicting with an agency regulation were nonnegotiable. Agencies had taken advantage of this situation and issued many regulations that served to restrict excessively the scope of bargaining. Executive Order 11,838 changed this by providing that, when a union proposal conflicted with a regulation issued by agency management, the proposal was negotiable unless a compelling need existed for the regulation and the regulation had been issued at agency headquarters level or at the level of a primary national subdivision.[7] Second, before Executive Order 11,838, if an unfair labor practice complaint alleging a unilateral change centered upon a negotiability dispute over whether the agency was obliged to negotiate the change, the union was required, before filing the complaint, to obtain a negotiability determination from the Federal Labor Relations Council. The negotiability procedure would lag for one to two years, and finally, after the council had issued a determination, the statute of limitation for seeking unfair labor practice recourse as to the unilaterally implemented change would have expired, thus leaving the union without remedy, or else, if the unfair labor practice had been held in abeyance, another year would lapse before a decision would be issued. Executive Order 11,838 sought to remedy this problem by authorizing the assistant secretary,[8] when

6. "Report and Recommendations on the Amendment of Executive Order 11,491" (June 1971), in *Labor-Management Relations in the Federal Service* (Washington, D. C.: GPO, 1975), p. 28.

7. Executive Order 11,491 *as amended*, § 11(a).

8. The assistant secretary of labor for labor-management relations was required, by section 6 of Executive Order 11,491, as amended, to render unit determinations, to

faced with the circumstance of an unfair labor practice alleging a unilaterally implemented change that could not be resolved without first resolving a negotiability dispute, to make a negotiability determination.[9]

During 1977 and before President Carter launched an effort pursuant to his campaign pledge to reform civil service, federal sector unions attempted to gain congressional enactment of a federal sector collective bargaining law. Several different union-backed bills were introduced before the Civil Service Subcommittee of the House Post Office and Civil Service Committee and elaborate hearings were held during the spring.[10]

On May 27, 1977, while these bills were pending before the Civil Service Subcommittee, the Carter administration commissioned the Federal Personnel Management Project to study the civil service system and to issue a report containing findings and recommended legislative proposals and options.[11] At this time the Carter administration had not yet formulated its position on proposed labor legislation. In an effort to gain enactment of a union-sponsored bill, the federal sector unions united in support of a single bill, but by the end of 1977 the bill remained unreported and locked in the subcommittee.[12]

By January 1978 the Federal Personnel Project had submitted its so-called Ink Report, named after Dwight Ink, executive director of the project. The Ink Report recommended, among other things, a centralized federal labor relations authority and a scope of bargaining similar in many respects to that which existed under Executive Order 11,491, as amended.[13] Thereafter, on March 2, 1978, the president presented his civil service reorganization proposals to Congress and to the nation in a televised address.[14] At this point, the federal sector unions were split in their support for the administration's plan. The largest of the federal unions, the American Federation of Government Employees, endorsed the general outlines of the president's package but with the qualification that specific amendments would have to be

---

supervise elections and certify their results, to make decisions on applications for national consultation rights, to decide unfair labor practice complaints, and to render grievability-arbitrability determinations. *See* section 6 of Executive Order 11,491.

9. Executive Order 11,491 *as amended*, § 11(d).
10. 705 GERR 3,29; 706 GERR 3; 707 GERR 9; 708 GERR 6.
11. 711 GERR 3.
12. 741 GERR 7.
13. 744 GERR 8.
14. 749 GERR 7.

made.[15] Other federal sector unions opposed the entire package and lobbied to defeat it.[16]

During the spring months of April and May civil service reform appeared to have stalled.[17] But by July, however, the prospect of passage of civil service reform improved. Several unions that had originally opposed the president's package recognized that a reform bill was becoming inevitable and shifted their efforts from total opposition to working to modify the administration's proposals. The civil service reform plan moved through the House Government Operations Committee, and by August the plan was moving through the Senate Governmental Affairs Committee.[18] On August 24, the Senate approved its version of S.2640,[19] and shortly afterward, the House passed its version.[20] The two versions were then considered by the House-Senate Conference Committee during September. As to the labor relations title of the reform bill, the conferees adopted the House version but with nine exceptions.[21] The conference issued its report with recommendation that the reported bill received approval from both houses. Both houses approved the conference report on S.2640, and on October 13, 1978, the bill, titled the Civil Service Reform Act of 1978, was signed into law.[22]

The Civil Service Reform Act of 1978 (CSRA of 1978) is composed of nine titles and amends Title 5, United States Code (Public Law 95-454, 92 Stat. 1192). Title VII of the CSRA of 1978 is headed "Federal Service Labor-Management Relations" and is essentially the law governing collective bargaining in the federal sector.[23]

As compared to Executive Order 11,491, as amended, the most striking organizational change wrought by Title VII of the CSRA of 1978 was that the Federal Labor Relations Council and the assistant secretary of labor became defunct in federal sector collective bargaining and were replaced by a new, independent agency named the

---

15. 749 GERR 9; 751 GERR 9; 791 GERR 5-6.
16. *Ibid.*
17. 757 GERR 6-7 and 34-35; 759 GERR 6 and 38.
18. 760 GERR 7; 761 GERR 6; 769 GERR 6; 771 GERR 9; 772 GERR 7.
19. 774 GERR 8.
20. 777 GERR 3.
21. *See* 779 GERR 6.
22. 781 GERR 7, 27, and 73.
23. Title VII of the Civil Service Reform Act of 1978 amends Title 5, United States Code, by adding to subpart F an amended chapter 7.

Federal Labor Relations Authority.[24] The staff of the Federal Labor Relations Authority (FLRA) is composed in substantial part of staff from the Federal Labor Relations Council and from the offices of the assistant secretary.[25] Unlike the Federal Labor Relations Council and the assistant secretary, which had no prosecutorial authority, the Federal Labor Relations authority is vested with authority to prosecute unfair labor practices.[26] Also, one of the authority's additional duties is to render negotiability determinations.[27]

While negotiability decisions issued under Executive Order 11,491, as amended, are not binding upon the FLRA, many of them and their analyses may serve to help predict what will and will not be declared negotiable under Title VII of the CSRA of 1978. Also, by applying an analysis of the CSRA's statutory language in combination with its legislative history, it is possible to predict how the FLRA negotiability decisions will compare and contrast with negotiability decisions that were rendered under the executive order. Several facts support these propositions. First, under the executive order negotiations with respect to many matters had to occur within the context of a preexisting legal framework created by statutes and governmentwide rules and regulations. For example, statutes and CSC regulations governed many facets of sick, annual, and administrative leave. Bargaining proposals could not conflict with the relevant statutes and regulations. Virtually all of this legal framework continues to exist under the CSRA, and bargaining proposals still may not

---

24. 5 U.S.C. § 7104.

25. The FLRA has nine regional offices and several satellite offices. A substantial part of the working field staff was initially composed of employees who were formerly employed in the regional and area offices of the Labor-Management Services Administration and who were offered and accepted the opportunity to transfer to the employment of the FLRA. The FLRA has now hired many employees who have had NLRB experience. On the national level, many of the FLRA officials have had experience under the executive order. Henry Frazier III, former executive director of the Federal Labor Relations Council, has been named, along with Ronald Haughton and Leon Applewhaite, to the Federal Labor Relations Authority. Steve Gordon, chief of the Office of Administrative Law Judges, which conducted hearings under Executive Order 11,491, as amended, has become the FLRA's general counsel. Samuel Chaitovitz, an administrative law judge before the CSRA, was named the FLRA's executive director. Influential decision makers under the executive order, such as Jesse Reuben and Jerome Hardiman, are in similarly high positions within the FLRA. Virtually all of the FLRA's administrative law judges had experience under the executive order.

26. 5 U.S.C. § 7105.

27. 5 U.S.C. §§ 7105(a)(2)(D) and (E).

conflict with relevant statutes and regulations. For example, the statutes and regulations governing leave remain unaffected. It logically follows that many of the FLRC negotiability determinations applying statutes and regulations to bargaining proposals may be applied to help chart the path that negotiability law will probably take under the CSRA. It is true that the CSRA has changed some of the legal framework within which bargaining must transpire. For example, the statutes and regulations governing discipline for both conduct and performance related reasons have been altered. All these changes in the legal framework, however, may be pinpointed, and careful analysis can ascertain what will be their effect upon negotiability under the CSRA.

Second, under Executive Order 11,491, as amended, the duty to bargain extended to personnel policies and practices and matters affecting working conditions. A rule of legal construction is that like language is usually to be accorded like legal construction. Under the CSRA of 1978, the duty to bargain extends to personnel policies and practices and matters affecting working conditions. It follows that decisions as to what comes within the scope of the duty to bargain under the CSRA should be similar to decisions on the scope of the duty to bargain under the executive order. This is not to suggest that there will be no differences, but to the extent that differences will eventuate, they may be predicted by reviewing the CSRA's legislative history and by examining the CSRA's language, which lists certain matters not within the scope of the duty to bargain.

Third, the executive order contained management rights language that served to prohibit bargaining about the substance of certain subject matters and other management rights language that vested an agency with the discretion to negotiate or not to negotiate the substance of certain other subject matters. Likewise, the CSRA of 1978 contains management rights language that serves to prohibit bargaining about the substance of certain subject matters and other management rights language that vests an agency with the discretion to negotiate or not to negotiate the substance of certain other subject matters. There are several differences between the management rights language of the CSRA and that of the executive order. These differences are readily recognizable, and careful analysis can predict any corresponding differences that will result in negotiability law. But most of the management rights language in the CSRA is identical to the language that was contained in the executive order. Since like language is normally accorded like legal construction, it logically follows that many of the executive order decisions and their analyses construing and applying management rights language should be helpful in predicting how the language will be construed and applied under the CSRA. Again, however, this is not to suggest that the construction and application of all management rights language in the CSRA will be identical to the constructions and applications that were rendered under the executive order. Legislative history clearly reflects that Congress intended that some of the CSRA's management rights language should be interpreted differently. These differences in interpretation can be reasonably identified by applying the CSRA's legislative history to the FLRC's negotiability decisions and determining how they would differ had they been decided under the CSRA.

Fourth, subjects within the management rights language of the executive order were not completely excluded from bargaining. While the exercise or nonexercise of the right was nonnegotiable, the procedures to be used in exercising the right and the adverse impact on employees were negotiable items. The same is true under the CSRA of 1978. Yet the CSRA's legislative history suggests a significant change. The FLRC held impact and implementation proposals non-negotiable if they substantially restricted or delayed the exercise of the management right. The CSRA's legislative history reveals that Congress intended that impact and implementation proposals are to be declared nonnegotiable only if they would prevent the agency from exercising the right at all. By applying this legislative history to proposals decided by the FLRC, one can identify the differences in negotiability that should eventuate under the FLRA.

The FLRA has already issued a number of negotiability determinations. These decisions, many of which serve to highlight the similarities and dissimilarities between negotiability under the CSRA and under the executive order, validate the correctness of this book's analytical approach and confirm many of its conclusions.

The benefit of the negotiability study and analysis presented in this book is threefold. First, by comparing and contrasting CSRA negotiability law to the law that existed under the executive order, the book will enable the reader to recognize and appreciate the subject areas in which the scope of bargaining has and has not been expanded. Second, by combining the determinations that the FLRA has issued with reasoned predictions of the conclusions the FLRA would have reached with respect to proposals that were before the FLRC, the book expands the base from which the reader can derive understanding of negotiability as it exists under the CSRA. This, in turn, should enhance the reader's ability to write negotiable proposals and to recognize nonnegotiable ones.[28] Third, the book presents a step-by-step analytical approach that can be applied to any negotiability question. This analytical approach will always be applicable regardless of how liberally or conservatively future FLRA decisions construe CSRA language affecting negotiability law.

---

28. Strictly speaking, many FLRC negotiability determinations remain in effect. Title 5, U.S.C., section 7135(b) provides that, "Policies, regulations and procedures established under and decisions issued under Executive Orders 11491, 11616, 11636, 11787 and 11838, or under any other Executive Order, as in effect on the effective date of this chapter, shall remain in full force and effect until revised or revoked by the President, or unless superseded by specific provisions of this chapter, or by regulations or by decisions issued pursuant to this chapter."

2.
The Duty
to Negotiate

Scope of the Duty to Negotiate

The basic duty to negotiate is grounded in Title 5, U.S.C., section 7114. Section 7114(a)(4) imposes upon an agency and the exclusive representatives the mandatory obligation to negotiate for the purpose of arriving at a "collective bargaining agreement."

Any agency and any exclusive representative in any appropriate unit in the agency, through appropriate representatives, shall meet and negotiate in good faith for the purposes of arriving at a collective bargaining agreement.[1]

Although section 7114 provides a partial definition of good faith,[2] neither section 7114 nor 7117 defines what specific matters are appropriate for inclusion in a "collective bargaining agreement." The def-

---

1. Section 7103(a)(16) of Title 5, U.S.C., defines an "exclusive representative" as, essentially, a labor organization that has been, and continues to be, recognized and certified as the exclusive representative for an appropriate bargaining unit. Section 7013(a)(4) defines "labor organization" as an organization composed in whole or in part of dues-paying employees and having the purpose of dealing with an agency concerning grievances and conditions of employment. Sections 7111(b)(c)(d)(e) and (g) establish election procedures by which a labor organization may be selected by bargaining unit employees as their exclusive representative. Section 7111(a) requires an agency to extend recognition to a labor organization so selected, and section 7111(d) provides, in part, that "a labor organization which receives the majority of the votes cast in an election shall be certified by the Authority as the exclusive representative."

Section 7112 of Title 5, U.S.C., established conditions and guidelines for the Federal Labor Relations Authority to apply in determining what is and is not an appropriate bargaining unit. A unit must be determined to be appropriate before an election may be conducted. Section 7123(a) provides that authority decisions regarding what are and are not appropriate units are not subject to judicial review. Section 7112(d) provides that, where within a single agency an exclusive representative already represents two or more appropriate units, upon petition by either the agency or the exclusive representative the smaller units may (with or without an election) be consolidated into a single larger unit, if the authority considers the larger unit to be appropriate.

2. 5 U.S.C. § 7114(b). *See also* section 7103(a)(12).

initions section of Title VII of the CSRA of 1978, however, defines
the phrase *collective bargaining* in terms of requiring union-management
negotiation over "conditions of employment":

'collective bargaining' means that performance of the mutual obligation of
the representative of any agency and the exclusive representative of employees
in an appropriate unit in the agency to meet at reasonable times and to
consult and bargain in a good-faith effort to reach agreement with respect to
the conditions of employment affecting such employees and to execute, if
requested by either party, a written document incorporating any collective
bargaining agreement reached, but the obligation referred to in this paragraph
does not compel either party to agree to a proposal or to make a conces-
sion. . . .[3]

In turn, the definitions section then defines the term *conditions of
employment*:

'conditions of employment' means personnel policies, practices, and matters,
whether established by rule, regulation, or otherwise affecting working conditions. . . .[4]

In essence, the section 7114(a)(4) obligation requires negotiation over
personnel policies, practices, and matters affecting working conditions.[5] If something is not a personnel policy, a personnel practice, or
a matter affecting working conditions, then the duty to negotiate does
not attach.

Lest there be any doubt, the section 7114(a)(4) obligation to
negotiate is a continuing duty. It is not limited merely to the negotiation of a master agreement.[6] The rationale underlying this construction is persuasive. The parties negotiating a master agreement cannot

---

3. 5 U.S.C. § 7103(a)(12).

4. *Id.* § 7103(a)(14).

5. The description of the section 7114(a)(4) duty to negotiate is identical to the
obligation that existed under Executive Order 11,491, as amended. Section 11(a) therein
imposed the following obligation to negotiate upon agency management and an exclusive representative: "An agency and a labor organization that has been accorded
exclusive recognition through appropriate representatives, shall meet at reasonable
times and confer in good faith with respect to personnel policies and practices and
matters affecting working conditions. . . ." The term *meet and confer* was intended to
mean to negotiate. "Report and Recommendations of the Federal Labor Relations
Council on the Amendment of Executive Order 11,491, as Amended," in *Labor-Management Relations in the Federal Service* (Washington, D.C.: GPO, 1975), p.41.

6. The language of CSRA of 1978 clearly indicates the contemplation of a continuing duty to negotiate. First, the explicit language of the act does not limit an
exclusive representative to the right to negotiate only one agreement. Rather, section
7114(a) provides that an exclusive representative is entitled to negotiate collective
bargaining agreements. Second, the language defining the duty to negotiate in good
faith does not suggest that parties meet for the purpose of negotiating a contract and
thereafterwards not meet. Section 7114(b)(3) requires the parties "to meet at reasonable

possibly envision every contingency and change that will arise during the life of the contract. Given the existence of the duty to bargain, bargaining should address new contingencies and mid-term changes not contemplated during the negotiation of the master agreement. This continuing bilateral effort to resolve problems enhances stability in the workplace. Bargaining over these new and different matters supplements or complements the master agreement, as distinguished from bargaining that modifies the terms of a master agreement.

Hence, absent a zipper clause[7] or a clear and unmistakable waiver,[8] the section 7114(a)(4) duty requires the parties to bargain not only during the negotiation of the master contract but also throughout the contract's life as well as during any other period when a labor organization is recognized as the exclusive representative.[9]

Matters Not within the Scope of the Duty to Negotiate

Five categories of personnel policies and practices and working conditions either do not come within the scope and meaning of the section

---

times and convenient places as frequently as may be necessary. . . ." Third, the act does not define "collective bargaining" as being a one-time affair. Section 7103(a)(12) defines collective bargaining as consisting, in part, of the obligation to meet "at reasonable times."

7. A zipper clause is a provision, in a master agreement, providing that the union surrenders all right to negotiate about new contingencies and changes that occur during the life of the agreement.

8. A contract waiver normally refers to the union's alleged surrender of the right to negotiate about a certain midterm issue not addressed in the master agreement. Such a waiver must be clear and unmistakable. NASA, Kennedy Space Center, Florida and American Federation of Government Employees, A/SLMR No. 223 (1972).

9. The same was true of the section 11(a) duty to negotiate under Executive Order 11,491, as amended. The Federal Labor Relations Council's 1975 report on the executive order addressed this point. "Section 11(a) of the Order requires that the parties . . . shall meet at reasonable times and confer in good faith with respect to personnel policies and practices and matters affecting working conditions. . . ." The term *reasonable times* is not further defined in the order. It is evident that at the very least the duty described requires that the parties avoid unnecessary delay in the process of negotiation. However, the question is raised as to whether the order requires, in addition, that a party must meet its obligation to negotiate before making changes in established personnel policies and practices and matters affecting working conditions during the term of an agreement. "The Assistant Secretary, when faced with this issue in a case, concluded that the Order does require adequate notice and an opportunity to negotiate prior to changing established personnel policies and practices and matters affecting working conditions during the term of an existing agreement. . . . We believe that the Assistant Secretary's conclusion on this matter is correct. . . ." "Report and Recommendations of the Federal Labor Relations Council on the Amendment of Executive Order 11,491."

7114(a)(4) duty or the duty is inoperable as to them.[10] First, as defined in section 7103(a)(14)(A), the section 7114(a)(4) obligation to negotiate specifically "does not include policies, practices and matters, relating to political activities prohibited under chapter III of chapter 73 of this title. . . ."[11]

The relevant provisions of chapter 73 of Title 5, U.S.C., are section 7322, which provides that a federal employee may not use his or her official authority or influence to coerce political action; section 7723, which mandates the discharge of a federal employee who requests, receives, or gives a political donation to another federal employee, a member of Congress, or a member of the armed services; and section 7324, which mandates discharge of a federal employee who has either used his or her authority to influence an election or has taken an active part in a political campaign.

Second, the section 7114(a)(4) obligation to negotiate, as defined in section 7103(a)(14)(A), specifically "does not include policies, practices, and matters . . . relating to the classification of any position. . . ."

Position classification has always been exempt from negotiation in the federal sector.[12] Position classification is governed by statute.

---

10. Similarly, Executive Order 11,491, as amended, described certain matters to which the obligation to negotiate did not attach. Section 11(a) provided, in part, that the obligation to negotiate extended only ". . . so far as may be appropriate under applicable laws and regulations, including policies set forth in the *Federal Personnel Manual*; published agency policies and regulations for which a compelling need exists under criteria established by the Federal Labor Relations Council and which are issued at the agency headquarters level or at the level of a primary national subdivision; a national or other controlling agreement at a higher level in the agency and this Order." In practical terms, this meant, among other things, that (1) chapter 73 of Title 5, U.S.C., as an applicable law within the meaning of section 11(a) of Executive Order 11,491, as amended, served to limit bargaining; (2) position classification, being set forth in the *Federal Personnel Manual* (*FPM*) and other regulations, was nonnegotiable; (3) any federal statute would have limited bargaining because a federal statute would have been an "applicable law" within the meaning of section 11(a) of the order and a bargaining proposal in conflict with such a statute would have been nonnegotiable; (4) governmentwide rules and regulations (e.g., General Services Administration regulations) were applicable regulations within the meaning of section 11(a), and hence a proposal could not conflict with such a regulation; and (5) a bargaining proposal could not conflict with an agency regulation for which there existed a compelling need and which had been issued at agency headquarters level or at the level of a primary national subdivision.

11. This same result would have issued under section 11(a) of Executive Order 11,491, as amended.

12. *Supra* note 10.

The Office of Personnel Management[13] is charged with the duty of promulgating standards for the classification of positions.[14]

Third, the obligation to negotiate, as defined in section 7103(a)(14)(A) specifically "does not include policies, practices and matters . . . to the extent such matters are specifically provided for by Federal Statute. . . ."

These matters specifically provided for by federal statute may, for the most part, be found in Title 5, U.S.C. The major ones include position classification;[15] pay rates;[16] merit pay and cash awards;[17] travel, transportation, and subsistence;[18] number of hours of work and holidays;[19] annual and sick leave;[20] adverse actions;[21] compensation for work injuries;[22] and retirement.[23]

The exclusion of these statutory matters, however, is not to imply that nothing about them is negotiable. The matters are negotiable to the extent that bargaining proposals do not specifically conflict with federal statute. For instance, criteria constituting prima facie evidence that an employee is entitled to a cash award should be negotiable. Parties should be permitted to negotiate that travel will ordinarily take place during normal working hours, conditions under which travel advances will be available, and any other travel matter not specifically provided by chapter 57 of Title 5, U.S.C. Parties should be permitted to negotiate starting and quitting times or even flexitime. Parties should be permitted to negotiate how much notice, if any, is required for use of sick and annual leave. Parties should be permitted to negotiate time limits for each statutorily provided step at an adverse action or even to negotiate steps in addition to those provided by statute. Parties should be permitted to negotiate that an employee may withdraw a submitted retirement letter. In essence, the parties should be permitted to negotiate anything that complements, supple-

---

13. 5 U.S.C. § 1101, *et seq.*
14. 5 U.S.C. § 5107.
15. 5 U.S.C. § 5101, *et seq.*
16. 5 U.S.C. § 5301, *et seq.*
17. 5 U.S.C. § 5401, *et seq.*
18. 5 U.S.C. § 5701, *et seq.*
19. 5 U.S.C. § 6101, *et seq.*
20. 5 U.S.C. § 6301, *et seq.*
21. 5 U.S.C. § 7501, *et seq.* Adverse actions, however, may be subjected to binding arbitration under a negotiated collective bargaining agreement. 5 U.S.C. § 7121.
22. 5 U.S.C. § 8101, *et seq.*
23. 5 U.S.C. § 8301, *et seq.*

ments, or explains the matter covered by federal statute as well as guidelines governing the exercise of discretionary authority that the federal statute vests with the agency. This same result would have issued under Executive Order 11,491, as amended.[24]

Fourth, section 7117(a)(1) serves to make the section 7114(a)(4) obligation to negotiate inoperable as to the substance of certain "governmentwide" rules and regulations.

[T]he duty to bargain in good faith shall, to the extent not inconsistent with any Federal law or any Government-wide rule or regulation, extend to matters which are the subject of any rule or regulation only if the rule or regulation is not a Government-wide rule or regulation.

Cast in comprehensible language, section 7117(a)(1) means that the obligation to negotiate does not require bargaining about a proposal that is inconsistent with a governmentwide rule or regulation, but the obligation does require bargaining of proposals that mirror or otherwise do not conflict with the governmentwide rule and regulation.[25] For example, if a governmentwide regulation of the General Services Administration (GSA) provides that the temperature in government buildings will not be below seventy degrees Fahrenheit, the parties could negotiate a proposal calling for the temperature to be seventy degrees or any higher temperature, but the parties could not negotiate a proposal calling for the temperature to be sixty-nine degrees or lower. If the GSA regulation were to provide that the temperature would be seventy degrees, then the parties could negotiate a proposal

---

24. *Supra* note 10. Also, on this subject, the CSRA's legislative history clearly reflects that the Committee on Conference considered that the pertinent provisions of both the Senate and House bills "authorize negotiations except to the extent inconsistent with law, rules and regulations." *See* Rep. No. 95-1717, 95th Cong., 2d Sess. 158 (1978). In proposal II in International Fire Fighters Local F-61 and Philadelphia Naval Shipyard, Case No. 0-NG-6, 3 FLRA 66, the union had proposed a list of holidays containing one that was not a recognized federal holiday. The authority held the proposal nonnegotiable to the extent that it violated Title 5, U.S.C., section 6103.

25. The bulk of the governmentwide regulations will be those issued by the Office of Personnel Management and found within the *Federal Personnel Manual*. The CSRA's legislative history reveals that the governmentwide rules and regulations language of the Senate bill specifically included policies set forth in the *Federal Personnel Manual*. The House bill contained no comparable wording. Regarding the language of what is now section 7117(a)(1), the Committee on Conference reported, "The conferees specifically intend, however, that the term 'rules or regulations' be interpreted as including official declarations of policy of an agency which are binding on officials and agencies to which they apply." *See* Rep. No. 95-1717, 95th Cong., 2d Sess. 158 (1978). Nevertheless, a labor organization may, under Title 5, U.S.C., section 7117(d), seek consultation rights with agencies that issue governmentwide rules and regulations.

that the temperature would be seventy degrees, but not a proposal providing for a temperature above or below seventy degrees. If the GSA regulation were to provide that the temperature would be "comfortable," the parties should be free to negotiate any temperature or temperature range deemed to be comfortable. This same result would have issued under Executive Order 11,491, as amended.[26]

Fifth, section 7117(a)(2) makes the section 7114(a)(4) obligation to negotiate inoperable as to proposals conflicting with an agency rule or regulation for which a compelling need exists and which has been issued at the agency headquarters or one of its primary national subdivisions.

The duty to bargain in good faith shall, to the extent not inconsistent with Federal law or any Government-wide rule or regulation, extend to matters which are the subject of any agency rule or regulation . . . only if the Authority has determined under subsection (b) of this section that no compelling need (as determined under regulations prescribed by the Authority) exists for the rule or regulation.

Before 1975 a proposal conflicting with any agency regulation was nonnegotiable, and this had served to excessively restrict the scope of negotiations. The compelling need concept, which was extracted directly from Executive Order 11,491, as amended,[27] was designed to inject reasonableness into the determination of when an agency regulation could restrict the scope of bargaining.[28] The CSRA of 1978

---

26. *Supra* note 10.
27. *Id.*
28. The compelling need requirement in Executive Order 11,491, as amended, was the result of the 1975 amendments to Executive Order 11,491, as amended. Before the 1975 amendments a proposal was rendered nonnegotiable if it conflicted with an applicable agency regulation. An applicable agency regulation was one issued to achieve a desirable degree of uniformity or one applicable to employees of more than one subordinate activity. National Association of Government Employees and U.S. Department of Commerce, National Oceanic and Atmospheric Administration, National Weather Service, FLRC No. 74A-20 (1973). The 1975 amendments were the result of the issuance of Executive Order 11,838 on February 6, 1975, which in turn had resulted from the "Report and Recommendations of the Federal Labor Relations Council on the Amendment of Executive Order 11,491, as Amended," (Jan. 1975), which in section V had enunciated the finding that "experience under the Order, as well as testimony during the current review, established that, while considerable progress toward a wider scope of negotiation at the local level had been effected, the exhortations of the (1969) Study Committee (which were supplemented by information activities under the Order by the Council and its constituent members) have fallen short of their objectives. As a result, meaningful negotiations at the local level on personnel policies and practices and matters affecting working conditions have been unnecessarily constricted in a significant number of instances by higher level agency

adds a new twist in that the compelling need concept is inoperable in one circumstance: An agency may not raise the compelling need concept to render proposals nonnegotiable where the level of recognition is at the same agency headquarters or subdivision level as the level of issuance of the rule or regulation and the exclusive representative represents a majority of the employees of the agency or appropriate subdivision.

Paragraph (2) of the subsection applies to any rule or regulation issued by an agency or issued by any primary national subdivision of such agency, unless an exclusive representative represents an appropriate unit including not less than a majority of the employees in the issuing agency or primary national subdivisions, as the case may be, to whom the rule or regulation is applicable.[29]

This should encourage unions to increase their efforts to consolidate units in order to obtain national bargaining rights.[30]

The FLRA has promulgated final compelling need standards under section 7105(a)(2)(D). With the exception that the goal of uniformity is no longer defined as constituting a compelling need, the FLRA's standards resemble the ones promulgated by the FLRC under Executive Order 11,491, as amended.[31] The FLRA's rules and regulations, found at section 2323.11 of Title 5 of the Code of Federal Regulations, provide the following "illustrative criteria":

A compelling need exists for an agency rule or regulation concerning any condition of employment when the agency demonstrates that the rule or regulation meets one or more of the following illustrative criteria:

---

regulations not critical to effective agency management or the public interest." In *Labor-Management Relations in the Federal Service* (Washington, D.C.: GPO, 1975), p. 38.

    29. 5 U.S.C. § 7177(a)(3).
    30. 5 U.S.C. §§ 7112 and 7105(a)(2)(A).
    31. Section 2413.2 of the rules and regulations of the Federal Labor Relations Council (5 C.F.R. § 2413) provided: "A compelling need exists for an applicable agency policy or regulation concerning personnel policies and practices and matters affecting working conditions when the policy or regulation meets one or more of the following illustrative criteria: (a) The policy or regulation is essential, as distinguished from helpful or desirable, to the accomplishment of the mission of the agency or the primary national subdivision; (b) The policy or regulation is essential, as distinguished from helpful or desirable, to the management of the agency or the primary national subdivision; (c) The policy or regulation is necessary to insure the maintenance of basic merit principles; (d) The policy or regulation implements a mandate to the agency or primary national subdivision under law or other outside authority, which implementation is essentially nondiscretionary in nature; or (e) The policy or regulation established uniformity for all or a substantial segment of the employees of the agency or primary national subdivision where this is essential to the effectuation of the public interest."

(a) The rule or regulation is essential, as distinguished from helpful or desirable, to the accomplishment of the mission or the execution of functions of the agency or primary national subdivision in a manner which is consistent with the requirements of an effective and efficient government.

(b) The rule or regulation is necessary to insure the maintenance of basic merit principles.

(c) The rule or regulation implements a mandate to the agency or primary national subdivision under law or other outside authority, which implementation is essentially nondiscretionary in nature.

The future application of compelling need will be inextricably tied to its past interpretation. The FLRC best defined compelling need by distinguishing between rules and regulations that are essential and those that are merely helpful or desirable.

[T]he compelling need provisions of the Order were designed and adopted to the end that internal "agency regulations not *critical* to effective agency management or the public interest" would be prevented from resulting in negotiations at the local level being "unnecessarily constricted". . . .

Thus, the Council's illustrative criteria for determining compelling need, while distinctive from one another in substance, share one basic characteristic intended to give full effect to the compelling need concept: They collectively set forth a stringent standard for determining whether the degree of necessity for an internal agency regulation concerned with personnel policies and practices and matters affecting working conditions warrants a finding that the regulation is "critical to effective agency management or the public interest" and, hence, should act as a bar to negotiations on conflicting proposals at the local level. This overall intent is clearly evidenced in the language of the criteria, several of which expressly establish that *essentiality*, as distinguished from merely helpfulness or desirability, is the touchstone.[32]

The significance of this is that, where compelling need is in issue, the prevailing party will be the one that best argues that the agency can or cannot conduct effective operations in the absence of the regulation.

Management Rights and Impact and Implementation

Illegal Bargaining Subjects

Title 5, U.S.C., section 7106(a) defines subject matter the substance of which the parties are prohibited from bargaining and entering agreement.

---

32. National Association of Government Employees, Local No. R14-87 and Kansas National Guard, FLRC No. 76A-16 and other cases consolidated therewith (1977) 11-12.

[N]othing in this chapter shall affect the authority of any management official of any agency—
(1) to determine the mission, budget, organization, number of employees, and internal security practices of the agency; and
(2) in accordance with applicable laws—
(A) to hire, assign, direct, layoff, and retain employees in the agency, or to suspend, remove, reduce in grade or pay, or take other disciplinary action against such employees;
(B) to assign work, to make determinations with respect to contracting out, and to determine the personnel by which agency operations shall be conducted;
(C) with respect to filling positions, to make selections for appointments from—
(i) among properly ranked and certified candidates for promotion; or
(ii) any other appropriate source; and
(D) to take whatever actions may be necessary to carry out the agency mission during emergencies.

Even though the parties may execute a contract provision encompassing section 7106(a) matters, such agreement is invalid and may not be enforced.

In contrast, when the parties agree to and enter a contract provision encompassing permissive subject matter, as defined by section 7106(b)(1), the agreement is valid and may be enforced.

Under the order, section 12(b) defined illegal bargaining matter,[33] and section 11(b) defined permissive bargaining matter.[34] There is much similarity and very little substantive difference between the management rights portion of Executive Order 11,491, as amended, and the management rights portion of Title 5, U.S.C., section 7106.[35]

---

33. Section 12(b) of Executive Order 11,491, as amended, provided: "Management officials of the agency retain the right, in accordance with applicable laws and regulations—(1) to direct agency employees; (2) to hire, promote, transfer, assign, and retain employees in positions within the agency, and to suspend, demote, discharge, or take any other disciplinary action against employees; (3) to relieve employees from duties because of lack of work or for other legitimate reasons; (4) to maintain the efficiency of the Government operations entrusted to them; (5) to determine the methods, means, and personnel by which such operations are to be conducted; and (6) to take whatever actions may be necessary to carry out the mission of the agency, in situations of emergency."

34. *Infra* note 72.

35. The executive order's section 12(b)(4)'s *efficiency of operations* language was deleted from the management's rights section of the CSRA of 1978. In *Little Rock*, the council ruled that, to sustain a 12(b)(4) argument, the agency had the burden of substantially demonstrating that (1) the proposal would increase costs or reduce effectiveness of agency operations, (2) the increase in costs or reduction in effectiveness

First, the "mission," "budget," "organization," "number of employees," and "security practices" language of section 7106(a)(1) of the CSRA of 1978 was preceded by identical language in section 11(b) of the order. Hence, while formerly permissive bargaining matter is now illegal bargaining matter, formerly nonmandatory bargaining subjects remain nonmandatory. The only change is that section 7106(a)(1) serves to narrow the scope of permissive bargaining matters.

Second, with respect to section 7106(a)(2)(A), the retained authority to direct employees is identical to the right reserved in section 12(b)(1) of the executive order, and the right to lay off employees was formerly contained in section 12(b)(3) of the order. Likewise, the right to discipline employees does not differ from the right to discipline that the agency had reserved under section 12(b)(2) of the executive order. The section 7601(a)(2)(A) authority to hire, assign, and retain employees finds its predecessor in section 12(b)(2) of the order, but this carry-over of reserved authority is imbued with a subtle, potentially significant difference. Section 12(b)(2) reserved to the agency the right to hire, assign, and retain employees in *positions* within the agency, whereas the right retained in section 7601(a)(2)(A) is to hire, assign, and retain employees *within the agency*—not within particular positions. This change creates the potential to expand the scope of bargaining. A fundamental rule of legal construction is that statutory or regulatory language must be interpreted in a manner that will give effect to every word; language should never be constructed in a manner that will render moot or meaningless a single word. Accordingly, since the phrase *in positions* has been removed from the CSRA and since the FLRC placed great emphasis on the words as contained in 12(b)(2) of the order, the logical conclusion is that section 7106(a)(2)(A) does not bar the negotiation of proposals providing that employees will or will not be assigned to particular categories of positions, proposals that employees will not ordinarily be involun-

---

would be inescapable and significant, and (3) other compensating benefits would not offset any increase in costs or reduction in effectiveness. This imposed a very heavy burden of proof upon agencies, and as a result agencies rarely, if ever, relied upon 12(b)(4) to declare union proposals nonnegotiable. For this reason, the CSR's removal of management's right to maintain efficiency of operations is insignificant. Local Union No. 2219, International Brotherhood of Electrical Workers, AFL-CIO, and Department of the Army, Corps of Engineers, Little Rock District, Little Rock, Arkansas, FLRC 71A-46 (1972).

tarily reassigned, or proposals providing that as long as employees are not laid off they will be retained or not retained in particular positions. Reinforcing this conclusion is the fact that, whereas section 12(b)(2) of the executive order reserved to the agency the right to *transfer* employees to positions within the agency,[36] this authority is not reserved to the agency under section 7106 of the CSRA. Preliminarily, however, the FLRA has signaled that it may not follow the aforegoing statutory analysis. In *Wright-Patterson Air Force Base*[37] the FLRA announced that it will interpret the agency's section 7106(a)(2)(A) right to assign employees in the agency as though the phrase *in positions* had not been removed.

The right to assign employees in the agency under section 7102(a)(2)(A) of the Statute is more than merely the right to decide to assign an employee to a position. An agency chooses to assign an employee to a position so that the work of that position will be done. Under section 7106(a)(2)(A) of the Statute, the agency retains discretion as to the personnel requirements of the work of the position, *i.e.,* the qualifications and skills needed to do the work, as well as such job-related characteristics as judgment and reliability. Therefore, the right to assign an employee to a position includes the discretion to determine which employee will be assigned. (Clearly, the assignment of an employee to a position is distinguishable from the assignment of an employee to a shift.) A procedure for selecting an employee for assignment solely on the basis of seniority removes that discretion which as indicated above, is an essential part of the decision to assign.[38]

While it is true that *Wright-Patterson* held that an agency retains the right to assign particular employees to particular positions, the

---

36. The *FPM* defines *transfer* as an employee leaving the employment of one agency and going to the employment of a second agency; the *FPM* definition of *reassignment* consists of an employee going from one position to another position in the same agency. Inasmuch as bargaining units do not cross agency lines (i.e., are not interagency), if the *FPM* definition of transfer were applied to transfer as used in section 12(b)(2) of the executive order, the word would never be operative and would be rendered meaningless; negotiations can address only bargaining unit positions and not positions outside the bargaining unit. A basic rule of legal construction is that a word appearing in statutory or regulatory language will not be given a construction that would render the word inoperable or meaningless. Accordingly, it is safe to assume that, as used in the executive order, the word transfer probably meant what *reassignment* meant in the *FPM* (as distinguished from *assignment*). Although the FLRC frequently quoted section 12(b)(2) in negotiability opinions, the council never addressed the meaning of transfer as used in section 12(b)(2) of the executive order.

37. AFGE and Air Force Logistics Command, Wright-Patterson Air Force Base, Case No. 0-NG-40, 2 FLRA 77 (1980).

38. *Id.* at 10.

authority added a twist that leaves the state of the law rather uncertain. The section 7106(a) rights are supposed to be absolute. Yet the authority held that the right to assign particular individuals is not absolute and that, if an agency elects not to use competitive procedures, then the agency essentially loses or waives the right to decide which particular individuals will be assigned to particular positions. Specifically, the FLRA held that the selection of which employee would be detailed to a position equal to or higher in grade than his or her original position could be based on seniority if the agency had decided not to use competitive procedures. The authority supplied the following rationale:

[C]ompetitive procedures reserve the agency's right to select the employee from . . . any appropriate source . . . the agency retains the option of exercising its discretion to select a particular individual for assignment. Only if the agency chooses not to use competitive procedures must it select the individual on the basis of seniority.[39]

In other words, *Wright-Patterson* presumably holds that a proposal is negotiable if it gives an agency the option to use competitive procedures, and if competitive procedures are not used, then the agency has forsaken its right to select which particular employee will be assigned to which particular position. The difficulty with the holding is that an agency may not forsake a 7106(a)(2)(A) right. In overview, it remains to be seen whether judicial review will let stand an interpretation that in effect reverses congressional legislation by reinserting the phrase *in positions* into 7106(a)(2)(A) and then allows waiver of this reinserted language.

Third, section 7106(a)(2)(B) of the act reserves to agency management the right to determine the personnel to conduct agency operations, assign work, and contract out. It contains some new language, but this is of no consequence because other language in Executive Order 11,491, as amended, had been construed to produce identical results. Under the executive order there was never any question that management retained the right to make the basic decision that particular work would or would not be assigned. To achieve this result, the FLRC interpreted and applied: the language in section

---

39. *Id.* This holding has been appealed to the Circuit Court of Appeals for the District of Columbia. AFGE v. FLRA, Case No. 80-1351, consolidated with Case No. 80-1358.

12(b)(2) reserving to management the right to assign and retain employees in positions within the agency;[40] the section 12(b)(5) right to determine the personnel to conduct operations;[41] and the right to determine which work will be encompassed within the job content of employees' positions.[42] Likewise, the section 7106(a)(2)(B) wording "to make determinations with respect to contracting out" is new language but not a new management right. Under the executive order, the Federal Labor Relations Council had achieved the same result through interpretation and application of the section 12(b)(5) right to determine the personnel by which agency operations were to be conducted.[43] This 12(b)(5) *personnel* language is, of course, now also embodied in section 7106(a)(2)(B).[44] *Personnel* does not mean the particular individual who will perform work, but rather, groups or categories of employees, each of which has its own unique identifying factors distinguishing it from the other groups or categories of personnel.

The FLRA has preliminarily indicated that it will give a very broad construction to the *assign work* language found in section 7106(a)(2)(B). In *Wright-Patterson Air Force Base* the FLRA interpreted the language as reserving to agency management not only the right to assign work but also the right to decide the particular employee to whom the work will be assigned.[45] The authority wrote, "The right to assign work includes discretion as to the particular employee to

---

40. NAGE Local R12-183 and McClellan Air Force Base, Calif., FLRC No. 75A-81 (1976); Immigration and Naturalization Service and the American Federation of Government Employees, FLRC No. 74A-13 (1975).

41. Association of Academy Instructors, Incorporated, and Department of Transportation, Federal Aviation Administration, FAA Academy, Aeronautical Center, Oklahoma City, Oklahoma, FLRC No. 75A-86 (1976).

42. This is by virtue of the staffing patterns language. *See* notes 20, 21, and 23 in Chapter 3.

43. Tidewater Virginia Federal Employees Metal Trades Council and Naval Public Works Center, Norfolk, Va., FLRC No. 71A-56 (1973); Philadelphia Metal Trades Council, AFL-CIO and Philadelphia Naval Shipyard, Philadelphia, Pa., FLRC No. 72A-40 (1973).

44. In *Tidewater* the Federal Labor Relations Council addressed the word *personnel* as used in section 12(b)(5)—"determine the . . . personnel by which . . . [agency] . . . operations are to be conducted"—and stated that it "means the total body of persons engaged in the performance of agency operations (i.e., the composition of that body in terms of numbers, types of occupations and levels) and the particular groups of persons that make up the personnel conducting agency operations (e.g., military or civilian personnel; supervisory or nonsupervisory personnel; professional or nonprofessional personnel; Government personnel or contract personnel)." FLRC No. 71A-56 at 6.

45. 2 FLRA 77 (1980).

whom it will be assigned."[46] If upheld on appeal, this broad construction of the *assign work* language will obfuscate much of the distinction between the agency's retained right to assign work and both the section 7106(a)(2)(A) right to assign employees and the section 7106(a)(2)(B) right to determine personnel by which agency operations will be conducted.

Fourth, with respect to the filling of positions, under section 12(b)(2) of Executive Order 11,491, as amended, the agency determined whether or not to fill a position, and whether to fill it with a new hire from a civil service roster or through a promotion action producing a list of candidates that included applicants from within the agency. The actual selection of the successful candidate was made nonnegotiable by a Civil Service Commission regulation.[47] Statutory analysis indicates that this is not changed under the CSRA of 1978. Section 7106(a)(2)(A) reserves to management the right to hire; while the right to promote or not to promote is not contained in section 7106, a proposal requiring an agency to promote—as opposed to hiring—would derogate from the agency's reserved right to hire under section 7106(a)(2)(A). Also, selection of the successful candidate for promotion or new hire is nonnegotiable. If on the one hand a vacant position is to be filled by a promotion action, then the actual selection from the list of candidates is nonnegotiable by virtue of section 7106(a)(2)(C)(i). If on the other hand a vacant position is to be filled with a new hire from the outside, then, by virtue of section 7106(a)(2)(C)(ii), the actual selection from the civil service roster or any other source is nonnegotiable. Hence, section 7106(a)(2)(C) makes no change in what is negotiable with respect to selection for the filling of vacant positions. Regardless of how arbitrary and capricious a selection from a properly ranked and certified list may be, it may not be challenged under a negotiated grievance procedure[48] on the ground

---

46. *Id.* at 28.

47. Veterans Administration Independent Service Employees Union and Veterans Administration Research Hospital, Chicago, Illinois, FLRC No. 71A-31 (1972).

48. In this respect the actual functioning of the CSRA of 1978 is not exactly consistent with the merit principles that the CSRA espouses. Section 2301 of Title 5, U.S.C., is titled "Merit System Principles," and provides that employees should receive fair and equal treatment in all aspects of personnel management, and section 2301(b)(1) provides that selection and advancement should be determined solely on the basis of relative ability, knowledge, and skills. Section 2302 of Title 5, U.S.C., which is titled "Prohibited Personnel Practices," proscribes personnel practices that violate any law, rule, or regulation implementing or directly concerning the merit

that the clearly best candidate was not selected. Such nonselection may be grieved only if some additional grievable factor is alleged, such as EEO discrimination, preselection,[49] or commission of a prohibited personnel practice.

It appears that, after some initial uncertainty, the FLRA is going to follow the above analysis with respect to whether a bargaining proposal may require an agency, when filling a position, to fill the position from within the agency, as distinguished from filling the position with a new hire from outside the agency. Initially, the authority issued two decisions containing reasoning that could not be satisfactorily reconciled. In *Perry Point* the negotiability of the following proposal was at issue:

It is agreed that an employer will utilize, to the maximum extent possible the skills and talents of its employees. Therefore, consideration will be given in filling vacant positions, to employees within the bargaining unit. Management will not call for a Civil Service Register of candidates if three or more highly qualified candidates can be identified within the minimum area of consideration. This will not prevent applicants from other VA field units applying provided they specifically apply for the vacancy being filled, and that they are ranked and rated with the same merit promotion panel as local employees.[50]

By precluding management from calling for a civil service register if three highly qualified candidates could be found within the agency, the proposal necessarily would have been determinative of the source that the agency could look to in filling positions. Nevertheless, the FLRA held the proposal negotiable and explained,

Congress intended to preserve management's right to select in filling a position, but to afford the parties an opportunity to negotiate concerning stand-

---

principles contained in section 2301. The problem, however, is that the merit principles virtually cannot be enforced. Section 7121(d) of Title 5 would on its face potentially allow a prohibited personnel practice to be grieved, but section 7121(c)(4) makes it clear that nonselection may not be grieved. The paradoxical result is that a negotiated grievance procedure may not, in this all-important regard, serve to enforce the merit system principles that are an integral part of the CSRA of 1978. When a selection has been arbitrary and capricious, an employee's recourse is to proceed under the Equal Employment Opportunity Act or to proceed under section 1206 and file an allegation of a prohibited personnel practice with the special counsel of the Merit Systems Protection Board.

49. FLRC No. 71A-56 (1973).

50. AFGE Local 331 and Veterans Administration Hospital, Perry Point, Maryland, Case No. 0-NG-17, 2 FLRA 59 (1980).

ards, criteria and procedures to the extent that bargaining on such matters would not prevent management from exercising the right *to make the actual selection.*[51]

But in *Wright-Patterson Air Force Base* the authority again addressed the question of whether section 7106(a)(2)(C) reserves to the agency the right to choose the source from which management will make a selection.[52] This time, relying explicitly on *Federal Personnel Manual (FPM)* chapter 335, subchapter 1-4, requirement 4, the FLRA held that section 7106(a)(2)(C) reserves to the agency the right to look to any appropriate source. The authority wrote that section 7106(a)(2)(C) "reserves to the agency the option of exercising its right to select an employee for assignment from among those available, through any appropriate source."[53]

Subsequently, in two separate opinions, the authority effectively reversed its holding in *Perry Point.* In *Delaware National Guard* the issue before the authority was the negotiability of the area of consideration. After reaching the obvious conclusion that negotiating with respect to the area of consideration would not violate management's section 7106(a)(2)(C) right, the authority exercised its judicial license to add a dictum claiming that the decision in *Perry Point* had actually dealt with the area of consideration.

See *American Federation of Government Employees, Local 331 and Veterans Administration Hospital, Perry Point, Maryland,* Case No. 0-NG-17, 2 FLRA 59 (January 17, 1980), wherein the Authority concluded that a proposal which would require only that *consideration* be given to employees within the bargaining unit in filling vacant positions but would not prevent management from considering other applicants, or expanding the area of consideration once bargaining unit employees were considered, or using any other appropriate source in filling such vacancies, did not prevent management from exercising its reserved right to select. In that case the Authority pointed out that the proposal was concerned only with limiting the area of such intensive search and would require only that consideration be given to employees within the bargaining unit in filling vacant positions. The Authority noted that the proposal would expressly permit agency employees from outside the minimum area of consideration to apply for positions covered by the provision, and would not limit management consideration of such applicants. Moreover, it would not prevent management from expanding the area of intensive search for eligible candi-

---

51. *Id.* at 3.
52. 2 FLRA 77 (1980).
53. *Id.* at 10.

dates or from making selections from any appropriate source once the minimum area of consideration was considered.[54]

In *Naval Administrative Command* the disputed proposal provided that consideration of outside applicants may be undertaken when there are less than three minimally qualified internal applicants being considered for the promotional vacancy and when the Qualification Screening Committee determines that no qualified candidates are among the applicants, external recruitment will be effected. This shall not exclude concurrent consideration of volunteer applicants or consideration of re-promotion or special consideration eligibles. However, vacancy announcements will be posted only in the minimum area of consideration.

The FLRA held the proposal nonnegotiable because it infringed the 7106(a)(2)(C) "right, with respect to filling positions, to make selections from among properly ranked and certified candidates for promotion or from any other appropriate source."[55] In *Naval Administrative Command*, the authority did not—as in *Delaware National Guard*—attempt to distinguish *Perry Point* by claiming that it had dealt only with the area of consideration. Instead, the authority distinguished *Perry Point* as standing for the proposition that a proposal may require that "consideration" be given to bargaining unit employees as long as the proposal does not prevent management from also considering any other sources.

It is essential to ascertain when section 7106(a)(2)(C) is and is not applicable. The language addresses filling positions, but it does not address the filling of all positions in any manner. Rather, it addresses the filling of positions by the making of selections for appointments. Thus section 7106(a)(2)(C) is operative only when agency management is filling positions by making selections. If a position is being filled by a method other than selection, then section 7106(a)(2)(C) cannot apply. An instance of this would be when a position is being filled by assignment only, as distinguished from

54. Association of Civilian Technicians, Delaware Chapter and National Guard Bureau, Delaware National Guard, Case No. 0-NG-104, 3 FLRA 9 (1980) 3.

55. NFFE Local 1451 and Navy Exchange, Naval Administrative Command, Orlando, Florida, Case No. 0-NG-160, 3 FLRA 60 (1980) 3. The FLRA rendered a similar legal conclusion in National Council of CSA Locals, AFGE and Community Services Administration, Case No. 0-NG-127, 3 FLRA 13 (1980), where the agency interpreted a union proposal as prohibiting the agency from selecting from sources outside the area of consideration. This interpretation was not controverted, and the authority declared the proposal nonnegotiable. This decision has been appealed to the Circuit Court of Appeals for the District of Columbia. AFGE National Council of CSA Locals v. FLRA, Case No. 80-1702.

selection. The word *select*—or *selection*—is not synonymous with the word *assign*.

Select is defined as "to choose in preference to another or others . . . carefully chosen."[56] *Selection* is defined as "a group from which a choice may be made . . . the state of being selected."[57] *Selection* entails a group and the act of choosing one or more in preference to others in the group.

In contrast, the word *assign* does not require a group; nor does it require the choosing of one or more in preference to others. The word *assign* is defined as "to designate, give or reserve (something) for a specific person or purpose; to appoint, as to a post of duty: *Assign to guard duty*; to name; specify . . . to ascribe; attribute. . . ."[58] One may be *selected*—i.e., formally chosen in preference to others in a group—and upon having been selected, *appointed* to a position. But one may also be *designated*—i.e., not formally chosen in preference to others in a group—and upon having been designated, appointed to a position. Section 7106(a)(2)(C) is limited to selections for appointments to positions; section 7106(a)(2)(C) does not apply to mere designations (i.e., assignments or reassignments) for appointments to positions.

In the federal sector, the elements of a selection procedure are well known, identifiable, and recognizable. First, the position to be filled is normally announced or advertised. Second, the people who are interested submit applications or else already have them on file, and this becomes a group. Third, the group members are compared in some fashion, and then the names of some or all of the group members are submitted to agency managers who will choose the successful candidate. Fourth, one or more of the group is chosen in preference to the other group members. The absence of these elements, particularly the group and the chosen in preference creates a prima facie case that no selection has occurred.[59]

---

56. *Random House College Dictionary*, rev. ed. (New York: Random House, 1975).
57. *Ibid.*
58. *Ibid.*
59. In the federal sector, personnel actions are supposed to be based upon merit principles. *FPM* chapter 335, subchapter 5-1(a) provides, in part, that "it is the objective of the competitive examining system to match skills against job requirements so as to insure consideration of competitors in relative order of merit. Inherent in this process is the basic assumption that participants in the examination are bona fide competitors for the type of employment for which the examination is held. The restrictions in this subchapter are designed to protect the competitive appointment principle. To avoid undue complexity and preserve needed flexibility, the Commission has established

Not every selection comes within the scope of section 7106(a)(2)(C). Subsections (i) and (ii) make it clear that to come within section 7106(a)(2)(C) the selection must be one that is from an "appropriate source."[60] Other selections are outside the scope of the section. Section 7106(a)(2)(C)(ii) does not define what the other appropriate sources are, but subsection (i) assists in this, since it is an appropriate source.[61] Thus, the only explanation of appropriate sources is a list of properly ranked and certified candidates for promotion. A promotion is a competitive action based on merit, and it is logical to conclude that other appropriate sources would be competitive actions based on merit.[62] The creation of a list of ranked and certified candidates for promotion consists of a series of recognizable, identifiable procedures that are formalized in regulation. It is logical to conclude that other appropriate sources would consist of a series of recognizable, identifiable procedures that are formalized in regulation. This interpretation is consistent with regulations issued by the Office of Personnel Management (OPM).[63] If the source does not require a competitive selection based on merit, or if the source does not consist of a series of identifiable procedures that are formalized in regulation, then the source is not appropriate. The prime example of an appropriate source would be an OPM register (roster) containing a list of names of eligibles for new hire; this would be a competitive

---

restrictions only to the extent that they are clearly needed to assure the integrity of examinations. Agencies should make certain, however, that appointments from competitive examination and subsequent noncompetitive actions are fully consistent with merit principles even in the absence of specific controls." Also, section 2301 of the CSRA establishes additional merit principles.

60. Subsection (ii) reads "other appropriate source," thus indicating that subsection (i) is an appropriate source, too.

61. *Id.*

62. *Supra* note 59.

63. The OPM has issued regulations for the express purpose of implementing section 7106. *See FPM* letter 335-12, dated December 29, 1978. Attached to this letter is a revised *FPM* chapter 335. Revised *FPM* chapter 335, 1-4, requirement 4, speaks to management's right to select or not to select from the best qualified candidates and to management's "right to select from other appropriate sources, such as reemployment priority lists, reinstatement, transfer, handicapped, or Veterans Readjustment eligibles or those within reach on an appropriate OPM certificate. In deciding which source or sources to use, agencies have an obligation to determine which is most likely to best meet the agency's affirmative action goals." Each of these consists of identifiable procedures that are formalized in statute, regulation, or both. It should also be noted that reassignment is conspicuously absent from requirement 4, ostensibly because a reassignment alone does not entail a selection from an appropriate source within the meaning of section 7106(a)(2)(C).

action, based on merit, consisting of a series of identifiable procedures formalized in regulation.

The above construction is extremely persuasive, and any other construction would be illogical.[64]

In final overview, when filling a position by making a selection from an appropriate source, under section 7106(a)(2)(C), an agency enjoys the reserved right to select any of the candidates. The parties may not even negotiate proposals requiring that the selection be objectively based on merit criteria and on employees' demonstrated performance.

The fifth and last illegal category of subject matter for bargaining is found in section 7106(a)(2)(D). The authority granted in this section for an agency to take necessary actions during emergencies is not new. It is almost identical to the right that existed under section 12(b)(6) of Executive Order 11,491, as amended.

Section 7106 does not except all matters that in any manner relate to the subjects mentioned therein from the obligation to nego-

---

64. This construction would produce a result that is both tolerable and healthy in the workplace. As long as employees in one job title, series, and grade are competent (if the employees are not competent, the proper recourse is for the agency to train the employee, proceed under Title 5, U.S.C., section 4301 *et seq.*, or both) and there are sufficient numbers to fill vacant positions, the agency's work and mission will be adequately accomplished and the agency has no legitimate interest in exercising unrestrained control over which particular employee occupies which particular position within the job title, series, and grade. Employees within one job title, series, and grade are presumptively able to perform competently. Too frequently when an employee has been involuntarily reassigned from one position within a job title, series, and grade to another position within the same job title, series, and grade, the underlying reason is that a manager either dislikes or has a personality conflict with the employee and wishes to harass the employee by sending him or her to some unpleasant geographical location. As long as there are qualified people available to fill positions, an agency has no legitimate interest in exercising unrestrained control whereby an employee is involuntarily reassigned from one job title and series to another job title and series that is at the same grade level as the first. This argues for the negotiability of any proposal that would vest an employee with a veto power over an involuntary reassignment to a position in circumstances where there are other available qualified personnel who may occupy that position. The only substantive counterargument is that this construction might result in the negotiation of proposals precluding management from transferring out an employee disliked by, or who has a personality conflict with, a manager or supervisor. But such an argument calls for extremely poor policy and practices. First, it calls for a back-door way of punishing an employee for an "offense" for which the employee may not legally be punished. This is not the posture that any federal agency should assume. Second, this argument would create undesirable policy in that it would transfer the problem. Better policy would require that the problem be resolved. Third, such an argument would allow for personnel actions based on a consideration other than merit. This would violate regulation. *Supra* note 59.

tiate as set forth in section 7114(a)(4); it reserves to management only the authority to make the basic decision. The procedures that will be used in implementing the basic decision, its impact on bargaining unit employees, or both must be negotiated. Section 7106(b) explicitly provides

Nothing in this section shall preclude any agency and labor organization from negotiating. . . .
  (2) procedures which management officials of the agency will observe in exercising any authority under this section; or
  (3) appropriate arrangements for employees adversely affected by the exercise of any authority under this section by such management officials.

Sections 7106(b)(2) and (3) find their heritage in Executive Order 11,491, as amended. Under Executive Order 11,491, as amended, the negotiation of such procedures and adverse effect[65] was customarily termed "negotiating over impact and implementation."[66] The Federal Labor Relations Council enunciated general guidelines governing impact and implementation negotiations, which remain relevant today.

The emphasis is on the reservation of management authority to decide and act on these matters, and the clear import is that no right accorded to union under the Order may be permitted to interfere with that authority. However, there is no implication that such reservation of decision making and action authority is intended to bar negotiations of procedures, to the extent consonant with law and regulations, which management will observe in reaching the decision or taking the action involved, provided that such procedures do not have the effect of negating the authority reserved.[67]

Several examples demonstrate impact and implementation negotiations under Title VII of the Civil Service Reform Act of 1978. Section 7106(a)(2)(A) reserves to an agency the authority to lay off employees. This entitles the agency to decide whether or not a layoff will take place; but the agency is nonetheless obligated to negotiate the procedures that will be used in informing the employees of the

---

65. The last sentence of section 11(b) of Executive Order 11,491, as amended, provided that "this does not preclude the parties from negotiating agreements providing appropriate arrangements for employees adversely affected by the impact of realignment of work forces or technological change."

66. See Puget Sound Naval Shipyard, Department of the Navy, Bremerton, Washington, A/SLMR No. 332 (1973).

67. Veterans Administration Independent Service Employees Union and Veterans Administration Research Hospital, Chicago, Illinois, FLRC No. 71A-31 (1972) 3. See also Lodge 2424, IAM-AW and Kirk Army Hospital and Aberdeen Research and Development Center, Aberdeen, Maryland, FLRC No. 72A-18 (1973).

layoff and in selecting which employees will be relieved of duties in effectuating the layoff. Similarly, section 7106(a)(2)(A) reserves to management the authority to take disciplinary action against an employee, which entitles the agency to decide whether or not a disciplinary action will take place; but the agency is nevertheless obligated to negotiate the procedures that will be followed in the imposition and appeal of a disciplinary action.[68]

Under the executive order, if an impact and implementation proposal would cause a substantial delay or constraint in the exercise of a right reserved to management, the FLRC would deem the delay or constraint equivalent to complete negation and thereupon hold the proposal nonnegotiable. Under the CSRA of 1978, it is most unlikely that the FLRA will treat constraint or delay as being synonymous with negation.

Persuasive evidence indicates that Congress did not intend to preclude negotiation of a proposal merely because it may severely constrain or even unreasonably delay the exercise of a reserved management right. The Committee on Conference considered and rejected section 7218 of the Senate bill, which provided in part that

(b) Nothing in subsection (a) of this section shall preclude the parties from negotiating—
  (1) procedures which management will observe in exercising its authority to decide or act in matters reserved under such subsection; or
  (2) appropriate arrangements for employees adversely affected by the impact of management's exercising its authority to decide or act in matters reserved under such subsection,
except that such negotiation shall not unreasonably delay the exercise by management of its authority to decide or act, and such procedures and arrangements shall be consistent with the provisions of any law or regulation described in 7215(c) of this title, and shall not have the effect of negating the authority reserved under subsection (a).[69]

The House bill required impact and implementation bargaining but contained no language barring negotiation of proposals that would unreasonably delay or negate the exercise of the authority reserved to the agency. The Committee on Conference adopted what now constitutes the present language of sections 7106(b)(2) and (3), and issued a joint explanatory statement, which provides that an impact-imple-

---

68. Such procedures, of course, could not be inconsistent with the adverse action procedures of the Civil Service Reform Act of 1978.

69. Section 7218 of the Senate bill contained language that is now in section 7106 of the CSRA of 1978.

mentation proposal is nonnegotiable only if it would preclude the agency from acting at all.

Senate section 7218(b) provides that negotiations on procedures governing the exercise of authority reserved to management shall not unreasonably delay the exercise by management of its authority to act on such matters. Any negotiations on procedures governing matters otherwise reserved to agency discretion by subsection (a) may not have the effect of actually negating the authority as reserved to the agency by subsection (a). There are no comparable House provisions.

The conference report deletes these provisions. However, the conferees wish to emphasize that negotiations on such procedures should not be conducted in a way that prevents the agency from acting at all, or in a way that prevents the exclusive representative from negotiating fully on procedures. Similarly, the parties may indirectly do what the section prohibits them from doing directly.[70]

The Federal Labor Relations Authority has already rendered decisions consistent with the interpretation that impact and implementation proposals are nonnegotiable if and only if they prevent the agency from acting at all.[71]

Permissive Bargaining Subjects

Title 5, U.S.C., section 7106(b), provides, in part:

Nothing in this section shall preclude any agency and any labor organization from negotiating—
(1) at the election of the agency, on the numbers, types and grades of employees or positions assigned to any organizational subdivision, work project, or tour of duty, or on the technology, methods and means of performing work. . . .

In contrast to section 7106(a), section 7106(b)(1) does not prohibit the parties from negotiating about the substance of the subject matters listed therein. Therefore subject matter within the purview of section 7106(b)(1) is neither mandatory nor illegal bargaining matter; rather, it is permissive bargaining matter. An employer may negotiate and enter a binding contractual agreement covering section 7106(b)(1)

---

70. Rep. No. 95-1717, 95th Cong., 2d Sess. 158 (1978).

71. AFGE, Local 1999 and Army-Air Force Service, Dix-McGuire Exchange, Fort Dix, New Jersey, Case No. 0-NG-9, 2 FLRA 16 (1979); National Treasury Employees Union Chapters 103 and 111 and United States Customs Service, Region VII, Case No. 0-NG-16, 2 FLRA 15 (1979).

subject matter, but the employer may also legally and with impunity refuse to negotiate section 7106(b)(1) subject matter.[72]

The staffing patterns language, "the numbers, types and grades of employees or positions assigned to any organization subdivision, work project or tour of duty . . .," and the label for it derive directly from Executive Order 11,491, as amended. The history of the staffing patterns language is extremely revealing. Wording in section 6(b) of Executive Order 10,988 (issued January 17, 1962) preceded the staffing patterns language of section 11(b) of Executive Order 11,491, providing that the bargaining obligation "shall not be construed to extend to such areas of discretion as the [agency's] organization and the assignment of its personnel." Unfortunately, the assignment of personnel clause was broadly construed as restricting negotiations on the procedures that would be used in the assignment of the employees. This problem was recognized, and when on October 29, 1969, Executive Order 11,491 was issued to supercede Executive Order 10,988, the language was amended to ensure that the employer could not refuse to negotiate assignment procedures. The history of Executive Order 11,491 puts this matter beyond reasonable doubt.

The words 'assignment of its personnel' have been interpreted by some as excluding from the scope of negotiations the policies or procedures management will apply in taking such actions as the assignment of employees to particular shifts or the assignment of overtime. This clearly is not the intent of the language. This language should be considered as applying to an agency's right to establish staffing patterns for its organization and the accomplishment of its work—the number of employees in the agency and the number, type, and grades of positions or employees assigned in the various segments of its organization and to work projects and tours of duty.

To remove any possible future misinterpretation of the intent of the phrase 'assignment of its personnel,' we recommend that there be substituted in a new order the phrase 'the number of employees, and the numbers, types, and

---

72. Except for the methods and means language which was classified as illegal bargaining matter before enactment of the CSRA of 1978, all the subject matters contained within section 7106(b)(1) trace their history directly to section 11(b) of Executive Order 11,491, as amended; see Executive Order 11,491, *as amended*, § 12(b)(5) with respect to the method and means language. Section 11(b) of the order provided, in part, that ". . . the obligation to meet and confer does not include matters with respect to the mission of an agency; its budget; its organization; the number of employees; and the numbers, types, and grades of positions or employees assigned to an organizational unit, work project or tour of duty or the technology of performing its work; or its internal security practices."

grades of positions, or employees assigned to an organizational unit, work project or tour of duty."[73]

The Federal Labor Relations Council interpreted the staffing patterns language in section 11(b) as not requiring an agency to negotiate the content of individual jobs or the duties that employees will and will not perform. A proposal relating to staffing patterns is, however, negotiable unless "integrally related to" and "determinative of" the actual staffing patterns. A proposal establishing starting times, the basic workday, and the basic workweek would not ordinarily be "determinative of" the agency's staffing patterns.

Like the staffing patterns language, section 7106(b)(1)'s *technology* language traces its history directly to section 11(b) of Executive Order 11,491, as amended, and it, too, generated extensive litigation under the order. This was due in part to the Federal Labor Relations Council's rather loose construction of the word.[74] The council broadly construed *technology* as encompassing at least as much as is encompassed by its generic and commonplace meanings and possibly more.[75] It is to be hoped that the independent Federal Labor Relations Authority will be able to pronounce reasonably identifiable perimeters for the word technology and also to distinguish it from *methods and means* now within section 7106(b)(1).

Methods and means traces its history to section 12(b)(5) of Executive Order 11,491, as amended. In the famous *Tidewater* decision, the Federal Labor Relations Council offered the following interpretations of *methods* and of *means*:

"Method" is "a procedure or process for obtaining an object" or "a way, technique or purpose of or for doing something." In other words, a method is the "procedure followed in doing a given kind of work or achieving a given end." Synonyms for method include mode, manner, way and system. The

---

73. "Study Committee Report and Recommendations, August 1969, Which Led to the Issuance of Executive Order 11491," (Aug. 1969) in *Labor-Management Relations in the Federal Service* (Washington, D.C.: GPO, 1975), p. 38.

74. Based upon the Federal Labor Relations Council's application of the term technology, it appears that it would encompass the processes, methods, means, materials, and equipment involved, directly or indirectly, in the performance of work. The council never sharply distinguished between section 11(b) *technology* and section 12(b)(5) *methods and means*. Indeed, the council defined *methods* as including technology.

75. *See* Charles Perrow, *Complex Organizations* (Glenville, Ill.: Scott, Foresman and Company, 1972), p. 166, where a distinction is made between the commonplace use of technology—in the sense of machines or sophisticated devices for achieving high efficiency—and the generic meaning of the word, which is the study of techniques and tasks.

term "methods," as used in the Order, therefore means the procedures, processes, ways, techniques, modes, manners and systems by which operations are to be conducted—in short, *how* operations are to be conducted.

"Mean" is "something by the use of help of which a desired end is attained or made more likely: an agent, tool, device, measure, plan or policy for accomplishing or furnishing a proposal." Synonyms for mean include instrument, agent, instrumentality, organ, medium, vehicle, and channel. The term "means," as used in the Order, therefore includes the instruments (e.g., an in-house, Government facility or an outside, private facility; centralized or decentralized offices) or the resources (e.g., money, plant, supplies, equipment or material) to be utilized in conducting agency operations—in short, what will be used in conducting operations.[76]

It is noteworthy that the council defined *method* as including procedures. Under the executive order this created confusion between negotiable implementation procedures and nonnegotiable methods and procedures.

It is to be hoped that the Federal Labor Relations Authority will strive to render reasonable and workable constructions of *means, methods,* and *technology.* At a minimum, the constructions of the terms should be sufficiently sharp to produce a reasonable semblance of mutual exclusivity among the terms; alternatively, the authority should acknowledge that meaningful, usable distinctions cannot be made and thereupon declare common definitions. Thus far, the FLRA has issued a definition of *mean.* In *U.S. Customs Service,* the authority defined *mean* as "any instrumentality, including an agent, tool, device, measure, plan or policy used by the agency for the accomplishing or the furthering of the performance of its work."[77]

Aside from being shorter, this definition does not substantively differ from the FLRC's interpretation of *mean.* In the future, will the FLRA treat materials and equipment as coming within the term mean and not within the term technology, or as coming within both? Having defined *mean* as inclusive of plan and policy, how can both *methods* and *technology* be defined as not also inclusive of the concepts of plan and policy? Will the authority construe *of performing work* as referring to work that is significant and requisite to the accomplishment of the agency's mission or as referring also to work that is insignificant or incidental to the accomplishment of the agency's mission? Will the authority require proof of an actual nexus between the mean and the performance of an agency's work or will the authority blindly accept

---

76. FLRC No. 71A-56 (1973) 5–6.
77. NTEU and U.S. Customs Service, Case No. 0-NG-3, 2 FLRA 30 (1979) 4.

an agency's allegation that such a nexus exists? Will the authority require a substantial nexus or simply require a nexus, however insubstantial or tenuous?

The early indication is that at the least the Federal Labor Relations Authority will require a nexus between the method or mean and the accomplishment of the agency's basic mission. In *Wright-Patterson Air Force Base* the authority addressed the question of what constitutes work within the meaning of section 7106(b)(1).[78] The authority looked to the CSRA's legislative history and examined the House-Senate conference report to find illustrations of work.

By inclusion of this language, however, it is not intended that agencies will discuss general policy questions determining how an agency does its work. It must be construed in light of the paramount right of the public to as effective and efficient a Government as possible. For example, the phrase "methods and means" is not intended to authorize IRS to negotiate with a labor organization over how returns should be selected for audit, or how thorough the audit of the returns should be. It does not subject to the collective bargaining agreement the judgment of EPA about how to select recipients for the award of environmental grants. It does not authorize the Energy Department to negotiate with unions on which of the research and development projects being conducted by the Department should receive top priority as part of the Department's efforts to find new sources of energy.[79]

Based on this legislative history, the authority declared that the term "performing work," as used in section 7106(b)(1), encompasses work that is "directly and integrally related to the accomplishment of the mission of the agency, *i.e.*, those particular objectives which the agency was established to accomplish."[80]

Whenever the subject matter of a proposal comes within the purview of section 7106(b)(1) and the employer elects not to negotiate the matter, this means that the employer may refuse to negotiate only the substance of the matter, i.e., the basic decision to take or not to take the action. The employer must nonetheless negotiate the procedures to be used in implementing the decision as well as its adverse impact upon employees.[81] For example, should an employer decide, while using the same number of employees, to expand from two shifts working only sixteen hours a day to three shifts working twenty-four

---

78. 2 FLRA 77 (1980).
79. S. Rep. No. 95-1272, 95th Cong., 2d Sess. 154 (1978).
80. *Id.* at 15.
81. 5 U.S.C. §§ 7106(b)(2) and (3). *Supra* notes 65, 66, 67.

hours a day, then the employer could refuse to negotiate regarding the basic decision to expand the number of shifts. This would be the substance of the change. The employer, however, would nonetheless be obligated to negotiate the impact and implementation of the change, i.e., the procedures to be used in implementing the basic change, such as the method of selecting which personnel will work the new shift and the starting and quitting times for the shifts.[82] To cite another example, the *tour of duty* language of section 7106(b)(1) excepts from the obligation to negotiate a proposal determining the number or types of employees who will perform overtime work; however, a proposal determining the processes for selection of personnel, from among the type that management has decided to use for overtime assignment, concerns only the procedures to be used in implementation of the decision that overtime will be performed and therefore would not come within this exception.[83]

Title 5, U.S.C., section 7114(c) provides that an agreement between an exclusive representative and an agency is subject to the approval by the head of the agency.[84] The distinction between permissive and illegal bargaining matter is of critical importance for purposes of this review. When making a section 7114(c) review, one of the grounds, among others, on which the agency head may disapprove an agreement is that it is not in accordance with the provisions of Title VII of the CSRA of 1978. Hence, an agency head may disapprove an agreement provision, the substance of which is a matter within the illegal bargaining matter of section 7106(a); since section 7106(a) matters may not be negotiated as to substance, any agreement thereon cannot be in accordance with the provisions of the CSRA of

---

82. *See* American Federation of Government Employees, National Joint Council of Food Inspection Locals and Office of the Administration, Animal, Plant and Health Inspection Service, U.S. Department of Agriculture, FLRC No. 73A-36 (1975).

83. *See* Federal Employees Metal Trades Council of Charleston and Charleston Naval Shipyard, Charleston, S.C., FLRC No. 72A-46 (1973).

84. "(1) An agreement between any agency and an exclusive representative shall be subject to approval by the head of the agency. (2) The head of the agency shall approve the agreement within 30 days from the date the agreement is executed if the agreement is in accordance with the provisions of this chapter and any other applicable law, rule, or regulation (unless the agency has granted an exception to the provision). (3) If the head of the agency does not approve or disapprove the agreement within the 30-day period, the agreement shall take effect and shall be binding on the agency and the exclusive representative."

1978.[85] But an agency head may not disapprove an agreement provision the substance of which is a matter within the permissive bargaining matter of section 7106(b)(1); since negotiation of the substance of those matters is permissive and not illegal, any resultant agreement thereon is in accordance with the provisions of the CSRA of 1978. This analysis is consistent with the manner in which such circumstances were treated under Executive Order 11,491, as amended.[86]

Negotiation Distinguished from Consultation

Under the CSRA of 1978, the duty to negotiate should not be confused with the duty to consult. There are two types of consultation in the federal sector. First, under Title 5, U.S.C., section 7113, "National Consultation Rights," an agency is required to grant national consultation rights to a labor organization that, although not recognized as exclusive representative on the agency level, has nevertheless been recognized as exclusive representative for a substantial number of employees of the agency. A labor organization that has been accorded national consultation rights is entitled to be informed in advance of any substantive change in conditions of employment proposed on the agency level and to present views and recommendations. The agency is not required to negotiate regarding the labor organization's views and recommendations, but rather to consider them. The agency is also

---

85. If an agency head fails to act within thirty days to declare that agreed language is in violation of section 7106(a), the agency may thereafter raise the same argument by declaring that any grievance that is based on the offensive language is nongrievable and nonarbitrable. NFFE Local 1862 and Department of HEW, Public Health Service, Indian Health Service, Phoenix, Arizona, Case No. 0-NG-195, 3 FLRA 25 (1980).

86. Under Executive Order 11,491, as amended, section 11(b) contained permissive bargaining subjects, and an agency head's act of approving or disapproving an agreement was called a section 15 review. The Federal Labor Relations Council definitively held that ". . . [M]atters which are within the ambit of section 11(b), although excepted from the obligation to negotiate, *may be negotiated* if management chooses to negotiate over them. In other words, while there is no requirement that matters within the ambit of section 11(b) be negotiated, the Order does permit their negotiation so that an agreement which results from the negotiation of such matters does not, thereby, fail to conform to the Order. Therefore, since the agency in the instant case, through its local bargaining representative, negotiated and reached agreement on the proposal in dispute as permitted by the Order, the agency cannot after that fact, change its position during the section 15 review process. Such an agreement conforms to the Order, and under section 15 it must be approved." AFGE Council of Locals 1497 and 2165, and Region 3, General Services Administration, Baltimore, Md., FLRC No. 74A-48 (1975). *See* NFFE Local 1485 and Coast Guard Base, Miami, Florida, FLRC No. 75A-77 (1976).

required to provide the labor organization with a written statement of the reasons for taking the final action.

Second, under section 7117(d) of Title 5, U.S.C., upon request a labor organization representing "a substantial number of employees" may request and be granted consultation rights by any agency that issues governmentwide rules and regulations. When the agency proposes a change in a governmentwide rule or regulation that will effect a substantive change in any condition of employment, the agency must inform the labor organization of the proposed change. In turn, the labor organization is entitled to submit views and recommendations to the issuing agency. The issuing agency is required to consider the views or recommendations before taking final action and then to provide the labor organization with a written statement of the reasons for taking the final action.

In contrast to consultation, wherein after an agency has considered a labor organization's views and recommendations it is then free to act unilaterally, the duty to negotiate requires an agency to do more than merely consider what the union might present; also, the agency may not act unilaterally. After the agency has notified the union of a proposed change in conditions of employment, the agency must, upon request, meet with the union at reasonable times and convenient places, as frequently as is necessary, in an effort to reach mutual, bilateral agreement.[87]

Analyzing Negotiability

Does the subject matter of the proposal come within the scope of section 7114(a)(4)? If yes, then something about the proposal is negotiable.

The proposal is negotiable in all respects that it does not specifically violate the Hatch Act; it does not specifically deal with the grade-level classification of a position; it does not specifically contravene federal statute, governmentwide regulations, or any agency regulation for which a compelling need exists and which was issued at a national level or national subdivision level that is higher than the

---

87. Section 7114(b) of Title 5, U.S.C., provides, in part, that "the duty of an agency and an exclusive representative to negotiate in good faith . . . shall include the obligation—(1) to approach the negotiations with a sincere resolve to reach a collective bargaining agreement . . . (3) to meet at reasonable times and convenient places as frequently as may be necessary. . . ."

level of recognition. To the extent that the proposal oversteps these boundaries, the proposal is nonnegotiable.

Does the subject of the proposal come within the scope of section 7106(a), which defines illegal subjects of bargaining? If not, then the substance of the proposal is negotiable (unless it comes within section 7106(b)(1)). If so, then only impact and implementation are negotiable, pursuant to sections 7106(b)(2) and (3), and even if the agency proceeds to negotiate and enter agreement on the substance, such agreement is illegal and as such is void and unenforceable.

Does the subject matter of the proposal come within the scope of section 7106(b)(1), which defines permissive subjects of bargaining, those about which an agency may, but is not required, to negotiate? If not, then the substance of the proposal is nonnegotiable. If so and the agency refuses to negotiate the subject of the proposal, then only its impact and implementation may be negotiated, pursuant to sections 7106(b)(2) and (3). If so, but the agency proceeds to negotiate and enter agreement upon the substance of the proposal, then the substance is negotiable and the agreement is valid and enforceable.

3.
Negotiability
of Specific Subjects

The Job

The following subsections entail an analysis of subject matter directly related to the job: who, what, where, how much, how many, and when.

Numbers of Employees

The clear language of section 11(b) of the executive order excepted from the obligation to negotiate matters with respect to the numbers of employees and with respect to the "numbers, types, and grades of positions or employees assigned to an organization unit, work project or tour of duty." Identical language is contained in the management's rights section of CSRA of 1978, with the sole change being that the number of employees is now illegal bargaining matter dealt with in section 7106(a)(1). The staffing patterns language is included in section 7106(b)(1). Given this carry-over of identical language, there is every reason to believe that the Federal Labor Relations Authority will construe section 7106(a)(1)'s *number of employees* and section 7106(b)(1)'s staffing patterns language as they were construed by the Federal Labor Relations Council.

On several occasions the FLRC applied this language to proposals relating to numbers of employees. In *INS-1975* the FLRC held that the staffing patterns language served to make nonnegotiable a union bargaining proposal directing that employees performing law enforcement duties work in pairs.[1] The proposal would have been determinative of the number of employees assigned to a work project or tour of duty. The union had contended that the proposal would

---

1. Immigration and Naturalization Service and American Federation of Government Employees, FLRC No. 74A-13 (1975).

promote the safety of employees performing dangerous work, but the FLRC rejected this argument on the ground that the fact that the proposal might promote safety did not make it negotiable.

INS-1975 also involved a second union bargaining proposal directing that an "appropriate" number of employees would be assigned to checkpoints. The FLRC reasoned that a requirement of an "appropriate" or "sufficient" number of employees is tantamount to a requirement that a specific number of employees be assigned to checkpoints. Consequently, the council held that the staffing patterns language served to make this second proposal nonnegotiable.

The staffing patterns language also serves to render nonnegotiable a proposal establishing staffing ratios. In INS-1974 the FLRC responded to a negotiability dispute over a proposal establishing staffing ratios (required manning levels) for various types of specified duties that bargaining unit employees performed.[2] The FLRC held that the proposal was nonnegotiable because the establishment of staffing ratios is "integrally related to" and "determinative of" the number of employees assigned to a work project or tour of duty. The FLRC pointed out, however, that a proposal providing procedures to be used in selection of individual employees for assignment to particular shifts, work projects, or tours of duty would be negotiable.

In Office of Dependent Schools the FLRC held nonnegotiable a union proposal providing that one teacher would have to teach no more than a specified number of students, depending on the type of class.[3] In Bureau of Indian Affairs the FLRC applied the staffing patterns language to hold nonnegotiable one union proposal providing a ratio of one teacher for a specified number of students and another union proposal providing a ratio of one teacher's aide for every seventeen students.[4]

Assignment of Employees

Under section 11(b) of Executive Order 11,491, as amended, management had the right to determine the types of positions or employees

---

2. AFGE (National Border Patrol and National Council of Immigration and Naturalization Service Locals) and Immigration and Naturalization Service, FLRC No. 73A-25 (1974).

3. Overseas Educ. Assoc., Inc. and Department of Defense, Office of Dependent Schools, FLRC No. 76A-142 (1978).

4. National Council of B.I.A. Educators, National Education Association and Department of the Interior, Bureau of Indian Affairs, Navajo Area Office, FLRC No. 77A-9 (1977).

assigned to any work project or tour of duty. Under section 12(b)(2) of the order management retained the right to assign employees and to retain them in particular positions within the agency. Under section 12(b)(5) management retained the right to determine the personnel by which the agency's operations were to be conducted. These combined to except from the obligation to negotiate substantive decisions regarding which particular group of employees would be assigned to perform work and to what positions employees would be assigned. The CSRA of 1978 carries over, in section 7106(b)(1), the management right to determine the types of positions or employees assigned to any work project or tour of duty. Section 7106(a)(2)(B) carries over the retained management right to determine the personnel by which the agency's operations (work) are (is) to be conducted. Section 7106(a)(2) retains with agency management the right to assign and retain employees within the agency.

The reserved right to determine the personnel by which agency operations or work will be conducted renders nonnegotiable a proposal containing language that limits the agency's discretion to decide the type of employee or the type of personnel to whom work will or will not be assigned. Based on this logic, the council held nonnegotiable proposals prohibiting the agency from contracting out work traditionally performed by unit employees.[5] The council's reasoning was that such language is inconsistent with management's retained authority to determine the personnel by which the agency's operations are to be conducted.

A proposal prohibiting the agency from assigning to nonunit employees work traditionally performed by unit employees is also nonnegotiable. In *McClellan Air Force Base*, the union had proposed the following:

The basic workweek will be five consecutive days with two consecutive days off. The hours of work for employees will be as follows:
  a. Full-time employees will have the opportunity to work a forty hour

---

5. Tidewater, Virginia Federal Employees Metal Trades Council and Naval Public Works Center, Norfolk, Va., FLRC No. 71A-56 (1973); Local 3, American Federation of Technical Engineers, AFL-CIO, and Philadelphia Naval Shipyard, Philadelphia, Pa., FLRC No. 71A-48 (1973); Federal Employees Metal Trades Council of Charleston, S.C., FLRC No. 72A-33 (1973); Federal Employees Metal Trades Council of Charleston AFL-CIO & Charleston Naval Shipyard, Charleston, S.C., FLRC 72A-35 (1973); Philadelphia Metal Trades Council, AFL-CIO and Philadelphia Naval Shipyard, Philadelphia, Pa., FLRC No. 72A-40 (1973). This result now flows from 5 U.S.C. § 7106(a)(2)(B).

week unless the workload is such that it will not support forty hours. However, in no instance will the full-time employees have their hours reduced by using part-time or intermittent employees. At no time shall the hours for full-time employees go below thirty-five hours per work-week.
  b. Part-time employees will have the opportunity to work a thirty-four hour week unless the workload is such that it will not support thirty-four hours. However, in no instance will the part-time employees have their hours reduced by using intermittent employees. At no time shall the hours for part-time employees go below twenty hours per workweek.[6]

The FLRC declared this proposal nonnegotiable on the stated grounds that it would be determinative of the numbers of employees assigned to an organizational unit or work project or tour of duty. The council reasoned that the proposal would be determinative of the numbers of part-time or intermittent employees who could be employed when their employment would reduce the hours of full-time employees below forty hours a week or part-time employees below thirty-four.[7] Subsequently, the FLRC applied *McClellan Air Force Base* to hold nonnegotiable a proposal in *Hill Air Force Base* providing that before using intermittents the employer would permit regular full-time employees to work forty hours per week and regular part-time employees to work thirty-four hours per week.[8] Still later the council applied *McClellan Air Force Base* to hold nonnegotiable a proposal in *McGuire Air Force Base* providing that

[t]he NAF Intermittent employee will not be regularly scheduled to more than 20 hours per workweek, and only used after the scheduling of the RPT [regular part time] employees have reached the maximum scheduled hours. . . .[9]

Under Executive Order 11,491, as amended, a proposal was non-negotiable if its effect was to direct which particular employee would be assigned to a position. For example, in *Office of Dependent Schools* the following proposal was in dispute:

---

6. NAGE Local R12-183 and McClellan A.F.B., Calif., FLRC No. 75A-81 (1976).

7. In a similar but not identical circumstance, AFGE, AFL-CIO, Local 1603 and Navy Exchange, Naval Air Station, Patuxent River, Maryland, Case No. 0-NG-200, 3 FLRA 1 (1980), the FLRA reached the same result by applying the agency's section 7106(a)(2)(A) right to remove employees.

8. American Federation of Government Employees, AFL-CIO, Local 1592 and Army-Air Force Exchange Service, Hill Air Force Base, Utah, FLRC No. 77A-123 (1978).

9. American Federation of Government Employees, Local 1778 and McGuire Air Force Base, N.J., FLRC Nos. 77A-18 and 77A-21 (1978).

When an involuntary reassignment must be made and more than one teacher within the same school is qualified for such assignment, then the teacher with the least amount of service in the DODDS system shall be involuntarily reassigned. Management may make exceptions to this rule under compelling circumstances.[10]

The FLRC held that this proposal infringed management's right to assign employees to particular positions within the agency.

We have consistently indicated that section 12(b)(2) manifests an intent to bar from agreements provisions which infringe upon management official's authority to decide and act concerning the personnel actions specified therein. In our opinion, the union's proposal here significantly infringes upon management's authority, within the meaning of section 12(b)(2), to assign an employee to a position within the agency. That is, the requirement that the agency assign the least senior of those teachers qualified for the position clearly interferes with management's authority to decide which particular individual will be reassigned once a decision has been made to fill a position by reassigning an employee. The proposal thus would deprive the management official involved of the discretion inherent in the reserved authority to make such a decision under section 12(b)(2).[11]

The FLRC, however, held negotiable proposals that established standards or procedures that would be applied in determining which particular employee or employees, from a group of employees, would be selected or designated to perform work. For example, in *INS-1975* the FLRC held negotiable one proposal containing a general provision that any rotation of employees would be fair and equitable and another proposal providing that, for employee development, the employer would rotate employees through the various phases of work that was available and within their job titles.[12] Similarly, in *U.S. Customs Service* the FLRC held negotiable proposals permitting employees to exchange shift, overtime, and placement assignments, provided qualified replacements approved by agency supervisors were ready and willing to accept the assignment and provided that work flow would not be impaired.[13]

Whereas the executive order had reserved to the agency the right to assign employees to positions, the CSRA of 1978 reserved to the agency only the right to assign employees. The deletion of the phrase

---

10. FLRC No. 76A-142 (1978).

11. *Id.* at 16.

12. Immigration and Naturalization Service and AFGE, FLRC No. 74A-13 (1975).

13. NTEU and Department of the Treasury, U.S. Customs Service, Region VII, FLRC No. 76A-28 (1979).

in positions suggested, based on rules of statutory construction, that management would retain only the right to assign employees in general to positions in general, as distinguished from the more specific right to assign a particular employee to a particular position. In *Wright-Patterson Air Force Base,* however, the FLRA rendered a contrary construction.

The right to assign employees in the agency under section 7102(a)(2)(A) of the Statute is more than merely the right to decide to assign an employee to a position. An agency chooses to assign an employee to a position so that the work of that position will be done. Under section 7106(a)(2)(A) of the Statute, the agency retains discretion as to the personnel requirements of the work of the position, *i.e.,* the qualifications and skills needed to do the work, as well as such job-related characteristics as judgment and reliability. Therefore, the right to assign an employee to a position includes the discretion to determine which employee will be assigned. (Clearly, the assignment of an employee to a position is distinguishable from the assignment of an employee to a shift.) A procedure for selecting an employee for assignment solely on the basis of seniority removes that discretion which as indicated above, is an essential part of the decision to assign.[14]

Based on this construction, the FLRA has held nonnegotiable most proposals that provide substitutes for management's right to select which particular employee will fill which particular position. In *Wright-Patterson Air Force Base,* the FLRA held nonnegotiable the following proposals:

IV. *Details to Lower Graded Positions*
Details to lower grade positions will be rotated among qualified and available employees in inverse order of seniority.

V. *Loans*
Selection of employees for loans will be equitably rotated among qualified and available employees with requisite skills in inverse order of seniority.

VI. *Temporary Assignments Outside the Bargaining Unit*
Where conditions are less at the receiving location than is provided for by this contract, the employee's wishes to decline such assignment will be considered. Selection for such assignments will be equitably rotated in accordance with Section (3) of this Article.

VII. *Mobility*
Prior to invoking the employment mobility requirement, the employer will seek volunteers from among employees of the same title, series and grade. If there are no volunteers, and the employer is required to unilaterally transfer

---

14. AFGE and Air Force Logistics Command, Wright-Patterson Air Force Base, Ohio, Case No. 0-NG-40, 2 FLRA 77 (1980) 10.

employees within the unit, the employee with the least amount of seniority shall be selected first. The remaining employees shall be transferred in ascending seniority order.[15]

The authority emphasized that its broad construction of the section 7106(a)(1)(A)'s *assign employees* language was necessary because of management's need to assign employees based on special needs, such as qualifications, skills, judgment, and reliability. This had suggested that, where no special needs existed, proposals could provide the selection procedure that would be utilized to determine which particular employee would perform certain work. This is not the case, however. In *U.S. Mint* the following proposals, among others, were in dispute:

Section 2. General Details
In situations where details of employees to positions outside their branch are expected to be regular or recurring and where no special skills or qualifications are required, the employee selected for the detail will be the senior employee within the branch who has volunteered for the assignment. When asking for volunteers, management will inform employees of the type of work to be performed and the duration of the assignment. If there are no volunteers, the least senior employee within the branch will be selected.

Section 3. Details Involving Special Qualifications
In situations where it is necessary to select an employee with specific qualifications for a detail outside his branch, the employees within the branch will be informed of the type of work to be performed, the length of the detail and the qualifications for the assignment. The senior qualified employee within the branch who has volunteered for the detail will be selected. If there are no volunteers, the least senior qualified employee within the branch will be selected.[16]

The FLRA determined that the proposals were nonnegotiable as violative of management's retained 7106(a)(2)(A) right to assign employees. Apparently it was inconsequential that the proposals satisfied management's need to make assignments based on special qualifications. The authority reasoned that the procedure contained in the proposals "mandates the selection of a particular employee for assignment to a detail solely on the basis of seniority and therefore

---

15. *Id.* The FLRA's broad interpretation of section 7106(a)(2)(A), as applied to proposals IV, V, VI and VII in *Wright-Patterson Air Force Base*, is currently under judicial review before the United States Circuit Court of Appeals for the District of Columbia. American Federation of Government Employees v. FLRA, Civil Case No. 80-1351.

16. AFGE, AFL-CIO, Local 695 and Department of the Treasury, U.S. Mint, Denver, Colorado, Case No. 0-NG-114, 3 FLRA 7 (1980).

removes from the activity any discretion in making such assignments."[17]

The authority has held nonnegotiable other proposals that would substitute a mandatory procedure for management's right to select which particular employee will perform work in which particular position. In *Air Force Contract Management Division* the FLRA held nonnegotiable a proposal directing that, when due to temporary incapacitation an employee was unable to perform his or her regular duties but could perform in other positions, then he or she would be detailed to a position compatible with his or her condition.[18] In *Scott Air Force Base* the FLRA held nonnegotiable the following proposal:

Any personnel downgraded as a result of the reclassification be given mandatory placement rights into a position for which they qualify in order of their standing on the Reduction-In-Force Retention Roster without consideration of Outstanding Performance Rating.[19]

In *Defense Contract Audit Agency* the FLRA held nonnegotiable a proposal that would have prohibited management from rotating employees to different positions or to different work assignments.[20]

A proposal mandating a selection procedure is not always nonnegotiable. It is negotiable if it provides that, before the selection procedure comes into effect, management first has the right to exercise or not exercise the right to select. In *Wright-Patterson Air Force Base*, the negotiability of the following proposal was at issue:

III. Unless the employer decides to use competitive procedures as outlined in Article ＿＿＿ (Promotions), temporary assignment to higher or same grade/ different duty positions shall be offered to qualified and available employees with requisite skills on the basis of seniority within the lowest organizational segment. If senior employees decline and it is necessary to detail an employee, the least senior employee shall be assigned.

The proposal was found to be negotiable because it

would allow the agency the option of utilizing competitive procedures to make the selection. Such competitive procedures reserve the agency's right to select the employee for promotion or reassignment from among those available through any appropriate source. Thus, under *Union Proposal III*, the

---

17. *Id.* at 5.
18. NFFE Local 1624 and Air Force Contract Management Division, Hagerstown, Maryland, Case No. 0-NG-74, 3 FLRA 20 (1980).
19. NFFE Local R7-23 and Department of the Air Force, Scott Air Force Base, Illinois, Case No. 0-NG-174, 3 FLRA 26 (1980).
20. AFGE, AFL-CIO, Local 3529 and Defense Contract Audit Agency, Case No. 0-NG-14, 3 FLRA 46 (1980).

agency retains the option of exercising its discretion to select a particular individual for assignment. Only if the agency chooses not to use competitive procedures must it select the individual on the basis of seniority.

As long as the actual selection remains with management, a negotiable proposal may establish criteria with which the selection must comport. In other words, a negotiable proposal may require management to assign work to employees fairly and without discrimination, but a proposal must not specify which employees will or will not be selected to perform the work. This conclusion may be derived from the decision in *Georgia National Guard* wherein the FLRA applied section 7106(a)(2)(B) to two proposals. Section 7106(a)(2)(B) did not bar negotiation of the following proposal:

When a general cleanup is required, assignment will be made on an equitable basis without regard to rank or grade or sex. Exception will be recognized for physical infirmities which may preclude participation or endanger the health of the Technician.

However, 7106(a)(2)(B) barred the negotiation of a proposal providing that

[t]echnicians . . . will not be utilized for grounds maintenance, or activities which are not job-related . . . technicians will not be directed to assignments outside his/her position duties without his/her consent.[21]

The same reasoning should apply to 7106(a)(2)(A)'s language regarding assignment of employees.

Job Content, Assignment and Distribution of Duties, and Classification

Assignment of duties, job content, and position description and classification are treated in a single section here because the decisions of the Federal Labor Relations Council tended to fuse and blur them together. In so doing, the council used language from the executive order that has been carried over into section 7106 of the CSRA of 1978. First, section 7106(b)(1) of the CSRA of 1978 provides that the agency is not obligated to bargain about the "numbers, types and grades of positions or employees assigned to an organizational unit, work project or tour of duty." The Federal Labor Relations Council consistently interpreted this language as not requiring the employer to bargain over the specific duties that will or may be assigned to a position or employees—i.e., job content, the content of individual jobs.[22] Any requirement that assignment of duties be consistent with the duties outlined in the employee's position description has been held to be nonnegotiable on the ground that it would be determinative of job content. Second, section 7106(a)(2)(A) retains to management the authority to assign employees, and section 7106(a)(2)(B) retains to management the right to assign work. In contrast, Executive Order 11,491, as amended, contained the right to assign employees, but did not contain a reserved management right to assign work. Yet the FLRC applied the executive order as reserving to the agency the right to assign work. This was accomplished by the rendering of the strained construction whereby the staffing patterns language was interpreted as meaning, in effect, assignment of work. Third, the FLRC construed the agency's right to "direct" employees as not requiring an agency to negotiate about the types or amounts of work that will be assigned to employees.

To be negotiable, a proposal relating to job content must aim at precision and completeness of the description of the employee's position, as distinguished from determining what duties may be assigned to the employee occupying the position. In *Navy Regional Finance Center* the union had submitted the following proposal:

It is agreed that each position description shall fully spell out the duties of the employees. When the catchall phrase, "and such other duties as may be assigned" is included in a position description, the employer agrees that it shall not except in unusual circumstances, be used as a basis for assigning duties to an employee which are unrelated to his principal duties.[23]

The FLRC determined that this proposal was negotiable. The proposal did not restrict the assignment of duties to employees or impose conditions determining which duties could be assigned to employees. The intent and effect of the proposal was to clarify and define the agency's position descriptions, and position descriptions do not determine assignment of duties but rather reflect such assignment for pay and classification purposes. The staffing patterns language excludes from the obligation to bargain only those proposals which direct or otherwise cause the agency to assign or not to assign certain duties to individuals or employees. In *IRS, Indianapolis District* the Federal Labor

---

22. International Association of Fire Fighters, Local F-111 and Griffiss Air Force Base, Rome, New York, FLRC No. 71A-30 (1973).

23. American Federation of Government Employees Local 53 and Navy Regional Finance Center, FLRC No. 73A-48 (1974).

Relations Council applied this analysis to hold negotiable the following proposal:

Those employees in the Indianapolis District who entered into the Revenue Representative position and were assigned IRS SPD No. 454N dated June 24, 1973, will retain that position description, together with an appropriate addendum to be drafted and attached thereto (the whole of which will be given a new district number as is required) until such time as they are promoted or transfer to a different position than that presently held or until such time as it no longer accurately reflects the duties being performed.[24]

Although the proposal required accuracy of the employee's position description, the proposal restricted neither assignment of duties to employees or positions nor modification of position descriptions to reflect such assignments. In accord is *Veterans Administration Hospital, Denver* wherein the FLRC held nonnegotiable the following proposal:

Employer agrees that assignment of duties will be consistent and related to the employee's position and to his qualifications. Other duties as assigned means other related duties. This does not change the employer's right to assign duties—consistent with the spirit and intent of this agreement.[25]

The first sentence of the proposal made the assignment of duties contingent on whether they are consistent with and related to the employee's position and qualifications. Thus it would have interfered with management's determination of job content. Rather than defining and clarifying the terms of the position description, the proposal established criteria determining duty assignment, and this would have constricted the agency's actual assignment of duties. The FLRC used the same rationale that was used in *Office of Dependent Schools* to hold nonnegotiable the following proposal:

Teachers shall not be assigned outside the scope of the North Central Association qualification standards unless very unusual circumstances exist justifying such assignment. In the latter case, such assignment shall be for no longer than required for such unusual circumstances.[26]

In *VA Atlanta Regional Office* the rationale was again employed to hold nonnegotiable the last sentence of the following proposal:

24. National Treasury Employees Union, Chapter 49 and Internal Revenue Service, Indianapolis District, FLRC No. 78A-100 (1978).

25. American Federation of Government Employees and Veterans Administration Hospital, Denver, Colorado, FLRC No. 74A-67 (1975). This case, as do many others, cites *Griffiss* as controlling authority, *supra* note 22.

26. FLRC No. 76A-142 (1978).

Each employee is entitled to a copy of his/her current position description which shall be reviewed annually. This position description must be accurate and should include all major duties that occur on a regular and recurring basis. Major duties are those of such weight that their inclusion is necessary for the proper classification of the position. The Employer will not routinely and chronically require the employee to perform substantial duties outside his/her regular field of work or which might result in injury to the employee or fellow employees due to lack of knowledge of task.[27]

This same result should accrue under the CSRA of 1978. Although the staffing patterns language has been carried over into section 7106(b)(1), this language had to be sorely strained to achieve the result. But under the CSRA of 1978, the result flows easily from the agency's reserved section 7106(a)(2)(B) right to assign work. Consistent with this reasoning, in *Georgia National Guard* the Federal Labor Relations Authority applied section 7106(a)(2)(B)'s assignment of work language to hold nonnegotiable a proposal providing that "technicians . . . will not be utilized for . . . activities which are not job related. . . . Technicians will not be directed to assignments outside his/her position duties without his/her consent."[28]

To be negotiable, a proposal must not prohibit assignment of duties not contained in the employee's position description. The *Wright-Patterson Air Force Base* petition contained a bargaining proposal providing that the agency's actual assignment of duties to employees would be within the "scope of the classification assigned" to the unit employees as defined in "appropriate classification standards."[29] The FLRC determined this proposal to be nonnegotiable because, by making the agency's authority to assign duties contingent on the content of each employee's respective position description, the proposal would have had the effect of constricting the agency's right to assign duties. To escape a declaration of nonnegotiability, a proposal must not proscribe or condition the assignment of specific duties to an employee or to a position.[30]

---

27. National Federation of Federal Employees, Local 122 and Veterans Administration, Atlanta Regional Office, Atlanta, Georgia, FLRC No. 77A-94 (1978).

28. Association of Civilian Technicians and State of Georgia National Guard, Case No. 0-NG-35, 2 FLRA 75 (1980).

29. FLRC No. 74A-2 (1974).

30. *See also* Local Lodge 830, International Association of Machinists and Aerospace Workers and Louisville Naval Ordinance Station, Department of the Navy, FLRC No. 73A-21 (1974); AFGE (National Border Patrol Council and National Council of Immigration and Naturalization Service Locals) and Immigration and Naturalization Service, FLRC No. 73A-25 (1974).

A negotiable proposal may define phrases and terms contained in position descriptions. In *Wright-Patterson Air Force Base* the FLRC was faced with a union proposal that defined the position description phrase "such other duties as may be assigned" as meaning "tasks which are normally related to the position and are of incidental nature."[31] The FLRC, reasoning that none of the management's rights serve to render a proposal nonnegotiable merely because it clarifies and defines general terms in a job description, determined the proposal to be negotiable. The FLRC's analysis of the proposal noted particularly that it restricted neither the agency's right to prescribe specifically in the job description any duties it wished to assign an employee or position nor the agency's right to change the job description without limitations. Consistent with this decision is the decision in *Fort Dix* wherein the authority held negotiable a proposal providing that when the phrase "other related duties as assigned" appeared in a position description, the phrase "will not be used to regularly assign work to an employee which is not reasonably related to his basic job description."[32] The authority's rationale was that the intended effect of the proposal was to ensure accuracy of position descriptions, that the proposal did not preclude the agency from assigning duties to an employee, but that if the agency regularly assigned to an employee duties unrelated to those spelled out in his or her position description, then the position description would have to be changed.

Proposals pertaining to assignment of duties may be declared nonnegotiable even though they do not address the position description. In *Veterans Administration Hospital, Montgomery* the FLRC found that the employer was not obligated to bargain about a union proposal directing management, upon occurrence of a stated set of conditions, to perform certain acts before assigning particular duties to unit employees.[33] According to the FLRC's viewpoint, such a proposal would restrict management's authority to determine how frequently unit employees would perform certain duties; thus the proposal was

---

31. FLRC No. 74A-2 (1974).

32. AFGE Local 1999 and Army-Air Force Exchange Service, Dix-McGuire Exchange, Fort Dix, New Jersey, Case No. 0-NG-20, 2 FLRA 16 (1979). The agency has appealed this decision to the Circuit Court of Appeals for the District of Columbia. Army Air Force Exchange Service, Dix-McGuire Exchange, Fort Dix, New Jersey v. FLRA, Case No. 80-1119.

33. American Federation of Government Employees Local 997 and Veterans Administration Hospital, Montgomery, Alabama, FLRC No. 73A-22 (1974).

declared to be an exception to the obligation to negotiate because it imposed conditions limiting management's authority to establish staffing patterns for its organization and for its accomplishment of work. In *Cherry Point* the FLRC again applied the staffing patterns exception to declare nonnegotiable the following proposal:

No journeyman or fourth year apprentice employee in the Unit shall be required to perform janitorial type duties, such as cleaning heads and urinals. However, journeymen and fourth year apprentices are responsible for the cleanliness of their immediate work area and any area the individual employee is responsible for being unclean. This responsibility includes the routine daily cleaning of machinery, tools, equipment, and floors. However, such cleaning will not include tasks requiring the use of solvents, paints or other chemical cleaning agents.[34]

The proposal would have been determinative of the work the employees would perform, i.e., job content. Similarly, in *Air Force Contract Management Division,* the FLRA applied section 7106(a)(2)(B)'s assignment of work language to hold nonnegotiable a proposal providing that duties would be tailored to the physical limitations of an employee who was incapacitated to perform regular duties but who was able to remain in a duty status. The proposal was determinative of what work would and would not not be assigned to employees.[35]

In *Philadelphia Naval Shipyard* the following two-section proposal was before the authority:

Section 1—The Employer and the Union agree that any given training session or drill will not exceed one (1) hour duration. It is further agreed that only one (1) training session or drill, of one (1) hour duration or less, will be assigned to any given workday. Training sessions or drills must be concluded by 1500 hours on weekdays. No training sessions will be held on Saturdays, Sundays or holidays.

Section 2—The Employer and the Union agree that no outdoor training sessions or drills will be held on days when the outside temperature exceeds 80 degrees fahrenheit, or drops below 45 degrees fahrenheit. It is further agreed that high humidity, high winds and precipitation shall be considered reason for cancellation of outdoor training sessions or drills. The Employer and the Union further concur that all on-duty personnel will participate in

---

34. International Association of Machinists and Aerospace Workers, Local Lodge 1859 and Marine Corps Air Station and Naval Air Rework Facility, Cherry Point, N.C., FLRC No. 77A-28 (1978).

35. 3 FLRA 20 (1980).

training sessions or drills with the exception of men on overtime status, completing ship inspection or extinguisher detail, whenever possible.[36]

The authority observed that assignment of training constitutes assignment of work within the meaning of section 7106(a)(2)(B) and then held both proposals nonnegotiable. Section 1 was held nonnegotiable to the extent that it imposed absolute limits on when training could be conducted during a fire fighter's workweek, which includes Saturdays, Sundays, and holidays.

Section 1 of the union's proposal, however, would place absolute limits on the ability of the agency to assign such training at all after the specified hours or on certain days of a firefighter's workweek. To that extent the proposal violates management's right to assign work.[37]

Section 2 was held nonnegotiable on the ground that, while a proposal may require management to entertain specified health and safety considerations in conducting work, a proposal may not impose arbitrary absolute limits, unrelated to health and safety, governing when the work will be conducted. In the same case the FLRA held nonnegotiable another proposal that, among other things, limited the particular duties management could assign on Saturdays, Sundays, and holidays. The authority stated that "there is nothing in the Federal Service Labor-Management Relations Statute or its legislative history which indicates that the right to assign work is limited to normal duty days."[38]

In contrast to the holdings in *Philadelphia Naval Shipyard*, in *Mare Island Station* the authority held negotiable a proposal that did not impose mandatory limits on when which work would be assigned but rather provided that management would endeavor to assign work in accordance with certain guidelines.

In view of seasonal changes in weather conditions, management will endeavor to schedule training so wintertime training will consist of those items that require class room sessions, i.e., hydraulics, first aid, rope and forcible entry practices, fire extinguisher practices, salvage, and pre-fire planning, etc. Sum-

---

36. International Association of Fire Fighters Local F-61 and Philadelphia Naval Shipyard, Case No. 0-NG-6, 3 FLRA 66 (1980). *See* Proposal I in International Association of Fire Fighters, Local F-48, AFL-CIO and Naval Support Activity, Mare Island Station, California, Case No. 0-NG-139, 3 FLRA 76 (1980).

37. 3 FLRA 66 (1980) 2.

38. *Id.* at 4.

mertime training requiring outdoor performance of skills such as hose lays, ladder practices, pump operation training, driver training, etc.[39]

The FLRC was so intent upon reserving to the agency the right to assign work that the council applied inconsistent reasoning. In *IRS, Indianapolis District* the negotiability of the first sentence of the following proposal was disputed:

Management agrees that they will use IRM 5200 which relates to Revenue Representatives' field procedures as a guideline as long as it is in effect and that Revenue Representatives on field duty will be assigned only manageable inventory work loads. Management further agrees to give proper consideration and make proper allowances when incompleted case assignments are the result of an interruption of a tour of duty in the field or an oppressive case inventory or for other reasons beyond the direct control of the affected employees.[40]

The parties had agreed to the language at the bargaining table, but upon reviewing the local agreement the agency head had disapproved the first sentence. Since the disputed portion had been agreed to locally and only been declared nonnegotiable upon the agency head's review, the Federal Labor Relations Council was unable to rely upon the staffing patterns exception, which is permissive bargaining matter, to declare the proposal nonnegotiable. Thereupon the council apparently scanned the illegal bargaining matter of section 12(b) of the executive order, searching for a reason to declare the language nonnegotiable. The council initially examined the meaning of section 12(b)(2) but then declared the disputed language nonnegotiable based on the agency's section 12(b)(1) right to direct employees. In a decision using uncertain logic, the council declared that an agency has the right to "accomplish" its mission by ordering employees to perform workloads so heavy that the employees are unable to perform all the work needed to accomplish the agency's mission.[41] Not only was this inherently contradictory, but the unreasonably expansive construction of the agency's right to "direct" employees muddied the water by infringing upon a management rights area that the council had previously held to be within only the staffing patterns language of section

---

39. International Association of Fire Fighters Local F-48, AFL-CIO and Naval Support Activity, Mare Island Station, California, Case No. 0-NG-139, 3 FLRA 76 (1980).
40. FLRC No. 78A-100 (1978).
41. *Id.*

11(b) of the order. Under section 7106(a)(2)(B) of the CSRA, however, the FLRA should be able to achieve this same result but with greater intellectual honesty.

Contrasting with the FLRC's determination in *IRS, Indianapolis District* are several other negotiability determinations. First, another proposal in *IRS, Indianapolis District* provided that

> when a Revenue Representative's field duty tour is interrupted for any significant period of time, their unresolves or incompleted cases may be 1) assigned to a Revenue Officer for further action; 2) assigned to another Revenue Representative in the field; or 3) returned to the Office for further processing or reassignment.

The proposal was declared negotiable. The council's stated reason for holding the proposal negotiable was that it did not require the agency to relieve an employee of assigned cases. The proposal "presents alternatives that management 'may,' but is not required to, follow."[42] Second, in *Charleston Naval Shipyard* the union had submitted two proposals, one that obligated management, for training purposes only, to assign journeyman-level work to apprentice employees, and another proposal that precluded management from assigning apprentice employees during their first year of apprenticeship to training off-station or otherwise away from the primary work location. The FLRC held that the executive order's section 11(b) staffing patterns language excepted both proposals from the obligation to negotiate. The FLRC expressed the view that training constitutes a part of job content.[43]

Third, in *Wright-Patterson Air Force Base* the union had proposed that

> [t]he employer will strive to utilize, under current requirements and circumstances, the present skills of each member of the workforce. . . . Procedures for skills utilization will include the redesigning of jobs where feasible.[44]

Job redesign entails, among other things, a determination of the work that will be assigned to the position or employee.[45] The Federal Labor

---

42. *Id.* at 6. The FLRC observed that "the impact of the quantity of work assigned on the performance evaluation of individual employees is, of course, negotiable." *See* FLRC No. 78A-100 (1978) note 6.

43. Federal Employees Metal Trades Council of Charleston and Charleston Naval Shipyard, Charleston, South Carolina, FLRC No. 72A-46 (1973).

44. 2 FLRA 77 (1980).

45. Edward E. Lawler III, *Motivation in Work Organizations* (Monterey, Calif.: Brooks/Cole Publishing Co., 1973), p. 148–70.

Relations Authority reasoned that if a proposal specified the particular manner in which a job was to be redesigned, it would be nonnegotiable as in conflict with management's 7106(a)(2)(B) right to assign work. But the proposal in question provided that the employer and not the union would redesign the job; in other words, the proposal did not require the agency to assign or refrain from assigning any particular work. Accordingly, the authority held the proposal negotiable on the ground that it merely provided that ". . . job redesign would be used as one of the procedures for best utilizing the present skills of unit employees, where this would be feasible."[46]

Not all duties may be categorized as neutral. For a multitude of reasons, some may be categorized as desirable, while still others may be categorized as unpleasant or difficult.[47] For this reason, employees have a direct job-related interest in the distribution of the duties and in the rotation of work assignments to such duties. This interest is primarily in ensuring fair and equitable distribution of duties and rotation of employee work assignments to the various duties. In *INS-1975*, the FLRC held negotiable one proposal providing that rotation of employees must be fair and equitable and another proposal providing that, for employee development, the employer would rotate employees through the various phases of work that is within their job title.[48] It is questionable whether the latter holding is good law under the CSRA of 1978. In *U.S. Mint* the authority held nonnegotiable two proposals requiring weekly rotation of work and position assignments, explaining that

even if the union intended only that employees be rotated to the various duties within their own position description, the specific language of the proposal at issue would require all employees to be rotated each week regardless whether any work were available which required the performance of such duties or whether the work previously assigned had been completed. In other words, management would be restricted in making new assignments, or in modifying, terminating, or continuing existing ones as deemed necessary or desirable. Accordingly, the specific proposal at issue herein is outside the duty to bargain under the Statute.[49]

---

46. 2 FLRA 77 (1980) 18.

47. For example, some duties may be desirable because they provide job enrichment or enhance promotability; duties may be undesirable because they detract from promotability, are overly difficult, or are unpleasant and tedious.

48. AFGE and Immigration and Naturalization Service, FLRC No. 74A-113 (1975).

49. 3 FLRA 7 (1980) 3.

In *McClellan Air Force Base* the union had submitted a proposal directing that "all work assignments will be equitably distributed among personnel within the same job classification."[50] The FLRC interpreted this proposal as requiring management to distribute equitably among only employees in the same job classification all work assignments, and from this point the council concluded that the proposal would restrict the employer from assigning to employees work not within the generic job classification of the positions occupied by the employees. On this basis, the proposal was declared nonnegotiable as violative of the agency's right to assign employees to positions within the agency. Ostensibly the proposal would have been declared negotiable had it read that, when the employer decides to assign work to an identifiable group of employees, the work will be equitably distributed among them to the greatest extent practicable. This would be consistent with the authority's decision in *Georgia National Guard,* which held negotiable a proposal requiring equitable distribution of cleanup duties.[51]

Employees have a vested financial interest in the grade of the position they occupy, and a position's grade level is a function of the grade of the assigned duties. Even where the grade level of the overall assigned duties does result in a change in grade of the employee's position, the portion of the duties graded higher or lower than the grade occupied by the employee results in a positive or negative effect on the employee's performance evaluation. The performance of lower graded work certainly is not promotion-building experience, while the performance of higher graded work most certainly is promotion-building experience. For these reasons employees have a vested interest in the grade level of assigned duties. Under the CSRA of 1978, the duty to bargain does not include matters "relating to the classification of any positions,"[52] and positions are to be classified by grade in accordance with criteria contained in governmentwide (nonnegotiable) regulations issued by the Office of Personnel Management.[53] Hence, position and duty classification will be nonnegotiable, and this result is consistent with the result that the Federal Labor Relations Council had achieved through interpretation and application of the staffing

50. NAGE Local R12-183 and McClellan Air Force Base, California, FLRC No. 75A-81 (1976).
51. 2 FLRA 75 (1980).
52. 5 U.S.C. §7103(a)(14)(B).
53. 5 U.S.C., ch. 54.

patterns language of Executive Order 11,491, as amended.[54] There remains, however, the matter of whether the grade level assigned to particular duties is negotiable as to substance and impact and implementation. In *Internal Revenue Service,* the union had proposed that "an employee who disagrees with the grade level assigned to a case may file a grievance pursuant to . . . [the negotiated grievance procedure]. . . ."[55]

The grade level of a case is supposed to be a function of the difficulty the employee encounters in processing the case. The agency did not dispute the fact that the subject matter of the proposal came within the basic obligation to negotiate, but rather, the agency contended that sections 11(b) and 12(b) of Executive Order 11,491, as amended, excepted the proposal from the obligation to negotiate. Nevertheless, the Federal Labor Relations Council declared that the proposal did not embody anything affecting personnel policies and practices and matters affecting working conditions of bargaining unit employees and ergo was outside the basic obligation to negotiate. The FLRC attempted to support its conclusion by writing that, since the supervisor made the initial determination of the grade level of a case before giving it to the unit employee, the case's grade level had no effect upon the unit employee. To demonstrate the questionable logic of the council's reasoning, an analogy may be offered: applying the council's reasoning, an employee could not grieve his or her performance evaluation because the employee's supervisor completes the evaluation before the employee receives it. Yet, this is unreasonable, and the law is clearly to the contrary.

Required Productivity, Production Criteria and Goals, and Measurement Thereof

The CSRA of 1978 has created substantial changes regarding performance expectations, productivity requirements, and measures of performance. Section 4302(a) of Title 5, U.S.C., requires each agency to develop one or more performance appraisal systems.[56] Each ap-

---

54. In *Office of Dependent Schools,* the FLRC, citing the staffing patterns language of the executive order, held nonnegotiable a proposal that would have obligated the agency to negotiate classification standards. FLRC No. 77A-130 (1978).

55. National Treasury Employees Union and Internal Revenue Service, FLRC No. 76A-132 (1977). *See also* FLRC No. 76A-157 (1977).

56. Title 5, U.S.C., section 4302(a) provides: "Each agency shall develop one or more performance appraisal systems which—(1) provide for periodic appraisals of job performance of employees; (2) encourage employee participation in establishing performance standards. . . ."

praisal system must provide performance standards and critical elements for each position.[57] The significance of performance appraisal systems is multiple. They may be used to evaluate employee performance during the appraisal period.[58] They may be used as bases for rewarding employee performance with monetary or other types of awards.[59] Failure to perform acceptably in a single critical element means ipso facto that an employee's performance is unacceptable,[60] and such an employee may be reassigned, demoted, or discharged.[61]

Critical elements and performance standards are not defined in Title II of the CSRA of 1978; however, their relationship may be discerned from the statute. Section 4301(3) of Title 5, U.S.C., clearly implies that performance standards are not elements, but rather, are categories within elements.[62] The OPM regulations address critical elements in terms of divisions among the employee's duties. The OPM regulations define critical element as

a component of an employee's job that is of sufficient importance that performance below the minimum standard established by management requires remedial action and denial of a within-grade increase, and may be the basis for removing or reducing the grade level of that employee. Such action may be taken without regard to performance on other components of the job.[63]

As used in section 4302(b)(1) of Title 5, U.S.C., a performance standard is supposed to permit accurate evaluation of job performance on the basis of objective criteria. To some extent this suggests specific measures of performance. Consistent with this approach, the OPM regulations define a performance standard as

the expressed measure of the level of achievement established by management

---

57. Title 5, U.S.C., section 4302(b) provides that "under regulations which the Office of Personnel Management shall prescribe, each performance appraisal system shall provide for—(1) establishing performance standards which will, to the maximum extent feasible, permit the accurate evaluation of job performance on the basis of objective criteria (which may include the extent of courtesy demonstrated to the public) related to the job in question for each employee or position under the system; (2) as soon as practicable, but not later than October 1, 1981, with respect to the initial appraisal periods, and thereafter at the beginning of each following appraisal period, communicating to each employee the performance standards and the critical elements of the employee's position. . . ."

58. 5 U.S.C. § 4302(b)(3).

59. 5 U.S.C. § 4302(b)(4).

60. 5 U.S.C. § 4301(3).

61. 5 U.S.C. § 4302(b)(6).

62. Title 5, U.S.C., section 4301(3) provides that " 'unacceptable performance' means performance of an employee which fails to meet established performance standards in one or more critical elements of such employee's position."

63. 5 C.F.R. § 430.202(e).

for duties and responsibilities of a position or group of positions. Performance standards may include, but are not limited to, elements such as quantity, quality, and timeliness.[64]

In overview, the OPM has issued regulations governing the implementation of the CSRA-mandated performance appraisal system.[65] The statutes and regulations combine to create a framework within which an employee's duties may be divided into various elements of which some are critical. Within each critical element are specific measures. These specific measures are called performance standards. The level of an employee's performance within any critical element is derived by comparing and contrasting the employee's actual performance against the element's performance standards.

Significantly, the CSRA framework makes no provision for elements that are merely desirable, as distinguished from ones that are critical.[66] It is thus conceivable that a performance appraisal system might include one set of elements that are critical and a second set

---

64. 5 C.F.R. § 430.202(d).

65. Title 5, C.F.R., section 430.102 provides, in part, that "(a) As required by 5 U.S.C. 4302(a), each agency shall establish one or more appraisal systems for appraising the work performance of employees during an appraisal period; (b) 5 U.S.C. 4302(a) and (b) require that each appraisal system shall provide for establishing performance standards based on the requirements of employee's positions, communicating the standards of performance and the critical elements of the position at the beginning of each appraisal period. An agency shall encourage participation of employees in establishing performance standards; (c) Performance standards and critical elements must be consistent with the duties and responsibilities contained in employees' position descriptions; (d) An appraisal system shall not permit any preestablished distributions of expected levels of performance (such as requirement to rate on a bell curve) that interfere with appraisal of actual performance against standards; (e) 5 U.S.C. 4302 requires that each appraisal system shall provide for periodic appraisals of performance. Employees shall generally be appraised on at least an annual basis. Agencies may provide for longer appraisal periods when duties and responsibilities of a position or the tour of duty of a position so warrant; (f) Critical elements and performance standards shall be in writing; (g) Periodic appraisals shall be in writing and shall be provided to the employee; (h) A system shall provide for obtaining information about performance of employees detailed or temporarily assigned to different positions when assignments are of sufficient duration to provide information about performance, and agencies shall give appropriate consideration to this information in making personnel decisions."

66. For example, an employee who wraps packages on a production line may also be required to submit periodic written reports that are sporadically used to cross-check the accuracy of the electric eye that counts the number of packages the employee has wrapped within a given time frame. The wrapping of packages might be a critical element, and the accuracy and punctuality of the written reports might be only a desirable element.

of elements that are desirable but not critical.[67] Since an employee may be discharged or demoted for unacceptable performance on one performance standard of a single critical element, other elements that are only desirable would not be relevant to discharges and demotions based on unacceptable performance. Desirable elements, however, might well be relevant and material to other personnel actions, such as promotion actions, performance awards, etc.

The above analysis of statute and regulation is a starting point for examining the negotiability of proposals regarding performance standards and critical elements. Proposals may not be inconsistent with the statutory or regulatory requirements. Proposals may not prohibit the establishment of performance standards or critical elements because these would conflict with the statutory language. For the same reason, a negotiable proposal may not provide that performance must be unacceptable in more than one element before an employee may be demoted or discharged. For example, a proposal could not provide that outstanding performance on nine critical elements would offset unacceptable performance on one element. But there should be no negotiability problem with proposals providing that performance standards and critical elements will be defined in terms of objective, job-related criteria or with proposals providing that standards and elements will be based on the requirements of each respective position, will be consistent with the duties contained in each respective position description, will be in writing, and will be communicated to each respective employee. Such proposals would essentially mirror the language contained in the regulations.

The extent to which performance standards and critical elements are negotiable is necessarily related to management's retained rights under section 7106 of Title 5, U.S.C. Are the actual standards and elements negotiable or are only their impact and implementation negotiable? Nothing in section 7106(a)(1) directly proscribes negotiations over standards or elements. At most, the decision as to what will and will not be standards and elements might be remotely determinative of the extent to which the agency's mission is accomplished, but the decision would not be determinative of what is and is not the agency's mission. Nothing in sections 7106(a)(2)(B) or (C) directly proscribes negotiations over the actual performance standards

---

67. Nothing in the CSRA prohibits the creation and use of elements that are merely desirable.

and critical elements. Nor does anything in section 7106(b)(1) directly proscribe negotiations over the actual standards and elements.

Section 7106(a)(2)(A) contains language that does not directly proscribe negotiations over the actual standards or elements but which may be not unreasonably construed as indirectly prohibiting negotiations. Section 7106(a)(2)(A) retains with the agency the right to remove, demote, or reassign an employee. It is not unreasonable to conclude that removal or demotion for unacceptable performance constitutes discipline within the meaning of section 7106(a)(2)(A). An employee being demoted or discharged for unacceptable performance must have failed to have satisfied one or more critical elements. If a particular performance deficiency is not part of a critical element, then the employee may not be demoted or discharged for that performance deficiency. If a particular performance deficiency within a critical element is at a level above the performance standard for the unacceptable level, the employee may not be discharged or demoted for unacceptable performance. Therefore, what is and is not a critical element and the measure of the performance standard will be determinative of whether an agency may demote or discharge an employee for unacceptable performance. If the conclusion is reached that the actual performance standards or critical elements are nonnegotiable, then under sections 7106(b)(2) and (3), impact and implementation should be negotiable.

Consistent with the above conclusions, albeit for different reasons, the authority has held that performance standards and critical elements are both nonnegotiable but that their impact and implementation are negotiable. In *Bureau of the Public Debt* the union had submitted two proposals.[68] The first proposed the following:

Accounts Maintenance Clerks, GS-502-3/5, must maintain the following minimum rates:

A. To retain his/her position incumbent must process 9.0 batches per hour.

In effect, the proposal assumed that processing batches would be a critical element and stipulated that nine batches an hour would be the quantitative performance standard.[69] If the employee processed nine batches per hour, he or she could not be demoted or discharged

---

68. National Treasury Employees Union and Department of the Treasury, Bureau of the Public Debt, Case No. 0-NG-56, 3 FLRA 119 (1980).

69. The authority offered definitions of performance standards and critical elements that are helpful: ". . . performance standards establish the minimum level of job performance required of an employee with regard to the duties and responsibilities

based on unacceptable quantitative performance. In reaching the decision that the proposal was nonnegotiable, the authority voiced several policy considerations. Performance standards and critical elements were created to promote governmental effectiveness and efficiency by making it easier for agencies to fire employees for unacceptable performance, and the authority was not oblivious to this congressional intent.

[T]he legislative history of the CSRA shows Congressional concern with promoting government effectiveness and efficiency, with the development of employee performance standards and critical elements to achieve this end. . . .[70]

In conjunction, the authority expressed concern that agencies should be able to assign work in a fashion that management deems necessary to accomplish its mission.

In assessing the work which must be done to accomplish its mission, the agency makes determinations based upon its resources as to the aggregate level of output required to meet the need for its services. An integral part of accomplishing this mission is assigning work and establishing priorities. These decisons, when expressed in terms of an individual's job, translate into performance standards, that is, the quality and amount of work needed from each employee in order to achieve the agency's mission and function.[71]

As a legal basis for its decision, the authority looked to and rendered expansive interpretations of the agency's reserved 7106(a)(2)(A) right to direct employees and 7106(a)(2)(B) right to assign work.[72] It is somewhat difficult to identify and articulate the precise considerations of each of the analytical steps underlying the decision in *Bureau of the Public Debt*. Obviously, the FLRA's major premise was that section 7106(a)(2) reserved to the agency the right to direct employees and to

---

of the employee's job. Critical elements are those components of the job which are of sufficient importance that failure to achieve the level of performance established in the performance standard requires remedial action." 3 FLRA 119 (1980) 6.

70. 3 FLRA 119 (1980) 8.

71. *Id.*

72. The authority defined the agency's right to direct employees as entailing the right "to supervise and guide them in the performance of their duties on the job." It defined the agency's right to assign work as entailing (1) the right to determine the particular duties to be assigned, (2) the right to determine which particular employee will be assigned which particular work, (3) the right to assign duties continuously or for a specific period of time, (4) the right to determine when work will or will not be assigned, and (5) the right to determine when assigned work will be performed. The actual decision in *Bureau of the Public Debt* served to expand these definitions to include the right to establish and identify critical elements and performance standards. 3 FLRA 119 (1980) 7–8.

assign work. It is the second or minor premise that is elusive.[73] Some language in the decision suggests that the authority possibly thought that assigned quantitative and qualitative levels of work would have to be the same as the levels prescribed in the performance standard or critical element.[74] It is unlikely, however, that the authority actually entertained such an assumption.[75] The authority reported no foundation supporting a conclusion that, when an agency assigns work or directs employees and establishes qualitative, quantitative, and timeliness targets, they must be identical to the performance standards or to the critical elements.[76] Whatever may have been the premise underlying its decision in *Bureau of the Public Debt,* the authority reached the conclusion that both performance standards and critical elements are nonnegotiable.

[S]ubsection A of the Union's proposal is not within the duty to bargain because it is within the framework of the right of management to direct

---

73. Performance standards and critical elements may be immediately related to matters such as evaluation of performance, promotion, demotion, discharge, and issuance of awards. But performance standards and critical elements are not, absent the addition of a nexus, immediately related to directing employees and assigning work. The language of the FLRA's decision makes it difficult if not impossible to ascertain what, if anything, constituted the nexus on which the FLRA relied. A reasonable suspicion would be that the authority deemed that the rights to assign work and direct employees become meaningful only when management also enjoys the right to identify critical elements and performance standards. Several agencies urged this position in their briefs.

74. The FLRA wrote, "While that [performance] standard could be significant in terms of evaluating the performance of individual employees, it also would establish a level of output which is required in terms of the agency's directing employees and assigning work." The FLRA also wrote that "negotiation of critical elements and performance standards would require an agency to bargain the quantity, quality and timeliness standards, which it must establish in making work assignments and in directing work employees . . . the negotiation of the number of batches an employee is required to process under the proposal would restrict the Agency's decision in establishing priorities for the performance of work." 3 FLRA 119 (1980) 8, 10.

75. For example, a critical element might be the assembly of widgets, and the performance standard nine widgets per hour. Nothing would prevent an agency from assigning work at a rate of ten or even fifteen widgets per hour. Indeed, employee performance at levels that exceed the standard is supposed to be a possible reason for rewarding the employee pursuant to Title 5, U.S.C., section 4302(b)(4). In *Bureau of the Public Debt,* the union stipulated that under its proposal management would be completely free to assign work at any rate exceeding the standard of nine batches per hour.

76. It is entirely possible, of course, that the members of the FLRA entertained the unarticulated opinion that employee performance would gravitate toward the lowest acceptable level. A necessary corollary to such an opinion would be that the federal government's incentive system cannot operate to motivate employees to perform at levels exceeding the lowest acceptable level.

employees and to assign work under section 7106(a), and is not a procedure or an appropriate arrangement within the meaning of section 7106(b)(2) and (3) of the Statute.[77]

In *Bureau of the Public Debt,* the authority went to great lengths to explain what matters within the performance appraisal system are negotiable. First, the FLRA explained that, except for performance standards and critical elements, everything about a performance appraisal system is negotiable as long as a proposal does not violate law or regulation.

[P]erformance appraisal systems, apart from the identification of critical elements and the establishment of performance standards, are within the duty to bargain, to the extent they are consistent with law and regulation. To the extent that an agency has discretion with respect to a given matter related to such systems the agency must upon request negotiate with an exclusive representative over that matter.[78]

If the authority in fact follows this dictum, it may logically lead to bargaining on a wide range of topics. For example, the union's first proposal in *Bureau of the Public Debt* addressed only a performance standard used, under section 4302(b) of Title 5, U.S.C., to remove or demote an employee for unacceptable performance. Since the authority held that all other aspects of performance appraisals are negotiable as long as consistent with controlling law, the FLRA's language may be read as implying that, except for critical elements used in determining whether an employee's performance is acceptable, negotiable proposals may specify other elements that will be used in other types of actions based on the appraisal system (e.g., promotion evaluations). The authority's language may also be read as implying that, except for performance standards used in determining whether an employee's performance is acceptable, negotiable proposals may specify other standards such as the ones that will be the basis for granting incentive awards, quality step increases, within-grade increases, etc.

The FLRA's analysis of the second proposal in *Bureau of the Public Debt* reinforces these conclusions. The proposal provided that, to receive a within-grade increase, an accounts maintenance clerk had to process nine batches an hour; this was the same hourly rate that, under the union's proposal, qualified the employee's performance as

---

77. 3 FLRA 119 (1980) 13.
78. *Id.* at 10.

being at an acceptable level. In analyzing the negotiability of the proposal, the authority noticeably did not rely upon the fact that the proposal identified a standard of performance that would serve as the basis for a personnel action. Rather, the authority's analysis focused upon an OPM regulation requiring that the standard of performance qualifying an employee for a within-grade increase must exceed the level qualifying an employee to be retained in his or her position or job.[79] Based on this governmentwide regulation, the authority declared the proposal nonnegotiable. The fact that the proposal was not held nonnegotiable on the ground that it identified a standard, when combined with the dictum that everything is negotiable except the critical elements and performance standard used to determine unacceptable performance, suggests that proposals may identify standards to be used for other purposes.

The second area in *Bureau of the Public Debt* that the authority identified as negotiable stems from a statutory requirement. Section 4302(a)(2) of Title 5, U.S.C., provides that employees may participate in the establishment of performance standards. The FLRA advised that the fashion and extent of employee participation is negotiable:

[T]he manner in which a particular agency provides for such employee participation is within the agency's discretion and, therefore, within the duty to bargain to the extent that it would not prevent the agency from establishing performance standards and critical elements pursuant to its statutory rights to direct employees and assign work.[80]

Third, in the same case, the authority observed that sections 7106(b)(2) and (3) of Title 5, U.S.C., serve to

authorize an exclusive representative to negotiate on such matters except to the extent that the establishment of procedures or appropriate arrangements through negotiations would prevent the agency from acting at all.[81]

The authority counseled that the right to engage in impact and implementation bargaining entitles union and management to

negotiate with regard to the process by which critical elements and performance standards are communicated to employees, periodic appraisals at least on an annual basis, the manner in which the performance of employees on detail will be appraised, the manner in which an employee's disagreement

---

79. 5 C.F.R. §531.407.
80. 3 FLRA 119 (1980) 10.
81. *Id.* at 11.

with his or her performance appraisal will be reviewed, and the process by which proposed performance standards will be reviewed within the agency.[82]

With specific reference to performance standards and critical elements, negotiable proposals may provide specific procedures to which management will adhere in the identification of critical elements and in the establishment of performance standards. According to the authority such procedures or criteria are exemplified by section 4302(b)(1) of Title 5, U.S.C., which "requires that performance standards be objective and job related."[83] It appears, however, that while the parties may negotiate such criteria, the question of whether the standards and elements comport with the criteria possibly may not be grievable or arbitrable at the time the standards and elements are enunciated. They possibly may not become grievable or arbitrable until applied against an employee.

[N]othing in this decision would preclude an exclusive representative from negotiating criteria for the application of performance standards which management has established. As the Authority determined with respect to a proposal requiring that performance standards be "fair and equitable" in *American Federation of Government Employees, AFL-CIO, Local 32 and Office of Personnel Management, Washington, D. C.,* 3 FLRA No. 120 (1980), decided this date, such a criterion would not interfere with the agency's discretion as to the identification of critical elements and the establishment of the content of a particular performance standard. This criterion would merely establish a general requirement by which the application of critical elements and performance standards established by management could subsequently be evaluated when they are challenged in a grievance filed pursuant to section 7121(e) of the Statute. This type of review would not preclude the Agency from initially determining the content of the standard, nor would it result in substitution of an arbitrator's judgment for that of the agency and setting a new standard. It would simply determine if the standard established by management as applied to the grievant complied with the requirements of the parties' agreement.[84]

The proposal from *Office of Personnel Management* cited in this passage provided that

[a]ll performance standards will be fair and equitable and consistent with the classification standards for the job. An employee who believes a standard

---

82. *Id.* at 12.
83. *Id.* at 12.
84. *Id.* at 13. The FLRA provided no rationale supporting the holding that the question of whether elements and standards comport with negotiated criteria is grievable only on a delayed basis. This is not to suggest, however, that no supporting arguments exist.

does not meet the above criteria may grieve under the procedures in Section _____.[85]

In holding negotiable the *fair and equitable* language contained in the proposal, the authority explained that

the proposal here does not impose on the Agency a particular decision as to the quantity, quality, and timeliness of production or the establishing of priorities, or otherwise establish the content of performance standards in derogation of management's right to direct employees under section 7106(a)(2)(A) of the Statute. Similarly, since the proposal does not prevent management from establishing performance standards and taking action under section 4303 of the CSRA against employees based upon such standards, it does not prevent management from taking disciplinary action against an employee pursuant to section 7106(a)(2)(A).[86]

The authority held negotiable the remainder of the proposal, including the portion providing that performance standards would be consistent with classification standards. The authority described the meaning and effect of this portion of the proposal.

In rare instances where an applicable classification standard uses a quantitative or qualitative performance criterion to distinguish among grade levels, the performance standard established would reflect this distinction.[87]

Hence the proposal was negotiable because it neither prevented the agency from establishing classification standards or performance standards, nor sought to negotiate over their substance.

Two other proposals in *Office of Personnel Management* supplied definitions for standards and elements and provided that all performance elements would be communicated in writing to an employee at the beginning of each appraisal period.

A performance standard is a statement of the expressed level of achievement in terms of quality, quantity, timeliness, etc., required for the performance of an element of an employee's job.

All performance elements identified for an employee's position, specifying those which are critical, will be communicated to the employee in writing at the beginning of each appraisal period. A critical element is one which is so

---

85. American Federation of Government Employees, AFL-CIO, Local 32 and Office of Personnel Management, 3 FLRA 120 (1980).

86. *Id.* at 9. The authority's mention of the agency's right to discipline, under Title 5, U.S.C., section 7106(a)(2)(A), suggests that the authority may consider this reserved right as pertinent to performance standards and critical elements.

87. 3 FLRA 120 (1980) 10.

important that inadequate performance of it outweighs acceptable or better performance in other aspects of the job.[88]

The agency alleged that the proposals were nonnegotiable to the extent that they provided definitions of critical elements and performance standards. The authority held the proposals negotiable. Although the language of the proposals was not identical to the definitions of elements and standards provided in the OPM regulations, the language was not inconsistent with the OPM definitions.

The FLRA's decision in *Bureau of the Public Debt* cited and distinguished the FLRC's decision in *U.S. Patent Office*.[89] The petition in *U.S. Patent Office* had contained three proposals. The first proposal established an equation for the computation of production goals to be used in connection with evaluations of performance. The avowed purpose of the proposal was to remedy alleged unreasonable and inequitable production goals assigned by management. In holding the proposal negotiable, the council analyzed the proposal as simply ensuring the statistical reliability, reasonableness, and equitability of the production goals against which individual productivity would be compared and evaluated. The council specifically rejected the arguments that the proposal violated management's retained rights to direct employees and to assign work. The council wrote that the proposal did not limit the amount or type of work that management might assign to individual employees and that the proposal would not necessarily prevent management from making "meaningful changes in work assignment procedures and processes" to increase efficiency.[90] The council also rejected the argument that the proposal imposed a production ceiling. According to the council, the proposal provided a "yard stick" for measuring work performance, but it did not serve to impose a "limitation on production."[91]

The authority's decision in *Bureau of the Public Debt* partially reverses the council's holding with respect to the first proposal in *U.S. Patent Office*. According to the authority's reasoning, a proposal may provide general criteria with which management must comply in establishing critical elements and their respective performance standards, but a proposal may not identify the actual elements or their

---

88. *Id.*
89. Patent Office Professional Association and U.S. Patent Office, Washington, D.C., FLRC No. 75A-13 (1975).
90. *Id.* at 6.
91. *Id.* at 7.

standards; however, it appears that standards or elements other than those used in determining whether performance is unacceptable may be negotiable. The interesting aspect of the authority's decision is that its interpretation of management's rights to assign work and to direct employees is in conflict with, and more expansive than, the council's interpretation of the same language. As the authority suggested in *Bureau of the Public Debt,* however, this conflict and expansion may be limited to performance appraisal practices concerning unacceptable performance, critical elements, and performance standards:

the precedent relied upon [*U.S. Patent Office*] is inapplicable in the circumstances of the present case. The performance standards and critical elements which are the subjects of the instant dispute are defined by and must conform to the requirements of chapter 43 of the CSRA, which differ appreciably from the performance appraisal practices which were in effect at the time of the Council's decision.[92]

The second proposal in *U.S. Patent Office* established several categories of specific levels of individual production that would qualify a patent examiner for a promotion, a within-grade increase, a quality step increase, a retention in grade, or a special achievement award. The agency took the position that this second proposal violated applicable law by making productivity the sole determinant of performance assessment. In examining this proposal the FLRC found that the agency's position was premised upon an untrue assumption. The proposal was worded so that attainment of the production goal would constitute only prima facie—not conclusive—evidence that promotion, within-grade increase, etc., was warranted. Under the CSRA of 1978, proposals establishing specific performance levels as prima facie evidence that an employee is entitled to a career ladder promotion, a within-grade increase, or an award, are likely to continue to be negotiable. Such actions are not mandatory. The agency is vested with discretion, and guidelines governing how management may exercise discretion are ordinarily negotiable. The remaining question, however, is whether negotiable proposals may establish specific performance levels constituting prima facie evidence that an employee's performance is not unacceptable within the meaning of section 4301(3) of Title 5, U.S.C. It would seem that such proposals, if operative, would be tantamount to identification of the critical elements and performance standards. They would conflict with the

---

92. 3 FLRA 119 (1980) 8.

FLRA's determination that management retains the right to identify critical elements and performance standards.

The third proposal in *U.S. Patent Office* provided that the production goal assigned to individual patent examiners could not be unrelated to the amount of time that the examiner spent in actually performing examination work. The agency argued that this proposal infringed upon the agency's right to assign work. The council rejected the agency's argument and held the proposal negotiable. This same result should ensue under the CSRA.

Equally important to production goals and criteria is the selection of the sample from which production readings and evaluations will be derived. When performance can be rated or measured on an in-depth analysis of only a portion of the total work product, which particular portion of the total work product will be rated or measured? A performance rating derived from a sample is dependent upon and can be no better than the integrity of the compositon of the sample on which the rating is directly based. Generally, an employee has a legitimate interest in ensuring that the sample is representative or skewed in favor of the employee's better performances—certainly an employee does not want the sample to be unfairly weighted by poorer performances.[93] The selection technique produces the sample, either representative or nonrepresentative, that will determine ratings on performance appraisals, whether the employee is denied or granted a within-grade increase, whether the employee is retained or discharged, whether the employee is denied or granted a career ladder promotion, and so forth. To the extent that an agency opts to base any of these on a sample of the employee's overall work product, the agency must negotiate the sample selection.[94]

Details and Temporary Duty Stations
A detail constitutes a temporary assignment of an employee to a different position for a specified period, with the employee returning

---

93. For example, Mondays and Fridays are traditionally low-quantity and low-quality days for employees. Hence, when an employee's overall evaluation is to be based upon only four days performance a month, the employee would not want those four days to be all Mondays and Fridays. Such a sample would ignore the better performances on Tuesdays, Wednesdays, and Thursdays, and the resultant evaluation would unfairly emphasize the poorer performances.

94. Internal Revenue Service, Fresno Service Center, A/SLMR No. 983; Internal Revenue Service, Southwest Region, A/SLMR No. 1106, FLRC No. 78A-135 (1978).

to the regular position at the end of the detail. Incidentally, a detail may be *de jure* (when written orders are issued) or *de facto* (when no orders are issued). Additionally , it is essential to realize that a detail requires an assignment to a different position, as distinguished from remaining in the same position while performing additional, different duties.[95] A detailed employee frequently performs different duties from those that he or she normally performs. Similar to a detail is a temporary change in the employee's duty station. A temporary change in an employee's duty station, however, does not entail the employee filling a position other than his or her regular one.

Since a detail is by definition an assignment to a position within an agency, under Executive Order 11,491, as amended, the basic decision of whether or not a detail would take place was a retained management right by virtue of the agency's section 12(b)(2) reserved right to assign employees to positions within the agency. At first blush, it would appear that the basic decision would be negotiable under the CSRA of 1978 because section 7106(a)(1)(A) reserves to an agency only the right to assign employees in an agency. Although the phrase *in positions* has been removed, the Federal Labor Relations Authority has interpreted section 7106(a)(1)(A) as though the phrase remained and clearly held that the basic decision of whether or not a detail will take place is nonnegotiable.[96]

A proposal may not determine when a detail will or will not take place.[97] The Federal Labor Relations Authority has interpreted management's right to assign employees as entailing the right to select the particular employee who will be detailed; hence, proposals may not require management to make selections using criteria such as seniority or inverse seniority or to take volunteers before resorting to involuntary methods.[98] Proposals may, however, provide that these criteria will be used if management does not use competitive procedures.[99] Possibly, proposals may provide that details will be equitably distributed and not be discriminatory.[100] The negotiability of the following proposal was in dispute in *General Services Administration, Baltimore*:

---

95. *Federal Personnel Manual*, ch. 300, subch. 8-1.
96. 2 FLRA 77 (1980); 3 FLRA 7 (1980); 3 FLRA 20 (1980).
97. 3 FLRA 20 (1980).
98. 2 FLRA 77 (1980), proposals IV, V, VI, VII. *See* 3 FLRA 7, proposal II.
99. 2 FLRA 77 (1980) proposal III.
100. 2 FLRA 75 (1980).

The Employer agrees to post temporary changes in the duty stations of employees at least 72 hours in advance. In the event that the required notice is not given, an employee may report to his normal duty station. In such cases, he will be transported to and from the temporary duty station by the Employer within the normal daily tour of duty, for a total number of days consistent with the number of day's notice not given, not to exceed three (3) days, (e.g., if the employee is given two (2) day's notice he would be supplied transportation for one (1) day).[101]

While the language of this proposal does not pretend to restrict the employer's retained authority to order employees to report to different duty stations, the agency contended the proposal was nonnegotiable because it "so closely prescribes the steps management must take in exercising its rights . . . that it invades those rights." The union countered with the argument that the proposal did not interfere with any exercise of management's reserved decision-making authority, but rather, provided procedures to be observed in reaching the decision and taking the action involved. The union also contended that management had failed to sustain its burden of demonstrating with evidence that the proposal's procedures were so constricting that they would have the effect of negating the reserved authority. The FLRC agreed with the union and held the proposal negotiable.

In our opinion, the obligation which the proposal would impose upon management—to provide 72 hours of advance notice of change in duty station or, in the alternative, to provide transportation to such changed duty station from the employee's normal duty station—would not prevent management from deciding and acting with respect to changing employee's duty stations. Furthermore, there is no showing that the procedures which the proposal would require management to follow in exercising its retained rights under section 12(b) of the Order would have the effect of negating or interfering with such reserved authority either by causing unreasonable delay in reassigning employees under emergency or non-emergency situations, or by imposing significant and unavoidable costs upon the agency.[102]

Under Executive Order 11,491, as amended, a proposal could be rendered nonnegotiable on the ground that, although it did not preclude management from making the decision to detail, it overly constricted the management right. In *Internal Revenue Service* the negotiability of the following proposal was at issue:

The detailing of personnel to lower graded positions is considered to be inconsistent with sound planning and management and will be kept to an

---

101. AFGE Council of Locals 1497 and 2165 and Region 3, General Services Administration, Baltimore, Maryland, FLRC No. 74A-48 (1975).

102. *Id.* at 8.

absolute minimum. However, the Employer may use details under the following circumstances:

A. when a temporary shortage of personnel exists;
B. where an exceptional volume of work suddenly develops and seriously interrupts the work schedule;
C. to fill temporarily the positions of employees on extended leave with or without pay; or
D. other conditions of a special and temporary nature.[103]

The FLRC held the proposal nonnegotiable on the ground that it overly limited management's right to detail employees to lower graded positions, because such assignments would essentially be prohibited if the number of them could not exceed the "minimum" limitation. Under the CSRA of 1978, proposals like this may well be negotiable. Under the CSRA, a proposal is negotiable unless it would so constrict the reserved right that management cannot act "at all," and proposals may do indirectly that which may not be done directly.[104]

In *Long Beach Naval Shipyard* the union had submitted a proposal providing that no unit employee would be detailed or assigned on a temporary basis to a position which he or she could not qualify to occupy on a permanent basis.[105] The FLRC held the proposal nonnegotiable, saying that the proposal would directly have constrained management's right to decide to assign certain employees to certain positions. While it is not certain, it is nonetheless more probable than not that the FLRA will uphold an agency's right to detail an employee to a position for which he or she could not qualify on a permanent basis. Any other holding would derogate from the authority's interpretation that section 7106(a)(2)(A) vests an agency with the reserved right to select the particular employee to be assigned to each particular position.

A detail, which entails an employee leaving his or her normal position and occupying a position other than his or her own, must be carefully distinguished from assignment of duties to an employee who remains in his or her normal position while performing other duties. In *VA Hospital, Salisbury* the union had submitted a bargaining proposal

---

103. National Treasury Employees Union and Internal Revenue Service, FLRC No. 77A-12 (1977).

104. *See* notes 68, 69, 70, 71 in Chapter 2.

105. Local 174 International Federation of Professional and Technical Engineers, AFL-CIO, and Long Beach Naval Shipyard, Long Beach, California, FLRC No. 73A-16 (1974).

providing that whenever an employee was given a duty assignment that was not compatible with his or her position description and that was expected to or did endure for more than two days, upon the employee's objection the supervisor would select for the assignment the least senior of the qualified employees within the group.[106] The FLRC held the proposal nonnegotiable, reasoning that it limited management's section 12(b)(2) right to assign employees to positions. This analysis was, of course, completely misguided, as the proposal did not, directly or indirectly, address assignment of employees to positions within agencies but rather the assignment of duties. A better analysis would have held the proposal nonnegotiable, under the staffing patterns language, as determinative of the employee's job content. Under the CSRA, section 7106(a)(2)(B)'s assignment of work language should produce the same result.

Relocation of Work or Reporting Sites
The duty to negotiate does not obligate the agency to negotiate about where a work site is located or at what location employees will report for work. The decision to relocate a work site or a work reporting site is not negotiable, and the agency may unilaterally make the decision to change these sites; however, the agency is obligated to negotiate about the impact of the decision upon employees and the procedures for its implementation.[107]

One recent FLRA opinion highlights the distinction between management's reserved right, which is nonnegotiable, and procedures that are negotiable. In *IRS, New Orleans District Office* the employees had for years performed during duty hours certain agency work within their respective private residences.[108] Employees had always decided whether and on what occasions they would or would not perform agency work at their homes. The agency decided to implement a change whereby employees could still perform agency work at home during duty hours, but employees could no longer decide whether to do so; instead, a supervisor would make the decision. The union proposed, among other things, that an employee could request daily

---

106. AFGE Local 1738 and Veterans Administration Hospital, Salisbury, North Carolina, FLRC No. 75A-103 (1976).

107. U.S. Air Force Electronics System Division (AFSC), Hanscom Air Force Base, A/SLMR, No. 571, October 31, 1975.

108. NTEU Chapter 6 and Internal Revenue Service, New Orleans District Office, Case No. 0-NG-9, 1 FLRA 102 (1979).

or continuous permission to perform during duty hours agency work at his or her home; that in deciding to grant or deny an employee's request the supervisor would consider the request's reasonableness, workability, and effect upon the efficiency of the service (as well as any other criteria that the supervisor wanted to consider); and that any decision would be fair, objective, and equitable. The union petitioned the FLRA after the agency had declared the proposals non-negotiable. The authority affirmed that section 7106(a) reserved to the agency the right to determine where employees would and would not perform work. But then the authority observed that the matter being negotiated was not whether employees could perform agency work within their homes; the agency had already exercised this reserved right and made the basic decision that employees could do so. The matter being negotiated was what procedures the agency's supervisors would follow in granting or denying an employee's request to perform agency work at home during duty hours. Accordingly, the authority held that the proposals were negotiable.

Reclassification

The Office of Personnel Management has, for each agency, an X-118, known as the qualification standards, which is a manual providing a general list of the basic duties of each position, some of the criteria on which the position's grade is determined, and the eligibility requirements that must be satisfied in order to qualify for placement into the position. Each agency has, for each position, a position description that is supposed to reflect accurately the responsibilities and duties actually performed by the incumbent employee filling the position. To determine the grade level of a position, a complex set of classification standards are applied to the duties and responsibilities and required qualifications. Based on these, the position is classified, and the classification is then graded.[109]

Before the CSRA of 1978, the Civil Service Commission, under

---

109. This applies only to positions graded GS-1 through GS-15. For positions GS-16, GS-17, and GS-18, *see* 5 U.S.C. § 5108. *Position* means the work, consisting of the duties and responsibilities, assignable to one employee. *See* 5 U.S.C. § 5102(a)(3). *Class* includes all positions similar in kind or subject of work, level of difficulty, and responsibility, and the qualification requirements of the work. *See* 5 U.S.C. § 5102(a)(4). *Grade* includes all classes of positions that, although different with respect to a kind or subject of work, are sufficiently equivalent in level of difficulty and responsibility and level of qualification requirements of the work to warrant their inclusion within one range of rates of basic pay in the General Schedule.

the authority of Title 5, U.S.C., section 5105, had issued standards that served as the basis for position classification and grading under section 5106 of the same title,[110] and what had been issued was called the Factor Evaluation System.[111] Under the Factor Evaluation System, a certain number of points were assigned for each of the following nine factors applied to the duties, qualification requirements, and responsibilities of the position: (1) knowledge required by the position; (2) supervisory controls; (3) guidelines; (4) complexity; (5) scope and effect; (6) personal contacts; (7) purpose of contacts; (8) physical demands; and (9) work environment. The points for each factor were totaled, the total was applied to a grade conversion table, and from this the position's grade was determined.[112] Before the CSRA of 1978, classification and grading of positions was excepted from the obligation to negotiate and was administered by the Civil Service Commission, but the agency was obligated to bargain over the impact and implementation of any decision to reclassify or regrade a position.[113] Also, since appeal of this constituted a statutory appeal, it could not be grieved under a negotiated grievance procedure.[114]

With respect to negotiability, the determinations made before the CSRA of 1978 will be like those of the future. The section 7114(a)(4)

---

110. Section 5106 provides:

"(a) Each position shall be placed in its appropriate class. The basis for determining the appropriate class is the duties and responsibilities of the position and the qualifications required by the duties and responsibilities.

(b) Each class shall be placed in its appropriate grade. The basis for determining the appropriate grade is the level of difficulty, responsibility, and qualification requirements of the work of the class.

(c) Appropriated funds may not be used to pay an employee who places a supervisory position in a class and grade solely on the basis of the size of the organization unit or the number of subordinates supervised. These factors may be given effect only to the extent warranted by the work load of the organization unit and then only in combination with other factors, such as the kind, difficulty, and complexity of work supervised, the degree and scope of responsibility delegated to the supervisor, and the kind, degree, and character of the supervision exercised."

111. *Instructions for the Factor Evaluation System* (May 1977), published by the U.S. Civil Service Commission, TS-27 (PM-F-240).

112. *Id.*

113. Army & Air Force Exchange Services, Pacific Exchange System, Hawaii Regional Exchange, A/SLMR No. 454 (1974).

114. Matters for which a statutory appeals procedure existed could not be raised in a negotiated grievance procedure under the executive order. *See* section 13 of Executive Order 11,491, as amended. An employee could appeal a reclassification directly to the Civil Service Commission or to the agency and then to the Civil Service Commission; but if an employee elected to appeal first to the Civil Service Commission, the appeal could not thereafter be lodged with the agency. *FPM*, chapter 511, subchapter 6.

duty to negotiate, as defined in section 7103(a)(14)(B), does not include the obligation to negotiate about the grade in which a position will be classified. The agency must nonetheless negotiate about the impact and implementation of a reclassification decision on any employee.[115] The decision to reclassify a position may not be grieved under a negotiated grievance procedure.[116] It is subject to a statutory appeal procedure. Depending on the circumstances, a General Schedule employee may appeal a reclassification directly to the OPM or first to his or her agency and then to the OPM (see subpart F of section 511, Title 5, C.F.R.). In contrast, a wage grade employee must always appeal within his or her agency before appealing to the OPM (see subpart G, section 532, Title 5, C.F.R.). Under the CSRA of 1978 the Factor Evaluation System may be reviewed and then left intact, modified, or replaced by a new system to be created by the Office of Personnel Management. Title 5, U.S.C., section 5105 provides

(a) The Office of Personnel Management, after consulting the agencies, shall prepare standards of placing positions in their proper classes and grades. The Office may make such inquiries or investigations of the duties, responsibilities, and qualification requirements of positions as it considers necessary for this purpose. The agencies, on request of the Office, shall furnish information for and cooperate in the preparation of the standards. In the standards, which shall be published in such form as the Office may determine, the Office shall—

(1) define the various classes of positions in terms of duties, responsibilities, and qualification requirements;

(2) establish the official class titles; and

(3) set forth the grades in which the classes have been placed by the Office.

(b) The Office, after consulting the agencies to the extent considered necessary, shall revise, supplement, or abolish existing standards, or prepare new standards, so that, as nearly as may be practicable, positions existing at any given time will be covered by current published standards.

In addition, section 5346(a) provides

The Office of Personnel Management, after consulting with the agencies and with employee organizations, shall establish and maintain a job grading system for positions to which this subchapter applies. In carrying out this subsection, the Office shall—

(1) establish the basic occupational alinement and grade structure or structures for the job grading system;

---

115. *See* 5 U.S.C. § 7106(b)(2) and (3).

116. *Id.* at (c)(5).

(2) establish and define individual occupations and the boundaries of each occupation;

(3) establish job titles within occupations;

(4) develop and publish job grading standards; and

(5) provide a method to assure consistency in the application of job standards.

A proposal that infringes upon section 5105 or 5346, or upon a subsequently promulgated OPM regulation, would be nonnegotiable.

Materials and Equipment

Employees have an understandable interest in the equipment with which they will perform their duties as well as in the office furnishings constituting the work environment. The FLRC issued one group of decisions supporting the proposition that materials and equipment are not negotiable, and another group of decisions supporting the proposition that materials and equipment are negotiable.

In three significant decisions the Federal Labor Relations Council determined that equipment and office furnishings fall within the technology of performing work language, now found in section 7106(b)(1) of the CSRA, and therefore are nonnegotiable. First, in *Yuma* the union had submitted a proposal requiring the agency to maintain drag roads (unpaved roads paralleling the United States-Mexico border) in a safe, reasonably level condition and free of excessive dust.[117] The agency contended that the proposal was nonnegotiable because under the executive order's technology of work language, the agency was not obligated to negotiate about the equipment or material that employees would use in the performance of work. In ruling that the proposal was negotiable, the FLRC carefully distinguished between a proposal that is determinative of the equipment to be used and a proposal requiring that, when equipment is used, it be maintained in compliance with a certain standard. The latter is negotiable, the former is nonnegotiable. In effect, *Yuma* sets forth a test. A proposal is nonnegotiable if it purports to decide whether or not, or to what extent, equipment will be used. A proposal is negotiable if it requires only that, when equipment is used, the agency must maintain the equipment according to a general standard. The proposal should not stipulate what actions the agency will take in order to comply with the standard. Given the fact that the executive order's section 11(b) tech-

---

117. AFGE Local 2595 and Immigration and Naturalization Service, U.S. Border Patrol, Yuma Sector, Yuma, Arizona, FLRC No. 70A-10 (1971).

nology language and the CSRA's section 7106(b)(1) technology language are virtually identical, this test in all likelihood will be applied by the Federal Labor Relations Authority.

The second significant case holding equipment and materials to be nonnegotiable is *INS-1975*, in which the council was faced with determining the negotiability of two proposals relating to equipment.[118] The first proposal, designed to promote safety, provided that "appropriate" communications equipment would be installed in the vehicles of employees working in remote areas. The second proposal provided that an "appropriate" number of vehicles would be assigned to checkpoints. Citing *Yuma*, the council determined that the section 11(b) technology language made both proposals nonnegotiable. By directing that certain equipment would be used by employees in performing their duties, the first proposal would have been determinative of the equipment to be used in the performance of agency work; likewise, the second proposal was nonnegotiable for the same reason. The proposal did not provide a general standard against which equipment, if used, would be maintained; instead, it would have been determinative of the dispositon and extent of use of equipment. The same determination should accrue under section 7106 of the CSRA of 1978.

The third significant case in which the council held equipment and materials to be nonnegotiable is *Internal Revenue Service*.[119] In this case, the agency was relocating from older premises with private offices to newer premises designed with an open-space concept. Mid-contract negotiations were being conducted. Negotiability disputes had developed over a number of bargaining proposals, six of them concerning equipment and office furnishing, and the council held that all but two union proposals were nonnegotiable. The first proposal provided that confidential office space would be provided whenever an IRS employee was required to meet with a taxpayer and that the number of conference rooms provided would be in accordance with a specific schedule outlined in the proposal. Citing *Yuma* and *INS-1975*, the FLRC declared that this proposal was nonnegotiable by virtue of the technology clause contained in section 11(b) of the executive order. The provision of conference rooms and office space

---

118. FLRC No. 74A-13 (1975).
119. National Treasury Employees Union, Chapter 010 and Internal Revenue Service, Chicago District, FLRC No. 74A-93 (1976).

are part of the means to be used in accomplishment of the agency's work, and the proposal did not present a standard of fairness or efficiency against which the agency's implementation of a chosen technology might be measured.[120]

A second proposal provided that one computer terminal would be provided to certain specified groups of employees, that employees in certain named positions would be given individual telephones, and that employees in certain named positions would be given individual calculators to use in the performance of their duties. The purpose of this proposal was to provide employees with ready means for achieving favorable performance evaluations. The proposal was nonnegotiable, however, because, rather than prescribing evaluative standards taking into account the provision or nonprovision of equipment necessary to enable employees to maximize performance, the proposal directly prescribed a specific technology that the agency would have been obligated to adopt.

A third proposal obligated the agency to situate employee work stations in the manner that would cause the least distraction. The purpose of this proposal was to minimize the distraction that can adversely affect performance. The council determined that this third proposal was negotiable because it spoke not to what technology the agency would adopt—nothing in the proposal would impede the agency's adoption of the open-space concept—but rather to the implementation of the technology. Incidentally, the council also held that this third proposal was not violative of the *methods and means* language in section 12(b)(5), now found in section 7106(b)(1) of the CSRA of 1978. The stated reason was that the proposal merely prescribed which standards were to be applied in determining placement of employee desks. The proposal did not prescribe how the agency was to achieve these standards.

A fourth proposal directed that waiting areas with chairs be made available for public visitors coming into the agency offices. The council held this proposal nonnegotiable because its subject matter was

---

120. FLRC No. 70A-10 (1971); FLRC No. 74A-13 (1975). As is readily apparent, the Federal Labor Relations Council did not sharply distinguish between the *methods and means* language of section 12(b)(5) of Executive Order 11,491, as amended, and the *technology* language of section 11(b) of the order. Under section 7106(b)(1) of the CSRA of 1978, *technology, method,* and *means* appear together in the same clause. It remains to be seen whether the Federal Labor Relations Authority will formulate sharp definitions that are mutually exclusive.

outside the scope of the obligation to negotiate, as it addressed members of the general public rather than bargaining unit employees.

The fifth union proposal called for maintenance of adequate lighting of work areas. The agency had argued that this fifth proposal was nonnegotiable because it conflicted with regulations promulgated by authority outside the agency, GSA regulations. The council deferred this issue to GSA. GSA replied that the proposal did not require the application of a standard inconsistent with GSA regulations. Therefore, the council, noting particularly that the proposal applied to the employer and not to GSA, held the proposal negotiable.

The sixth proposal called upon the employer to secure parking spaces for bargaining unit employees. The council held that this sixth proposal was nonnegotiable because under law the Internal Revenue Service is not authorized to obtain parking spaces. The law authorizes only GSA to obtain parking spaces, and the union's bargaining relationship was with the Internal Revenue Service, not with GSA. The council advised, however, that the Internal Revenue Service would have to negotiate the assignment of parking spaces made available to the agency by GSA. Moreover, if GSA has made spaces available to the agency, it is entirely possible that the agency would have to negotiate the substance of the decision of whether the agency will or will not, acting on its own initiative, return the spaces to GSA.

In contrast to *Yuma, INS-1975*, and *Internal Revenue Service*, the FLRC issued another group of decisions supporting the irreconcilable proposition that materials and equipment are negotiable. First, in *Food Safety and Quality Service*, the union had proposed that the employer would furnish all necessary protective clothing such as gloves, coats, frocks; meat thermometers; and other equipment that the employer determined necessary for performance of duties.[121] Contrary to the *Yuma* doctrine, this proposal specified certain equipment that the employer was required to furnish. Nevertheless, the FLRC declared the proposal negotiable. Second, in *GSA, Baltimore* the union had submitted a proposal providing, in effect, that the employer was prohibited from requiring employees to work unless the employer first provided protective equipment and safety devices.[122] This pro-

---

121. AFGE, National Council of Meat Graders, and Department of Agriculture, Food Safety and Quality Service, FLRC No. 77A-63 (1978).
122. AFGE Council of Locals 1497 and 2165 and Region 3, General Services Administration, Baltimore, Maryland, FLRC No. 74A-48 (1975).

posal, too, effectively required the use of certain equipment, and the FLRC declared it negotiable.

One of the initial FLRA decisions regarding material and equipment suggests that the authority may follow *Food Safety and Quality Service* and *GSA, Baltimore*. In *Naval Air Development Center*, the authority was faced with the issue of the negotiability of the following proposal:

[C]ivilian and officer personnel who are engaged in foot hazardous operations and who wear foot protection [shall] be provided with safety shoes without charge.[123]

Curiously, the agency argued neither that the proposal violated section 7106(b)(1)'s technology, methods and means language nor that the proposal's subject was not a "working condition." Rather, the agency argued that the union had failed to prove the absence of a compelling need for an agency regulation that allegedly conflicted with the proposal. The difficulty with the agency's position, however, was that the agency, not the union, was encumbered with the duty of proving the existence of a compelling need. Since the agency had neglected to offer evidence or argument proving the existence of a compelling need, the FLRA held the proposal negotiable.

Promotions and Placements into Higher Grades

Promotions

By virtue of section 11(a) of Executive Order 11,491, as amended, any negotiable proposal regarding promotions could not be inconsistent with promotion procedures contained in the *Federal Personnel Manual*.[124] Section 12(b)(2) of the executive order reserved to agency management the right to decide whether a promotion action would or would not take place and whether or not to fill a position by an internal promotion or with a new hire from outside the agency. Under the impact and implementation doctrine, an agency was obligated to negotiate the procedures used in filling a unit position or conducting a promotion action.[125] Due to these constraints and limitations on bargaining,

---

123. AFGE Local 1928 and Department of the Navy, Naval Air Development Center, Warminster, Pennsylvania, Case No. 0-NG-13, 2 FLRA 62 (1980).

124. In part, section 11(a) prescribed that the parties shall negotiate "so far as may be appropriate under applicable laws and regulations, including policies set forth in the Federal Personnel Manual."

125. Department of Agriculture and Office of Investigation and National Federation of Federal Employees Local 1375, A/SLMR No. 555, August 29, 1975.

negotiated contractual promotion procedures normally consisted of four distinct steps designed to implement the *FPM*'s merit promotion requirements.[126]

First, the vacancy announcement was posted, applications were submitted, and a determination was made as to which applicants met the basic eligibility requirements. Second, each applicant who met the minimum eligibility requirements was evaluated by his or her respective supervisor. This evaluation was based upon the employee's past twelve-month performance in light of the requirements of his or her assigned position description. Thus an employee detailed to a different position would be evaluated not on performance in the different position but rather on performance of the duties required by the position description of his or her regular job. Third, a ranking panel was appointed and convened. Its purpose was to evaluate candidates based on how they were expected to perform in the position to be filled, i.e., potential in the target position. After evaluating candidates, the panel ranked them and created a highly qualified list (HQL). Then top candidates were selected from the highly qualified list and their names placed on the best qualified list (BQL). Fourth, the names on the best qualified list were submitted to the selecting official. Based upon an investigation that was supposed to be sufficiently deep to enable the official to make an intelligent, objective decision that was supposed to be based on principles of merit, the selecting official then had carte blanche authority to choose any of the BQL candidates as the selectee. The selecting official recorded the selectee's name on a promotion certificate. Regardless of how arbitrary and capricious the selection may have been, regardless of how inconsistent with true merit, the selecting official's decision could not be challenged or in any way curtailed.

Despite political rhetoric from the White House and other advocates of civil service reform, very little substantive difference will emerge under the Civil Service Reform Act of 1978. The Office of Personnel Management will issue regulations and other policies with respect to the filling of positions. The OPM is vested with a very broad grant of authority to promulgate rules and regulations governing, among other things, the filling of positions.[127] Agencies must

---

126. *See FPM* chapter 335, prior to issuance of *FPM* letter 335-12 dated December 29, 1978.

127. 5 U.S.C. §§ 1103 and 1104.

develop performance appraisal systems that will produce employee performance appraisals that, in turn, will be used in personnel actions.[128] Like the defunct Civil Service Commission, the OPM has the duty of assisting in the creation and administration of agency appraisal systems while also monitoring those systems that the OPM helped to create.[129]

Under the CSRA of 1978, the scope of the duty to bargain is virtually identical to the limited scope that existed under the executive order. First, by virtue of section 7117(a)(1) of the CSRA of 1978, the section 7114(a)(4) obligation to negotiate does not permit the negotiation of any proposal that is inconsistent with governmentwide rules or regulations; therefore, any bargaining proposal is nonnegotiable if it is inconsistent with any OPM rule or regulation, as interpreted and applied by the OPM.[130] The subordination of the bargaining obligation to OPM regulations is virtually identical to the executive order's section 11(a) subordination of the scope of the duty to bargain to the *FPM* provisions issued by the Civil Service Commission. Second, under section 7106(a)(2)(A) of the CSRA, agency management is vested with the reserved right to decide whether or not to fill a position with a new hire; in effect, this means that an agency may decide to fill a position by a new hire, and if the agency elects to fill the position by other means, then the agency will probably conduct a promotion action.[131] This reservation of rights is identical to the reservation that existed under section 12(b)(2) of the executive order. Third, section 7106(a)(2)(C) reserves to agency management the right

with respect to filling positions, to make selections for appointments from—
    (i) among properly ranked and certified candidates for promotion; or
    (ii) any other appropriate source.

This is the reserved right that management enjoyed under the executive order.

The Office of Personnel Management has issued a revised *Federal*

---

128. *Id.* § 4302.

129. Title 5, U.S.C., § 4304(a) provides that the OPM is obligated to assist agencies in the development of performance appraisal systems, and section 1103(a)(5) provides that the OPM is obligated to enforce civil service rules and regulations, and section 4304(b)(1) obligates the OPM to review those performance appraisal systems—which the OPM helped to create under section 4304(a)—to ensure compliance with law and regulation.

130. *See* 5 U.S.C. §7105(i).

131. The agency could fill the position by lateral reassignment.

Personnel Manual chapter 335 on merit promotion.[132] The revised *FPM* chapter purports to represent "a major change in policy." The revised *FPM* chapter 335 contains five merit promotion requirements.[133] None of these represents a major change in policy. Requirement 1 is simply reiteration of the principle that promotion actions should be based on merit. This does not represent a change. Requirement 2 merely provides that the area of consideration must be sufficiently broad to ensure the availability of high-quality candidates; this requirement represents no change. Requirement 3 merely reiterates the previous requirements that employees must meet the minimum eligibility requirements, that evaluation methods must be valid, and that due weight must be given to other factors such as awards. The only possible change wrought by requirement 3 is that the *FPM* no longer spells out precisely what procedure will be employed to rank employees comparatively. Requirement 4 provides that, in filling a position, management is free to select from any appropriate source, regardless of whether or not a promotion action has been commenced:

Selection procedures will provide for management's right to select or not select from among a group of best qualified candidates. They will also provide for management's right to select from other appropriate sources, such as reemployment priority lists, reinstatement, transfer, handicapped, or Veterans Readjustment eligibles or those within reach on an appropriate OPM certificate. In deciding which source or sources to use, agencies have an obligation to determine which is most likely to best meet the agency mission objectives, contribute fresh ideas and new viewpoints, and meet the agency's affirmative action goals.[134]

Requirement 5 merely carries over the requirement that records be maintained for two years in a fashion that safeguards individual privacy and that also is sufficiently detailed to allow reconstruction of the promotion action, including documentation of how candidates were rated and ranked. In effect, the five merit promotion requirements do not represent a major change in policy, as claimed by the OPM. Nor are any major changes wrought by the elimination of requirements that were contained in *FPM* chapter 335 before issuance of *FPM* letter 335-12, December 29, 1978, and the revised *FPM* chapter 335.

---

132. *FPM* letter 335-12, dated December 29, 1978. Attached to the letter is revised *FPM* chapter 335.

133. These are located in items 1-4 of the revised *FPM* chapter 335. *Supra* note 132.

134. *Id.* at requirement 4.

That letter states that the following requirements have been eliminated:

—competition for upgraded positions resulting from planned management action;

—the stipulation that Federal employees selected from registers must also be among the best qualified on internal promotion lists;

—fixed limits on the number of best qualified candidates referred to a selecting official;

—competition in noncompetitive moves to position with higher promotion potential;

—priority and repromotion consideration; and

—acceptance of voluntary applications.

In addition, the present requirement for competition for details of more than 60 days to higher graded positions has been changed to 120 days.[135]

Despite elimination of the requirements, some but not all remain negotiable.[136]

It is against the entirety of this background that one must analyze the law of negotiability as it applies to promotion actions in the federal sector. Federal sector unions cannot legally control the pool of applicants available for federal employment. Hence, hiring has not been, and will not be, a highly negotiated subject except to the extent that when a job is being filled federal sector unions have an interest in obtaining promotion opportunities for current federal employees.

A promotion action comes within the scope of the obligation to negotiate only if the target position to be filled is a bargaining unit position.[137] It is of no consequence if it is a bargaining unit employee

---

135. Item 6 of *FPM* letter 335-12. *Supra* note 132.

136. In *FPM* letter 335-12, the OPM advised agency management that "elimination of the above requirements would not, for the most part, preclude agencies from adopting or negotiating similar provisions in their own plans. For example, an agency might find it desirable to include a provision on acceptance of voluntary applications or priority or repromotion consideration for persons who have been denied proper consideration. However, it would be inappropriate for an agency to establish its own requirement that Federal Employees selected from registers must also rank among the best qualified on internal promotion lists. Experience has shown that this provision placed employees at a serious disadvantage in competing for positions, and also restricted agency discretion to select from other appropriate sources. Agency authority to select from any appropriate source of candidates is specifically cited in the Civil Service Reform Act (5 U.S.C. 7106(a))."

137. AFGE (National Border Patrol Council and National INS Council) and Immigration and Naturalization Service, U. S. Department of Justice, FLRC No. 76A-68 (1977); FLRC No. 77A-28 (1978).

who is applying for a position outside the bargaining unit; any proposal addressing promotion to a nonunit position is nonnegotiable. In *Corpus Christi Army Depot*, the union had submitted the following proposals:

Promotional Selection Panels. The Employer agrees to grant Union participation on all job promotion selection panels for all positions classified as professional by the Civil Service Commission. The Employer also agrees to permit the Union to participate in selection panels for positions on which a professional employee has applied for.

Positions Qualification Crediting Plan. The Union will be allowed to participate as a full partner in the process of determining the Qualification Crediting Plan for the qualification criteria of any position to be filled for which professional employees are qualified.

Criteria for Highly Qualified Candidates. The Union will be allowed to participate as a full partner in the process of determining the criteria for Highly Qualified Candidates for any position to be filled for which professional employees are qualified.[138]

Each of the proposals would have applied to promotions to bargaining unit as well as non-bargaining-unit positions. The council held that the proposals were nonnegotiable because they would apply to promotion to the non-bargaining-unit positions. But it would seem that the council need not have declared the proposals wholly nonnegotiable. It may be logically concluded that the proposals were nonnegotiable only to the extent that they applied to promotions to non-bargaining-unit positions and that the proposals were negotiable to the extent that they applied to promotions to unit positions.

A bargaining proposal must not obligate an agency to fill or not to fill a vacant position. In *Keesler Air Force Base* the union had submitted a bargaining proposal stating that "management agrees to adopt a policy of filling vacancies where they organizationally and functionally exist. . . ."[139] Despite the fact that the language did not specifically require that a vacancy be filled by a promotion action, the FLRC held this proposal nonnegotiable on the ground that section 12(b)(2) of the executive order reserved to management the right to determine whether or not a promotion action would be instigated, and that the proposal, by directing when and under what conditions a promotion action must be conducted, would have negated manage-

---

138. American Federation of Government Employees, Local 3632 and Corpus Christi Army Depot, FLRC No. 77A-140 (1978).

139. NFFE Local 943 and Keesler Air Force Base, Mississippi, FLRC No. 74A-66 (1975).

ment's retained 12(b)(2) right to make the basic decision whether to promote and to fill a position. This same reasoning made nonnegotiable a bargaining proposal in *USDA* that would have required the agency to fill vacant positions on a specified date.[140] In *Blaine Air Force Base* the FLRC held nonnegotiable a proposal that, when a formal grievance had been filed under the agency grievance procedure, would have prevented the filling of any vacancy on a permanent basis until either the grievance had been resolved or the employee had exercised any statutory or mandatory placement rights, whichever occurred first. According to the FLRC, the proposal would have unreasonably delayed or impeded the agency's 12(b)(2) right to conduct a promotion action.[141]

Under the CSRA of 1978, the agency does not retain the right to promote, although the right to hire is retained by virtue of section 7106(a)(2)(B). For this reason, the FLRA cannot logically apply the reasoning that the FLRC applied in *Keesler Air Force Base, USDA*, and *Blaine Air Force Station.* The authority may, and in all likelihood will, reach the same result through application of the number of employees language found in section 7106(a)(1). Any proposal that directs or prohibits the filling of a vacant position would be determinative of the number of employees.

Once management has decided to fill a position, the parties should be able to negotiate several types of proposals. The parties should be able to negotiate that the agency would notify the union as soon as a decision had been made to fill a position and before the agency had decided where to search to fill the position. The parties should be able to negotiate a provision providing that, upon having decided to fill a position, management would conduct promotion action procedures extending only up to the submission of a list of ranked and certified candidates to a selecting official; such a proposal would not preclude exercise of the agency's section 7106(a)(2)(B) right to hire or the agency's section 7106(a)(2)(C) right to select from any source when filling a position. Alternatively, the parties might

---

140. NFFE Local 1555 and Tobacco Division, AMS, USDA, FLRC No. 74A-32 (1975).

141. Local 631, American Federation of Government Employees, AFL-CIO and Blaine Air Force Station, Blaine, Maine, FLRC No. 74A-33 (1975). *But see* AFGE Local 1999 and Army–Air Force Service, Dix-McGuire Exchange, Fort Dix, New Jersey, 2 FLRA 16 (1979) and National Treasury Employees Union Chapters 103 and 111 and United States Customs Service, Region VII, 2 FLRA 15.

negotiate a provision providing that management, when considering filling a position from names on a list of potential new hires, would give equal consideration to current agency employees qualifying for the position. Such a proposal would entail a procedure that would not detract from the agency's right to hire or the agency's right to select from any source; a necessary corollary would be a procedure that would advise current agency employees that a position was going to be filled, a procedure whereby employees can express interest by submission of an application, and a procedure whereby their names can be submitted to the selecting official for consideration. As long as such proposals address the filling of a bargaining unit position and neither preclude the hiring of a new employee nor require the agency to promote from within, the proposal should be negotiable. The case in favor of negotiability of these proposals is extremely persuasive. The CSRA of 1978 was intended to ensure that positions are filled based on merit. Requirement 1 of the OPM's merit promotion plan in *FPM* chapter 335, as revised, reiterates the marriage to merit principles. It is axiomatic that a system functioning on merit must provide for consideration and potential selection of all qualified, interested candidates. Witness revised *FPM* chapter 335, requirement 4. Any system that precludes applicants who happen to be current agency employees from receiving consideration equal to that given to non-agency applicants is not based on merit but rather is based on source or status. Any system that is based on source or status is antithetical to merit principles, and any proposal that contributes to consideration based on merit serves to support merit promotion principles.

A more difficult question would be presented by a proposal requiring a selecting official, in considering all candidates, first to give consideration to current agency employees. If such a proposal requires the selecting official to decide not to select any of the current agency employees before giving any consideration to new hires, then it would probably be nonnegotiable. But such a proposal should be negotiable if it required the selecting official, in considering candidates, to commence in a procedural order that would cause him or her to look first at the candidates who are currently agency employees, and thereafter, if a new hire rather than a current agency employee is selected, to write a long narrative that lists all resource information examined, that applies a list of objective criteria to each candidate, and that explains in detail all reasons the new hire was selected and why each current agency employee was not selected.

When all or any part of an action under the merit promotion procedure is to be conducted, the parties must negotiate how employees will be informed of the forthcoming event. This could conceivably entail personal notices to employees, posting of vacancy announcements on all bulletin boards, announcements on public address systems, or any other methods to communicate the message. The parties may negotiate the length of the period within which management will communicate the message and the contents of the message. For example, a vacancy announcement should, at the least, contain the following: announcement number; opening date; title, series, and grade of position; geographical location of position; minimum qualifications required; selective placement factors, if any; brief summary of the duties of the position, together with an indication of where additional information may be obtained; evaluative methods to be used in ranking and selection, including all factors to be considered by the selecting official; closing date; and statement of equal employment opportunity.

Before *FPM* letter 335-12 of December 29, 1978, *FPM* chapter 335, subchapter 3-3(a) had defined *area of consideration* as

the area in which an agency makes an intensive search for eligible candidates during a specific promotion action. It must at least include the minimum data designated in the promotion plan.

It had also defined *minimum area of consideration* as

the area designated by the promotion plan in which the agency should reasonably expect to locate enough highly qualified candidates to fill vacancies in the positions covered by the plan. The agency must include this area in its initial search for candidates.

These definitions are not disturbed by revised *FPM* chapter 335, which provides in 1-1(E) that

[t]he area of consideration is the area in which the agency makes an intensive search for eligible candidates in a specific promotion action. The minimum area of consideration is the area designated by the promotion plan in which the agency should reasonably expect to locate enough high quality candidates, as determined by the agency, to fill vacancies in the positions covered by the plan. (When the minimum area of consideration produces enough high quality candidates and the agency does not find it necessary to make a broader search, the minimum area of consideration and the area of consideration are the same.)

Since there is no change in the meaning and use of either area of consideration or minimum area of consideration, the area of consideration under the CSRA of 1978 should be no less negotiable than it was under Executive Order 11,491, as amended.[142]

Area of consideration was negotiable under Executive Order 11,491, as amended, and accordingly, it should be negotiable under the CSRA of 1978. This allows negotiation of proposals that may virtually ensure selection of bargaining unit employees as opposed to most non-bargaining-unit employees or applicants from other geographical proximities. *Social Security Administration* brought before the FLRC the question of the negotiability of a bargaining proposal limiting, in promotions to grade 13 positions, the area of consideration to those employees with bureau experience at the grade 12 level.[143] The essence of this negotiability dispute centered upon the extent to which the area of consideration is negotiable, as the council reported in quoting from the union's brief.

The only issue in dispute is whether existing GS-13 positions in the Bureau of Health Insurance will be filled by employees with Bureau experience at this GS-12 level (Union's proposal) or whether these GS-13 positions will be open to Headquarters wide competition (management's unilateral determination). Thus, in essence, the real dispute is over the area of consideration for GS-13 level positions in the Bureau of Health Insurance.[144]

The agency argued that the proposal would restrict the area of consideration to "a mere 6 percent" of the employees in the bargaining unit and that such limitation would conflict with the *FPM*. The FLRC pointed out that the area of consideration simply defines the "area in which an agency makes an intensive search for eligible candidates during a specific promotion action." This does not mean that other candidates are precluded from submitting applications, which they may do if they somehow learn of the vacancy announcement and promotion opportunity. Thereupon the council held that the union proposal was negotiable and explained,

---

142. *FPM* chapter 335, as revised and attached to *FPM* letter 335-12, December 29, 1978, provides in 1-4, requirement 2, that "areas of consideration must be sufficiently broad to ensure the availability of high quality candidates, taking into account the nature and level of the positions covered. Agencies must also ensure that employees within the area of consideration who are absent for legitimate reason, e.g., on detail, on leave, at training course, in the military service, or serving in public international organizations or on Intergovernmental Personnel Act assignments, receive appropriate consideration for promotion."

143. AFGE Local 1923 and Social Security Administration, Headquarters, Bureaus and Offices, Baltimore, Maryland, FLRC No. 71A-22 (1973).

144. *Id.* 6-7.

To repeat, the union's proposal, according to that organization's express intent, speaks only to that "area of consideration" for filling vacant GS-13 positions, that is, the area in which the agency makes an intensive search for eligible candidates during a specific promotion action. The proposal, as so limited by the union and as we therefore so construe it for purposes of this decision, does not establish BHI experience at GS-12 level as a qualification for GS-13 positions. Moreover, nothing in the proposal limits consideration of candidates to those within BHI at the time of the vacancy. Nor does the proposal negate in any manner the need to comply with other pertinent FPM requirements, e.g., the need to extend the minimum area of consideration if it does not produce at least three highly qualified candidates; to allow employees outside the minimum area to file voluntary applications who meet the position qualifications.[145]

In *Cherry Point*, the following proposal was also found to be negotiable:

The Employer agrees to use to the maximum possible extent the skills of employees in the bargaining unit. The area of consideration for internal placement announcements shall be the Naval Air Rework Facility, Marine Corps Air Station and U.S. Naval Hospital, Cherry Point, N.C., unless this area will not supply sufficient candidates for the vacancy. The Employer will discuss with the Union the need for extending the area of consideration before it is in fact extended. Consideration may also be made of voluntary application of employees outside the area of consideration. [Every reasonable effort will be made by the Employer to obtain identical information on non-unit candidates as is obtained for unit candidates. Non-unit candidates shall be evaluated as nearly as possible by the same criteria used to evaluate unit candidates.][146]

A proposal must not, however, go so far as to bar nonunit employees from being eligible for consideration for promotion. In *McGuire Air Force Base*, the following proposal was in dispute:

In order to be eligible for Merit Promotion, an employee must be a regular employee of the unit and meet the minimum qualifications of the Merit Promotion Announcement.[147]

Although the council held this proposal nonnegotiable, it failed to provide any clear reasoning, but instead lumped this proposal with another and held both to be nonnegotiable because the other one was nonnegotiable. But the two were not inherently intertwined. A more rational approach, and an approach consistent with other decisions would have been to have held the cited proposal nonnegotiable on

---

145. *Id.*
146. FLRC No. 77A-28 (1978).
147. FLRC No. 77A-18 (1978) and FLRC No. 77A-21 (1978).

the basis that it would have violated merit promotion principles by basing eligibility on status, i.e., being a member of the bargaining unit, and not on qualifications and demonstrated ability.

The parties to the collective bargaining relationship are obligated to negotiate the procedures and forms and contents thereof that the respective supervisors will utilize in evaluating the various candidates for promotion to bargaining unit positions. For example, proposals may direct that the evaluating supervisor will be the one who assigns, reviews, and directs the employee's work and that no other manager will directly or indirectly inject influence into the appraisal, that the evaluation will cover a specific period of time unless a shorter period is noted on the face of the evaluation, that the evaluation will constitute a specific numerical percentage of the total point score ultimately assigned to each respective candidate, and that the employee may attach written comments to the evaluation.[148] In addition, the parties are obligated to negotiate definitions and objective standards against which the candidates will be compared on each evaluative factor on the evaluation form that the supervisor prepares.

In a promotion action there are two major evaluative steps. The first is the supervisor's evaluation of the employee's performance, and the second is the evaluation of the employee by a ranking panel or ranking official.[149] Revised *FPM* chapter 335, 1-4, requirement 3 provides that the evaluative procedure must be consistent with instructions in *FPM* supplement 335-1. Section S3-1(a) provides that procedures must be approved by the OPM or by the agency; this is no bar to negotiations because an agency can approve the evaluative procedures specified in bargaining proposals (or the OPM would approve the promotion procedures of a negotiated agreement). Section S3-1(c) provides that any procedure used for in-service placement must meet the "minimum requirements for acceptability" that are listed in section S3-4 of the supplement:

a. Demonstration of content, construct, or criterion—related validity, or a combination of these, for the procedure according to professionally accepted standards to the extent feasible and appropriate. . . . In circumstances where

---

148. International Association of Fire Fighters Local F-61 and Philadelphia Naval Shipyard, Case No. 0-NG-6, 3 FLRA 66 (1980), proposal III.

149. Revised *FPM* supplement 335, S4-1(b), provides that "agencies must use multiple measures in ranking employees to determine the best qualified unless otherwise authorized by the OPM." Thus, the supervisory evaluations may not ordinarily be used as the sole basis for ranking candidates.

it is not appropriate to validate an evaluation procedure or not feasible, the procedure, nevertheless, must be job related. Where validation is appropriate, the OPM will evaluate agency plans and evidence of effort and achievement in bringing selection procedures into compliance within a reasonable period of time.

b. Standard directions for administering the procedure.

c. Standard scoring or rating instructions which enhance or ensure objectivity and reliability of scoring or rating.

d. A method for interpreting and combining results of the various methods and instruments in a manner consistent with (a) above.

e. A method for recording results of evaluative procedures so that the record is meaningful and usable in the future.

f. Provisions for reporting the results of evaluative procedures in meaningful terms to individual employees and operating officials.

g. Assurance that the procedure has not been compromised where disclosure would give an undue advantage to some candidates over others and provisions to maintain the level of security appropriate to each instrument or procedure.

Logically there exists no reasonable bar to the negotiation of evaluative factors, weights that may be attached to each evaluative factor, the various ratings (numerical or otherwise) that may be assigned to the various evaluative factors, and distinguishing definitions for the various ratings. Whatever is negotiated, however, must not be so vague and lacking in meaning that it fails to comport with the minimum *FPM* requirements for promotion appraisals. For example, in *Norton Air Force Base* the following proposal was disputed:

The annual performance rating will be substituted for the Air Force "Supervisory Appraisal" of current performance in ranking employees for Merit Promotion.[150]

An annual performance rating is composed of only a single word: *unsatisfactory, satisfactory,* or *outstanding.* One word does not describe adequately the "significant factors of the employee's present job that are significant in the job to be filled."[151] A single word cannot normally suffice to make "meaningful distinctions" between candidates

---

150. American Federation of Government Employees, Local 1485 and Department of the Air Force, Norton Air Force Base, California, FLRC No. 77A-110 (1978).

151. Recently superseded *FPM* supplement 335-1, section 4-5(1). Revised *FPM* supplement to chapter 335 at S4-2(b)(1) contains similar language: ". . . the procedure measures an element important for success in the higher level. . . ."

for promotion.[152] In effect, while latitude exists, it is not so great as to defeat the purpose for having supervisory appraisals and a ranking process. Furthermore, there should be no question whatsoever about the negotiability of a proposal providing that a supervisor, as well as each ranking official, will justify the rating for each evaluative factor by writing a narrative containing objective documentation that includes specific examples.

As to the ranking panel or official, the parties may negotiate the makeup and precise procedures that, both individually and collectively, the panel and its members, or the official, will follow in evaluating candidates. For example, the parties may negotiate the size of the panel and at least some of the composition of the panel,[153] and that the ranking panel's, or official's, score assigned to an employee will constitute a specific numerical percentage of the total points ultimately assigned to and used in numerically ranking the employee as a candidate.

To be considered by the selecting official, a candidate must be determined to be one of the best qualified candidates.[154] Best qualified candidates are determined by comparative evaluation of all candidates, as opposed to the top rated from each of the various sources supplying candidates.[155] The best qualified candidates are the ones having numerical scores ranking at the top of the list of candidates.[156] The number of candidates who will be designated as best qualified

---

152. Recently superceded *FPM* chapter 335, section 3-6. Revised *FPM* supplement to chapter 335 at S4-2 (b)(2) contains similar language: ". . .makes meaningful distinctions among employees. . . ."

153. In *Veterans Administration Hospital, Montgomery,* the council declared negotiable a proposal obligating the employer to appoint a unit employee to the promotion board, with the provision that the appointment would be made from a list, provided by the union, of unit employees meeting the employer's criteria for being on the promotion board. The council reasoned that the proposal merely established a procedure providing that a unit employee would serve on the board evaluating candidates for promotion; the proposal did not interfere with management's retained section 12(b)(2) right to decide whether or not a promotion action will take place. FLRC No. 73A-22 (1974).

154. Revised *FPM* chapter 335, 1-1(g) provides, "*Best qualified candidates* are measured against other candidates. They are qualified candidates who rank at the top when compared with other eligible candidates for a position. A reasonable number of the best qualified candidates are referred for selection."

155. In *INS-1977,* the FLRC held nonnegotiable a proposal providing that the best qualified list would be composed of the top two candidates seeking demotion and the top two candidates seeking promotion. FLRC No. 76A-68 (1977).

156. *Supra* note 154.

is negotiable. The only limitation is that the number be "reasonable."[157]

The actual selection of the successful candidate for promotion, i.e., the selectee, from the best qualified list was held to be nonnegotiable under Executive Order 11,491, as amended.

The Commissioner's regulations clearly make the actual selection of a candidate for promotion nonnegotiable. Section 3-7c of FPM Chapter 335 provides that the selecting official is entitled to choose any of the candidates on a promotion certificate. Section 5-1d of that chapter identifies the decision of which candidate among the best qualified to select for promotion as a reserved management right and, consequently, not appropriate for negotiation.[158]

This language is from the response that the CSC had made to an FLRC referral; the FLRC quoted the language in its opinion. Furthermore, under the executive order the selecting official enjoyed the carte blanche authority to select whoever he or she wished to select; the selecting official could not be required to show preference to any group or type of employee on the best qualified list.[159]

Under the CSRA the selecting official enjoys an even more unfettered and unreviewable discretion. Section 7106(a)(2)(C) vests a selecting official with the right to fill a position with a selection from a properly ranked and certified list of candidates or from any other appropriate source. Revised *FPM* chapter 335, requirement 4, provides that in filling a position the selecting official enjoys the right to select or not select from the best qualified list or to select from priority lists, reinstatement lists, transfer lists, lists of new hires, or any other "appropriate" list. Although a nonselected employee may challenge whether the list of candidates was properly ranked and certified, a nonselected candidate may not challenge nonselection from a properly ranked and certified list of candidates. This is true regardless of how unreasonable, arbitrary, and capricious the selection may have been.[160]

Several types of proposals may serve to temper a selecting official's absolute right to select from a best qualified list. First, a negotiable proposal should be able to require that, for every candi-

---

157. *Supra* note 154.

158. FLRC No. 71A-31 (1972) 4.

159. FLRC No. 77A-18 and 77A-21 (1978); FLRC No. 76A-79 (1977); FLRC No. 77A-28 (1978) 9.

160. 5 U.S.C. §7121(c)(4); *see also* revised *FPM* chapter 335, 1-6.

date, the selecting official review a prescribed list of information that would normally be necessary to render an objective and intelligent decision and, after having reviewed the prescribed list of information for each candidate, to write a priority schedule showing the relative importance of each type of information and the reasons therefore. Second, a negotiable proposal should be able to require that a selecting official draft a long narrative stating with specificity all reasons the nonselectees were not selected, all reasons the selectee was selected, and a complete comparison between the selectee and each nonselectee. The FLRA has held negotiable a proposal providing that "when the selecting official, for a valid reason, requests additional name(s) be added to a Referral and Selection Register because an employee named on the original register cannot be selected, and other names are added, a copy of selecting official's reason(s) for which the individual cannot be selected will be made available to the Union, upon written request of the employee."[161]

A proposal is negotiable although it may have the effect of determining who will or will not be the selecting official. In *Kirk Army Hospital* the FLRC determined that the following proposal was negotiable:

Should any personal relationship exist between the selecting supervisor and any referred candidates the supervisor shall refer the certificate to the next higher supervisor for selection.[162]

The council rejected both the agency's section 12(b)(2) argument and its section 11(b) staffing patterns argument.

In a like case, *Veterans Administration Research Hospital*, the negotiability of the following proposal was in dispute:

Positions will normally be filled from within the Hospital structure when there are three highly qualified candidates available. Prior to notifying the Personnel Division of a proposed selection the selecting official shall advise the VAISEU steward of the proposed selection. If the steward desires, the selecting official shall provide him with information concerning the reasons for the proposed selection and the written materials used in making said selection (written materials concerning an employee shall only be provided with his consent.) Notification to the Personnel Division shall not be made until the steward has had until the end of the steward's second tour of duty following receipt of notice of the proposed selection from the selecting officer

---

161. NFFE Local 1671 and Adjutant General, Arkansas National Guard, 1 FLRA 11 (1979).

162. Lodge 2424, IAM-AW and Kirk Army Hospital and Aberdeen Research and Development Center, Aberdeen, Maryland, FLRC No. 72A-18 (1973).

to request review by the next highest level supervisor who has not participated in the proposed selection under review. The decision by this supervisor will be final and not subject to further review. If the steward has decided not to seek review of the decision he shall immediately notify the selecting officer so that the Personnel Division may receive notice of the decision.[163]

In rejecting the agency's arguments based on section 12(b)(2) of the executive order and on Civil Service Commission regulations, the council held the proposal negotiable, deferring the argument based on CSC regulations to the commission. The CSC answered that no commission regulation "puts any mandatory requirement on the level at which the selecting authority should rest. We view this as a matter that is subject to management discretion." Based on this, the council ruled that the proposal was not inconsistent with mandatory CSC requirements. The council went to great length in explaining its rejection of the agency's 12(b)(2) argument:

Section 12(b) dictates that in every labor agreement management officials retain their existing authority to take certain personnel actions, i.e., to hire, promote, etc. The emphasis is on the reservation of management authority to decide and act on these matters, and the clear import is that no right accorded to unions under the Order may be permitted to interfere with that authority. However, there is no implication that such reservation of decision making and action authority is intended to bar negotiation of procedures, to the extent consonant with law and regulations, which management will observe in reaching the decision or taking the action involved, provided that such procedures do not have the effect of negating the authority reserved.

Here, the union's proposal would establish procedures whereby higher level management review of a selection for promotion may be obtained before the promotion is consummated. The proposal does not require management to negotiate a promotion selection or to secure union consent to the decision. Nor does it appear that the procedures proposed would unreasonably delay or impede promotion selections so as to, in effect, deny the right to promote reserved to management by section 12(b)(2). Under these circumstances, we find that the union's proposal is not rendered nonnegotiable by section 12(b)(2) of the Order.[164]

Temporary Promotions

The grade of the position that an employee occupies, not the grade of the duties that the employee actually performs, determines the grade at which an employee is paid. If a GS-5 employee is officially placed in a GS-6 position, then the employee is entitled to GS-6 pay, even if

---

163. Veterans Administration Independent Service Employees Union and Veterans Administration Research Hospital, Chicago, Illinois, FLRC No. 71A-31 (1972).

164. *Id.* at 3.

all the work that the employee actually performs is below the GS-6 level. If the same GS-5 employee performs all GS-6 work but the employee is not officially placed in a GS-6 position, then the employee will be paid at the GS-5 level. If, however, the GS-5 employee is unofficially placed in a GS-6 position and performs GS-6 work, then the employee is entitled to be paid at the GS-6 level if he or she is in the position for more than one hundred twenty days or for any lesser period of time as provided by contract or agency regulation.[165]

In *VA Atlanta Regional Office*, the union had submitted one proposal addressing both temporary promotion and temporary performance of higher graded duties.

An employee temporarily placed in a higher grade position or assignment to a group of duties warranting a higher grade will be temporarily promoted, if the assignment is to exceed 60 days.[166]

The agency contended that the agency's reserved right to promote or not promote, under section 12(b)(2) of the executive order, rendered nonnegotiable the portion of the proposal requiring a temporary promotion for an employee temporarily placed in a higher grade position. In dismissing this argument and in holding this portion of the proposal to be negotiable, the FLRC reasoned that:

[t]he "temporary promotion" called for by the disputed provision is simply a ministerial act which implements the decision and action taken by the agency itself in selecting and assigning the particular employee to the higher grade position. Nothing in the provision interferes in any manner with the right of the agency to make such decision or accomplish such action, and thus nothing in the provision impairs the agency's right to determine whether and whom temporarily to promote. Accordingly, we find that the disputed provision is not violative of section 12(b)(2) of the Order.[167]

But the council held nonnegotiable the portion of the proposal that required a temporary promotion for an employee assigned to a group of duties warranting a higher grade than the grade of the position that the employee occupied. The council's decision was based upon a comptroller general's decision that an employee may not be paid at the higher grade until the position has been officially classified upward.[168]

In contrast to the FLRC's decision in *VA Atlanta Regional Office*,

---

165. Comptroller general decision No. B-180010.08 (May 4, 1976).
166. FLRC No. 77A-94 (1978).
167. *Id.* at 10.
168. *Supra* note 165.

in *Wright-Patterson Air Force Base* the FLRA held negotiable a proposal containing language subtly but significantly different.[169] The proposal did not address merely the assignment of higher graded duties generally, but rather, higher graded duties *of a position.*

When an employee is temporarily assigned the duties of a higher graded position for 30 consecutive days, the employee will receive the rate of pay for the higher position to which assigned, commencing on the 31st day.

The authority reasoned,

[T]he requirement that the employee receive the higher rate of pay is tantamount to a requirement that the employee who has been selected by management be temporarily promoted to the higher graded position . . . the requirement that an employee temporarily serving in or performing the duties of a higher graded position be paid the rate of pay of the higher graded position must be interpreted as consistent with applicable law, that is, as requiring that the employee be temporarily promoted to that position.[170]

In *Pearl Harbor* the negotiability of the following proposal was disputed:

When an employee is detailed to a higher level position in excess of 20 work days within a calendar year, the employee will be temporarily promoted to the higher level position commencing with the 21st day if he/she is eligible and otherwise qualified for a temporary promotion.[171]

The council held the proposal negotiable to the extent that it applied to positions within the bargaining unit; the proposal was nonnegotiable to the extent that it applied to supervisory positions outside the bargaining unit. In *Arkansas National Guard,* the authority held negotiable a proposal providing that "an employee detailed to a higher grade position for over sixty (60) days will be given a temporary promotion on the 61st day of the detail."[172] In two similar decisions, the Federal Labor Relations Authority held negotiable the following proposals:

The Employer agrees that an employee who is detailed to a bargaining unit position of a higher grade for over thirty (30) consecutive calendar days and who meets the appropriate qualifications and time-in-grade requirements as set forth by statute or Civil Service regulations will be temporarily promoted and receive the rate of pay for that position. The Employer agrees to refrain

169. 2 FLRA 77 (1980).

170. *Id.* 26–27.

171. Service Employee's International Union, Local 556, AFL-CIO and Submarine Force, U.S. Pacific Fleet and Naval Submarine Base, Pearl Harbor, Hawaii, FLRC No. 78A-65 (1978).

172. 1 FLRA 11 (1979).

from rotating details of employees solely to avoid compensation at the higher level.[173]

and

When an employee is temporarily assigned to an encumbered, but temporarily vacant bargaining unit position of a higher grade for 30 days, the employee will receive the rate of pay for the higher position to which assigned, commencing on the 31st day.[174]

In *Cherry Point* the union had submitted a merit promotion proposal that, among other things, would have required use of competitive merit promotion procedures for temporary promotions for 120 days or less.[175] Use of competitive merit promotion procedures would have required anyone receiving a temporary promotion to meet the minimum eligibility requirements for the position being filled and to have been rated best qualified. The agency contended that the proposal violated the reserved management right to promote and assign employees to positions within the agency. The council concluded that the proposal was nonnegotiable.

Similarly, the section 12(b)(2) right to promote includes the right to temporarily promote without resort to competitive procedures. The disputed proposal, however, in effect would deny management the authority to temporarily promote employees to positions unless those employees had been determined, competitively, to be among the top three or fewer qualified candidates. The effect of this denial of authority would be to prevent management from temporarily promoting qualified employees without resort to competition.

These limitations imposed by the proposal on management's right . . . without use of competitive procedures to temporarily promote bargaining unit employees would so constrict management's discretion in the exercise of its right to . . . promote personnel under section 12(b)(2) as to effectively deny that right. Accordingly, insofar as the proposal would in effect negate management's right to . . . temporarily promote employees noncompetitively, it is nonnegotiable.[176]

FLRA decisions on the issue of merit procedures for temporary positions should differ from those of the FLRC. First, section 7106(a)(2)(C) of the CSRA simply reserves to agency management the right to make, from appropriate sources, selections for appointment. Unlike section 12(b)(2) of the executive order, section

---

173. NTEU and U.S. Customs Service, Region IX, 2 FLRA 8 (1979). *See also* AFGE Council of Prison Locals and Department of Justice, Bureau of Prisons, FLRC No. 78A-122 (1979), a case that arose under the FLRC but was decided by the FLRA.

174. 2 FLRA 77 (1980).

175. FLRC No. 77A-28 (1978).

176. *Id.* 5–6.

7106(a)(2)(b) does not reserve to the agency the right to promote to positions within the agency, or even the basic right to promote or not promote. Accordingly, the retained management rights do not prevent negotiation of a proposal requiring that all temporary promotions be conducted according to competitive merit promotion procedures. Second, under the CSRA, the fact that a proposal might significantly or even greatly constrict a right reserved to management is no longer sufficient reason to render the proposal nonnegotiable. Under the CSRA, a proposal is negotiable unless it would prevent management from acting "at all."[177] Third, as revised by *FPM* letter 335-12, *FPM* chapter 335, subchapter 1-5(C)(4) provides that, at the agency's discretion, competitive procedures may or may not be used for temporary promotions of 120 or fewer days, and subchapter 1-5(A)(1) provides that competitive procedures must be used for temporary promotions of more than 120 days to higher graded positions. Note carefully that the agency is not prohibited from using competitive procedures for temporary promotions of 120 or fewer days. The agency may in its discretion use competitive procedures and still be in full, absolute compliance with OPM regulations; how its discretion will be exercised is ordinarily negotiable. It follows that the issue of whether competitive procedure will be used for promotions of 120 or fewer days should be fully negotiable. Consistent with this reasoning, in *Bureau of Prisons* the authority held negotiable a proposal providing that competitive procedures would be used for the making of "temporary promotions of employees to a higher grade for a period longer than 60 days."[178]

Assignment of Employees to Higher Graded Positions

Under Executive Order 11,491, as amended, the Federal Labor Relations Council supported the right of agency management to place unqualified employees in higher graded positions. In *Pearl Harbor* the union had proposed that "when available, qualified employees only will be assigned to higher level positions."[179] The council first reasoned that the agency's section 12(b)(2) right to assign employees to positions within the agency encompassed both "temporary assignments" and "details." The second step in the council's analysis was

---

177. Rep. No. 95-1717, 95th Cong., 2d Sess. 158 (1978).
178. FLRC No. 78A-122 (1979).
179. FLRC No. 78A-65 (1978).

to observe that *FPM* chapter 300, subchapter 8-3, permits an agency to detail an employee to a higher graded position for fewer than sixty days without regard to whether or not the employee meets the minimum qualifications standards for the higher graded position. The council's third step was to conclude that the proposal would overly restrict an agency's right to assign unqualified employees to higher graded positions.

The union's proposal would require that, when the agency decides to fill a vacant "higher level position" by temporarily assigning or detailing an employee to that position, it must assign only an employee it has determined is qualified to fill that position, if such an employee is available. That is, the agency would be precluded from detailing an employee who may not be qualified to fill the vacant position until it has determined if there are unit employees who are qualified to fill that position and if any of those employees are available. In our opinion . . . by thus requiring the agency to determine the qualifications and availability of its employees as a precondition of its decision to detail an employee, particularly in circumstances where such a decision must be expeditiously made, would impose constraints upon agency management's exercise of its authority under section 12(b)(2) to temporarily assign or detail employees so as, in effect, to negate that authority.[180]

This decision, however, is most unlikely to govern under the CSRA of 1978. *FPM* chapter 300, subchapter 8-4(3) provides that details to higher graded positions for more than sixty days are required to be made according to competitive procedures. Among other things, this means that to be assigned to the higher graded position, an employee is required to meet the minimum eligibility standards for the position. In effect, there is no bar to use of competitive procedures to select which employees will be detailed, and in some instances Civil Service Commission regulations mandate use of such procedures. This makes the FLRC's decision in *Pearl Harbor* untenable. The Civil Service Commission had already decreed in regulation that use of competitive procedures to select which employee will be detailed for over sixty days to a higher graded position does not negate an agency's right to assign employees and is in fact required.[181]

The synthesis is that in *Pearl Harbor* the council relied upon

---

180. *Id.* at 5.

181. *FPM* chapter 300, subchapter 8-4(e) provides that, "except for brief periods, an employee should not be detailed to perform work of a higher grade level unless there are compelling reasons for doing so. Normally, an employee should be given a temporary promotion instead. If a detail of more than 60 days is made to a higher grade position, or to a position with known promotion potential, it must be made under competitive promotion procedures."

invalid reasoning. As documented by *FPM* chapter 300, subchapter 8-4(e), use of competitive procedures does not ipso facto overly restrict an agency's right to assign employees. A proposal is no longer non-negotiable merely because it constricts or delays exercise of a reserved management right. Except in emergencies where a detailee cannot be timely selected using competitive procedures or in very short details where it would be unreasonably inefficient and costly to use competitive procedures, there is no bar to requiring that competitive procedures be used to select which employee will be detailed to a higher graded position.

Under section 7106(a)(2)(C) of the CSRA of 1978, an agency may select from an appropriate source to fill a position, and while under 7106(a)(2)(A) an agency continues to possess the right generally to assign employees within the agency, an agency no longer retains the right to decide unilaterally that a particular employee will be assigned to a particular position within the agency. As revised by *FPM* letter dated December 29, 1978, *FPM* chapter 335, subchapter 1-5(A)(2), provides that competitive procedures must be used for selection of an employee to be detailed more than 120 days to a higher graded position. As the OPM has intimated, however, although the 60-day requirement has been increased to 120 days, there is no bar to the negotiation of a proposal providing that competitive procedures will be used to select which employee will be detailed for 60 days.[182] In other words, there is no bar to negotiation of a proposal providing that competitive procedures will be used to select which employee will be detailed to a position for a period of 120 or fewer days. Of course, such a proposal should contain a proviso to accommodate emergencies and very short details where it would be unreasonably inefficient and costly to conduct a competitive procedure.

Career Ladder Promotions

As revised by *FPM* letter 335-12, December 29, 1978, *FPM* chapter 335, subchapter 1-5(C)(1)(a), provides that, when an employee has been competitively placed into a position on a career ladder, then at the agency's discretion promotion up the ladder may or may not be competitive. The only limitations would be that to be promoted the employee must meet the minimum qualification standards for the

---

182. *See* revised *FPM* chapter 335, subchapter 1-5. *Supra* note 136.

higher graded position and comply with any time-in-grade restrictions. The time-in-grade restrictions result primarily from the civil service regulations that were promulgated to implement the Whitten Amendment and that continue to survive despite the long overdue death of what was a rider to the 1951 National Emergency Act.[183]

The interest that unions have in career ladder promotions is to ensure that employees are promoted to the next higher grade as soon as legally possible. In *SSA, Denver* the following proposal was before the council:

All employees in career ladder positions will be promoted when the employer has certified that the employee is capable of satisfactorily performing all aspects of current level and demonstrated ability to perform at the next higher level, provided time-in-grade requirements have been met.[184]

In a decision using curious logic, the FLRC held that the proposal did not violate section 12(b) of the executive order, but rather it violated the organization language of section 11(b).[185] The FLRC asserted that the proposal purported "to assign the particular agency function . . . to the Denver District Manager. . . ." This assertion, however, is completely unsupported by any language actually contained in the proposal, and the council's opinion neither supplied nor cited any factual evidence to support it. Accordingly, the decision in *SSA, Denver* would unlikely withstand the scrutiny of judicial review that is provided for by section 7123 of the CSRA of 1978. No such review could have been had under Executive Order 11,491, as amended.

Notwithstanding the lack of reasoning and evidence plaguing the FLRC's determination in *SSA, Denver*, it nonetheless follows from the decision that there should be no negotiability problem with a proposal providing that when any time-in-grade requirement has been met, the employee is capable of doing higher-graded work, and such work is available, then an employee in a career ladder position "will be

---

183. *See* 5 C.F.R. § 300.601 *et seq.* The Whitten Amendment was actually a rider to the 1951 National Emergency Act that Congress enacted during the Korean War. It provided that an employee could not be promoted to a higher grade until after the employee had served twelve months in the lower grade. *See* 5 U.S.C. § 3101 as it existed before the 1978 amendment. On September 14, 1978, the Whitten Amendment terminated under section 101 of Public Law 94-412, September 14, 1976 (90 Stat. 1225).

184. AFGE Local 1802 and Department of Health, Education and Welfare, Social Security Administration, Denver District, FLRC No. 77A-148 (1978).

185. The same language is contained in Title 5, U.S.C., section 7106(a)(2)(A).

promoted, regardless of which manager at whatever level may be assigned the function of authorizing career ladder promotions." Consistent with this conclusion, in *U.S. Customs Service, Region IX* the FLRA held negotiable the following proposal:

All employees in identified career ladder positions working below the full (journeyman) level will be certified and promoted on the first day of the first pay period after a period of one (1) calendar year or whatever lesser period may be applicable provided that the employee has demonstrated the ability to perform at the next higher grade level and there is sufficient higher level work to be performed.[186]

In this opinion, which applied executive order law because the negotiability dispute had arisen before the effective date of the CSRA of 1978, the FLRA recognized the reality that once an employee has been placed within a career ladder, promotion on the ladder is usually automatic. In effect, an employee has a right to the reasonable expectation that he or she will be promoted, provided administrative requirements are met. Certification of such a promotion is normally a de facto ministerial act not involving an independent decision that a promotion action will or will not transpire. For collective bargaining purposes, this decision effectively repudiated the fiction, created and perpetrated by the Civil Service Commission before the CSRA of 1978, that promotion within a career ladder is never automatic, that an employee has no right to reasonably expect that he or she will be promoted if administrative requirements are met, and that certification is always a discretionary act encompassing an independent decision that a promotion action will or will not transpire.

Hours of Work and Overtime

Regular Duty Hours and Starting and Quitting Times
Title 5, U.S.C., chapter 55 defines the regular workweek as consisting of forty hours and the regular workday as consisting of eight hours. Naturally, no proposal about the regular workweek or workday may conflict with this statute.[187] Starting and quitting times are not speci-

---

186. National Treasury Employees Union and United States Custom Service, Region IX, FLRC No. 78A-29, 2 FLRA 8 (1979).

187. *But see* Public Law 95-390, September 29, 1978, "Federal Employees Flexible and Compressed Work Schedules" (5 U.S.C. § 6101).

fied in the U.S.C., and, with one minor exception, daily starting and quitting times are negotiable.

The definitive case on the negotiability of hours of work and duty hours is *Department of Agriculture*, in which the negotiability of the following proposal was at issue:

Work week: It is agreed that the basic work week is forty (40) hours and the basic work day is eight (8) hours. This work week shall commence at 6:00 A.M. . . .[188]

In finding that the proposal was negotiable, the FLRC held that work schedules and particularly duty hours and starting time are negotiable subject matter and that negotiation is not barred by the tour of duty language of the staffing patterns exception now found in section 7106(b)(1) of the CSRA of 1978.

The dispositive nature of this holding can be fully appreciated upon review of the background of the case. The case was originally decided on December 27, 1973, when the FLRC held negotiable the proposal as it specified the number of days in a workweek, the number of hours in a workday, and starting time. Specifically, the council held: that no applicable statutes barred negotiation of work schedules and starting time; that section 12(b)(4) of the executive order did not bar negotiation of work schedules and starting time; that neither section 11(b) nor 12(b)(5) of the executive order barred negotiation of hours of work and duty hours; and that under section 11(a) of the executive order, the parties were obligated to negotiate work schedules and starting time.[189]

Subsequently, the case was appealed to United States District Court for the Eastern District of Virginia, Alexandria Division. The appeal sought review and reversal of the council's decision.[190] The court remanded the case for further consideration. Thereupon the FLRC requested additional information, carefully reconsidered the case, and issued a supplemental opinion and decision on June 10,

---

188. American Federation of Government Employees, National Joint Council of Food Inspection Locals and Office of the Administrator, Animal Plant and Health Inspection Service, United States Department of Agriculture, FLRC No. 73A-36 (1973) and FLRC No. 73A-36 (1975).

189. FLRC No. 73A-36 (1973).

190. National Broiler Council Inc. v. Federal Labor Relations Council, 382 F. Supp. 322, 328 (April 24, 1974). *See also* FLRC No. 73A-36 (1975) 4–5.

1975.[191] That decision held that a proposal concerning work hours, and particularly duty hours or starting time, is negotiable under section 11(a) of the order and is not made nonnegotiable by the tour of duty language found in section 11(b). Noting that the proposal at issue specified duty hours and a starting time, the council reasoned,

[T]herefore, as decided by the Council in *Plum Island, Charleston*, FLRC No. 71A-52, and related cases, a proposal relating to basic work week and hours of duty of employees is not excepted by an agency's bargaining obligation under section 11(b) unless, based on the special circumstances of a particular case (as in *Plum Island*), the proposal is integrally related to and consequently determinative of the staffing patterns of the agency, i.e., the numbers, types and grades of positions or employees assigned to the organizational unit, work project or tour of duty of the agency.[192]

Previously, the council had held that the number of days in a week, the number of hours in a workweek, and the specific days of the workweek were negotiable. In *Naval Supply Center, Charleston* the union had proposed that "the basic work week shall consist of five (5) eight (8) hour days, Monday through Friday. . . ."[193] The agency had contended that the proposal was nonnegotiable under section 12(b)(4)'s efficiency language and the staffing patterns language. The council disagreed and held that the proposal was negotiable. According to the council, the proposal would boost morale and enhance physical and mental well-being, and these benefits outweighed the agency's section 12(b)(4) efficiency claim that the proposal would cause the government to pay avoidable overtime. As to the staffing patterns exception, the proposal in *Naval Supply Center, Charleston* was not integrally related to or determinative of staffing patterns because it would not require the agency to bargain on numbers, types, and grades of positions or employees assigned to any organizational segment or tour of duty; nor did the proposal pretend to be determinative of the number of shifts the agency would use in accomplishing its mission.

The only exception to the obligation to negotiate the substance of hours of work and duty hours is a narrow one. This narrow exception, the "*Plum Island* exception," occurs where special circumstances create the "integral relationship" between hours of work and duty

---

191. FLRC No. 73A-36 (1975).

192. *Id.* at 18.

193. Federal Employees Metal Trades Council of Charleston and U.S. Naval Supply Center, Charleston, South Carolina, FLRC No. 71A-52 (1972).

hours and staffing patterns that allows hours of work to determine these patterns.[194] The narrowness of the *Plum Island* exception is best explained by the reasoning of the FLRC in *Department of Agriculture*.

As will be recalled, the agency in *Plum Island* operated a research facility and, in order to provide for round-the-clock operation and maintenance, it employed four crews of 11 men each, who worked on three rotating, weekly shifts and who supplemented a regular, one-shift crew of maintenance employees. The agency had decided to eliminate the entire third shift in one of its two laboratory buildings and to establish two new fixed shifts working on a five day basis. . .However, the union proposed that any such changes in tours of duty (and hence the staffing of the new fixed first and second shifts and the restaffing of the rotating shifts) be proscribed unless negotiated with the union.

The Council held (in *Plum Island*) that the union's proposal was excepted from the agency's obligation to bargain under section 11(b), and, more particularly under the exclusion in that section relating to "the numbers, types, and grades of positions or employees assigned to an organizational unit, work project or tour of duty." As observed by the Council, this language of the Order, according to section E.1. of the Report accompanying Executive Order 11,491, clarified the right of the agency to determine the "staffing patterns" for its organization and for accomplishing its mission. The Council found that the number and duration of the work shifts, or tours of duty, as intended to be changed by the agency in that case, were *integrally related to and determinative of the numbers and types of employees assigned to those tours of duty of the agency*; and therefore that, under the facts of that case, the union's proposal to bargain on such changes was nonnegotiable under section 11(b).[195]

This reasoning corresponds with the actual language of the staffing patterns exception as it existed within section 11(b) of the executive order and as it now exists in section 7106(b)(1) of the CSRA of 1978. The language of the staffing patterns exception does not state that tour of duty is excepted subject matter from the agency's obligation to bargain; it does state that an agency is not obligated to negotiate about "the numbers, types and grades of positions or employees" assigned to an organizational unit, work project, or tour of duty. Therefore, the council's holdings may be phrased as a presumption: any proposal regarding work schedules and duty hours is negotiable, and this presumption can be overcome only by a demonstration that the bargaining proposal has the effect of directing the numbers, types, and grades of positions or employees to be assigned to a tour of duty.

---

194. AFGE Local 1940 and Plum Island Animal Disease Laboratory, Department of Agriculture, Greenport, New York, FLRC No. 71A-11 (1971).

195. FLRC No. 73A-36 (1975) 15–16.

The burden of making this showing rests upon the agency.[196] Nothing less than clear and unmistakable evidence will suffice to satisfy this burden of proof.[197]

Consistent with the *Plum Island* exception, the FLRC and the assistant secretary held nonnegotiable other proposals that would have been determinative of the number of shifts or the number of employees assigned to a shift. In *Department of the Navy*, the union had submitted a proposal that, in effect, would have required the agency to use three shifts rather than two in conducting operations.[198] The assistant secretary held the proposal nonnegotiable under the staffing patterns exception. Similarly, *Federal Employees Metal Trades Council* makes it clear that the staffing patterns exception makes nonnegotiable a bargaining proposal either restricting the number of employees or positions that may be assigned to shifts or determining the number of shifts, as long as each shift is sufficiently distinguishable from other shifts so that each constitutes a separate, identifiable tour of duty.[199] For example, in *Plum Island*, the union proposal prohibited a third shift; since the third shift was to work during nights and without it the nights would not have been worked, the shift constituted a separate, identifiable tour of duty. But in *IRS, Kansas City Service Center*, one particular unit, a taxpayer assistance section, worked from 6:30 a.m. to 3:50 p.m. Within these duty hours, the agency wanted one shift to work from 6:30 a.m. to 3:00 p.m. and a second shift to work from

---

196. In *AFGE Local 1966 and Veterans Administration Hospital, Lebanon, Pennsylvania*, the council stated that "there was no showing *by the agency* that the basic work week for employees involved was integrally related to the numbers and types of employees in question. . . ." FLRC No. 72A-41 (1973) 3.

197. "It is clear from the Council's ruling that the matter of the basic work week and duty hours of employees are bargainable subjects where an activity may not act unilaterally with regard thereto absent 'special circumstances showing the subject to be integrally related to and consequently determinative of the staffing patterns of the agency.' I interpret the Council's decisions to place the burden on an agency to affirmatively show the existence of the 'special circumstances and integral relationship,' and, as is with the case with the claimed waiver of rights granted by the Order . . . such should not be lightly inferred and should be 'clear and unmistakable.' " Administrative law judge Salvatore J. Arrigo, Southwest Exchange Region, AAFES, Rosewood Warehouse, South Carolina and NFFE Local 1613, Case No. 40-5987 (CA), recommended decision and order, October 10, 1975, affirmed on these grounds as to these matters, reversed in part on other matters on different grounds, A/SLMR No. 656 (May 29, 1976).

198. Department of the Navy, Naval Plant Representative Office, Baltimore, Maryland, A/SLMR No. 486 (February 28, 1975).

199. Federal Employees Metal Trades Council of Charleston, AFL-CIO, and Charleston Naval Shipyard, Charleston, South Carolina, FLRC No. 72A-35 (1973).

7:20 a.m. to 3:50 p.m. The union proposed a third shift which would work from 7:00 a.m. to 3:30 p.m.[200] The FLRA ruled that, inasmuch as the unit worked only nine hours and twenty minutes, from 6:30 a.m. to 3:50 p.m., this period constituted a single tour of duty. From this perspective, the union proposal simply provided different starting and quitting times within the single tour of duty, which did not call for creation of a shift that would have an identity separate and apart from the basic hours of 6:30 a.m. to 3:50 p.m. Since the union proposal was not determinative of the numbers, types, or grades of employees assigned to the 6:30 a.m. to 3:50 p.m. tour of duty, it was declared negotiable.

On infrequent occasion, unusual circumstances may make it impossible to assign employees to permanent, fixed shifts or to shifts that rotate on a fixed basis. In such circumstances, the parties may negotiate standards and guidelines governing the scheduling of days-on and days-off. Proposals must not, however, go so far as to determine the numbers or grades of personnel that may be assigned to any particular tour of duty. For example, in *Wright-Patterson Air Force Base*, the last sentence of the following proposal was disputed:

Nurses shall have their tours of duty arranged to permit each person to have two consecutive days off in each calendar work week. Any nurse may request to waive the right in writing. Days may be split preceding or following a weekend off. Saturday and Sunday will not normally be scheduled off unless both are scheduled off. Nurses will have every other weekend off.[201]

A direct effect of the proposal would have been to have required the agency to hire additional, qualified nurses to meet the medical staffing necessary to render adequate patient care. Hence the proposal was integrally related to numbers and types of employees and accordingly declared nonnegotiable.

One type of proposal that is negotiable is one calling for a modified form of flexitime, staggered working hours. Under this concept, there is a "core time" within which all employees must be present at their job, and attached to the starting and ending points of the core time are flexible "bands" within which the employee may vary starting and quitting times; the number of hours worked, how-

---

200. NTEU Chapter 66 and Internal Revenue Service, Kansas City Service Center, 1 FLRA 106 (1979).
201. 2 FLRA 77 (1980).

ever, must be eight a day. For example, in *Marshall Space Flight Center*, the negotiability of such a proposal was disputed.

Each daily tour of duty will include a core period to be worked by all employees from 9:00 a.m. to 2:30 p.m. The additional three (3) hours to be worked within the flexible time bands during the 6:00 a.m. to 5:30 p.m. time period.[202]

In other words, an employee would be required to work the five and a half hours from 9:00 a.m. to 2:30 p.m. Two and a half hours could be worked entirely from 6:00 a.m. to 9:00 a.m., or split, as from 7:30 a.m. to 9:00 a.m. and 2:30 p.m. to 4:00 p.m., or any other combination that, with a half-hour lunch period, would produce an eight and one-half hour day. According to the FLRC's reasoning, the proposal did not encroach upon management's reserved right to direct employees because it did not give any employee the right to "refuse to perform work assigned to him, to refuse a direct management order, or to refuse to appear for work when ordered to do so"; it did not encroach upon means and methods because it did not give employees the right to "refuse work when ordered to do so" or "to require that individual employees or groups of employees be assigned specific terms of duty outside the flexible allowances when such assignment is necessary to accomplish the mission"; and it would not be determinative of staffing patterns. The council's treatment of the staffing patterns contention is noteworthy because the agency had argued that the proposal would create an extended period (potentially from 6:00 a.m. to 5:30 p.m.) during which full support services (e.g., administrative, clerical, and technical) would have to be provided. This would either require management to increase the numbers of support personnel in order to staff the extended period—make the proposal determinative of the number of personnel—or require management to create a new shift for support personnel for the extended period. In a decision that will establish no record for incisive reasoning addressing the actual issues, the FLRC rejected the agency's staffing patterns argument on the ground that

it would appear that, if certain support facilities were available only at certain hours of the day and such facilities were needed by unit personnel,

---

202. Marshall Engineers and Scientists Association, Local 27, International Federation of Professional and Technical Engineers, AFL-CIO and National Aeronautics and Space Flight Center, Huntsville, Alabama, FLRC No. 76A-81 (1977).

the proposal would not limit management's ability to assure that the work schedules of those personnel included hours when such facilities were available.[203]

Although the council planted the innuendo that the starting and quitting times of bargaining unit personnel may be virtually required to coordinate with the starting and quitting times of nonunit personnel, the FLRC's decision constituted rejection of the argument that a proposal concerning starting and quitting times may be rendered nonnegotiable by the fact that an agency will be forced to increase its staff of nonunit support personnel.

Overtime

Work in excess of eight hours a day or in excess of forty hours a week is usually classified as overtime.[204] Overtime is a matter affecting working conditions and therefore one which management must negotiate.[205] Numerous statutes and regulations control overtime, however, and any proposal regarding overtime must not conflict with these. In *Adjutant General of New Mexico*, the council found a union proposal nonnegotiable because it conflicted with statute prescribing compensatory time, as opposed to pay, for overtime.[206] In *U.S. Marshals Service*, the FLRC held a proposal nonnegotiable because it employed definitions of administratively uncontrollable overtime and premium pay that did not comport with the statutory definitions.[207]

Management retains the right to determine whether overtime will or will not be performed; however, management must negotiate the procedures to be observed in reaching or implementing the decision,

---

203. *Id.* at 5.

204. As used in this subsection, the term *overtime* refers only to overtime within the meaning of Title 5, U.S.C. It does not include, and is separate from, overtime within the meaning of the Fair Labor Standards Act. Public Law 93-259 (April 8, 1974) made FLSA applicable to the federal sector. *See* FPM letter 551-1 (May 15, 1974) and FPM letter 551-9 (March 30, 1976).

205. Local Union No. 2219, International Brotherhood of Electrical Workers AFL-CIO and Department of Army Corps of Engineers, Little Rock District, Little Rock, Ark., FLRC No. 71A-46 (1972).

206. National Federation of Federal Employees Local 1636 and Adjutant General of New Mexico, FLRC No. 73A-23 (1976). The union's proposal provided that National Guard technicians would be paid time-and-a-half for overtime. This proposal conflicted with Title 32, U.S.C., section 709(g)(2), which prohibits paying overtime to technicians and requires that they be granted compensatory time off from regular duties in lieu of overtime.

207. Department of Justice, U.S. Marshals Service, and International Council of USMS Locals, AFGE, FLRC No. 78A-105 (1978).

provided such procedures do not have the effect of negating the re-served authority. For example, management's reserved rights to de-termine methods, means, and the personnel by which work will be accomplished do not prohibit negotiation of proposals affecting the assignment of overtime. In *Philadelphia Naval Shipyard*, the bargaining proposal at issue provided that the employer would not assign to nonunit employees the overtime duties of unit employees, where such assignment would be for the sole purpose of eliminating the need for unit employees.[208] The council reasoned that such a proposal was negotiable because it concerned only the assignment of overtime and did not restrict management's right to decide that overtime would or would not be performed. The agency had also argued that negotiation of assignment of overtime was also restricted by the staffing patterns exception. The FLRC firmly rejected this contention, observing that an overtime proposal is negotiable unless integrally related to staffing patterns and holding that the overtime assignment proposal in dispute was not integrally related to staffing patterns.

The FLRC held negotiable a number of other proposals address-ing the assignment of overtime. It found negotiable one proposal requiring that overtime be assigned fairly and equitably[209] and another proposal necessitating agreement on when overtime shifts would be scheduled.[210] In still another case, *VA Hospital, Altoona*, the FLRC held that management's reserved rights did not bar negotiation of the following proposal:

Section 1. The parties agree that it is the intent of this article that overtime shall be equitably distributed among interested employees (by job categories) on a calendar year basis, insofar as possible. In those services where overtime may be required, the overtime rosters will be maintained in the Service Chief's office, in the following manner: . . .

b. Those employees desiring to be included on the voluntary overtime roster will notify the Service Chief in writing.

c. When it is determined that overtime will be required, the official as-signing the overtime will begin by contacting the most senior (SCD) em-ployees on the voluntary list, and will continue this procedure in descending order (SCD) and continue in descending order until the overtime require-ment is satisfied.

d. In the event the voluntary procedure does not satisfy the overtime re-quirements, the official will then assign the overtime to the remaining non-

---

volunteer employees beginning with the least senior (SCD) and continue in ascending order until the overtime requirement is satisfied.

e. For purposes of this article, when an employee on the voluntary list is given the opportunity to work overtime and does not wish to do so, he will be considered to have worked the overtime for "equitable distribution purposes". . . .

Section 3. When assigning non-voluntary overtime, management will upon request, relieve an employee from overtime assignment if his reason is an emergency, and there is another qualified employee available for that overtime assignment. . . .

Section 5. When it is known in advance that there will be an overtime requirement, employees assigned overtime work will be given as much advance notice of such assignments as possible. The Supervisor shall make a reasonable effort to provide a minimum of 4 hours of work to an employee who is requested to perform work on an overtime basis on a non-scheduled work day.[211]

In holding this proposal negotiable, the FLRC expressly relied upon the decision in *U.S. Customs Service, Region VII*.[212] That decision had held negotiable proposals providing a procedure whereby an employee could swap overtime assignment with another employee and a procedure whereby an employee could be relieved of an overtime assignment if another employee was available and willing to work.

The council's decisions with respect to overtime assignment were not fully consistent with the council's decisions regarding assignment of work within regular duty hours. For example, in *Coast Guard Base, Miami* the FLRC held that the *personnel by which agency work will be accomplished* of section 12(b)(5) of the executive order did not bar negotiation of a proposal providing that

[t]he employer shall not assign normal scheduled overtime to the employees who do not perform this job description during the week except in emergency situations.[213]

This ruling contrasts with the rulings in *VA Hospital, Denver, Office of Dependent Schools, Wright-Patterson Air Force Base, Long Beach Naval*

---

211. American Federation of Government Employees, Local 1862 and Veterans Administration Hospital, Altoona, Pa., FLRC No. 76A-128 (1977). The FLRC remanded the case for an agency determination of whether the proposal violated an agency regulation for which a compelling need possibly existed.

212. FLRC No. 76A-28 (1977).

213. Local 1485, National Federation of Federal Employees, and Coast Guard Base, Miami, Florida, FLRC No. 75A-77 (1976).

Shipyard, and *VA Hospital, Salisbury.*[214] The council declared the proposal in *Coast Guard Base, Miami* negotiable because

[u]nder the disputed provision in the present case, if management determines that "normal scheduled overtime" performed "during the week" by particular employees at the base, then management shall not assign the same tasks to other employees to perform on *overtime,* "except in emergency situations." Thus it is clear that the instant provision, unlike the proposal in *Tidewater:* (1) is concerned only with the type of work which management has previously assigned to unit employees to perform on a regular-time basis, i.e., "during the week"; (2) relates to such work only when the agency has specifically designated it to be performed as scheduled *overtime;* and (3) would not restrict management in any way in otherwise assigning to unit or non-unit employees work to be performed during periods which have not been designated as scheduled overtime.[215]

Presumably, the FLRC determined that job content is based on duties performed within the course of the regular workweek, as distinguished from duties performed during overtime.

The issue in *Little Rock* was whether section 12(b)(4) barred negotiation of a union proposal that would have precluded the employer from reducing costs by reducing the amount of premium pay (administratively uncontrollable overtime).[216] The council reasoned that the efficiency exception in section 12(b)(4) could not be invoked to deny negotiations unless the agency demonstrated substantially that increased costs or reduced effectiveness would be inescapable and significant and would not be offset by compensating benefits. The council determined that the agency had not sustained this heavy burden and therefore found the union proposal negotiable. Inasmuch as the CSRA of 1978 does not carry over the efficiency language that appeared in section 12(b)(4), Executive Order 11,491, as amended, this result should remain good law.

Standby Time and On-Call Duty

Standby time (status) is usually defined as time outside regular duty hours during which an employee is required to remain at his or her regular duty station or residence ready to respond to calls for his or

---

214. Respectively, FLRC No. 74A-67 (1975), FLRC No. 76A-142 (1978), FLRC No. 74A-2 (1974), FLRC No. 73A-16 (1976), FLRC No. 75A-103 (1976).
215. FLRC No. 75A-77 (1976) at 6.
216. FLRC No. 71A-46 (1972).

her services; an employee may be paid for standby time.[217] On-call duty is usually defined as time outside regular duty hours during which an employee is required to leave word at the duty station so that he or she may be called to work if needed; an employee is not ordinarily paid for on-call duty.[218]

In *Public Health Service Hospital*, the negotiability of the following proposal was in dispute:

In areas where twenty-four (24) hour coverage is required those who are utilized will have their homes designated as the official stand-by duty station.[219]

The FLRC found the proposal nonnegotiable on the ground that it would be determinative of the methods by which agency operations are to be conducted. In reaching this decision, the council reasoned that, in administering health care, use of employees standing by at the hospital, or use of employees standing by at their homes who must take time to travel to the hospital whenever called, would be determinative of the methods used by the hospital to administer emergency care.

In contrast to its ruling on standby time, in the same case, the FLRC held negotiable the following proposal concerning on-call duty:

In those positions where twenty-four (24) hour coverage is required and it is the Employer's decision that "on call" rather than standby will be used, the parties agree that each individual employee assigned to "on call" status is strictly voluntary and that they have the right to refuse. It is further agreed that an employee assigned to "on call" may not be required to remain within a specified distance or time of the duty station and that no restriction will be placed on their movements. Further, refusal to serve in an "on call" status may not be considered in the annual performance evaluation or acceptable level of competence for a within grade increase. The Employer will not impose any restraint, interference, coercion, discrimination, or take any retribution against any employee who refuses to serve in an "on call" status or who when assigned "on call" should not be available when called.[220]

The council expounded at length on the fact that the proposal addressed not the agency's right to assign work and to assign and direct employees but rather the question of whether on-call would be vol-

---

217. 5 U.S.C. § 5545.
218. AFGE Local 1170 and DHEW, Public Health Service Hospital, Seattle, Washington, FLRC No. 76A-92 (1977).
219. *Id.*
220. *Id.*

untary or mandatory. According to the council, the agency would be better off to use employees in standby status. One cannot avoid the suspicion that the council held the proposal negotiable because the council took a dim view of the idea of requiring employees, without compensation, to serve in an on-call status.

Standby time served by employees at their duty stations must be compensated pursuant to law. On the other hand, it is equally clear that on-call time, as defined in agency personnel instructions, need not be compensated. Further, standby status is frequently characterized by various authorities as time spent predominantly for the employer's benefit, and on-call time is characterized as that time spent away from the worksite predominantly for the employee's benefit; thus, since standby time is for the employer's benefit it is clearly related to the operations of the agency. However, on-call time, which is uncompensated time spent by the employee away from the worksite pursuing activities predominantly in his own interest, clearly cannot be regarded as part of the operations of the agency.

Thus, it is our view that management does not retain the right under the Order to determine, unilaterally, to use on-call time as a method of carrying out agency operations. Hence, where, as here, a union proposes to negotiate with respect to the use of on-call time, section 12(b)(5) may not be asserted as a bar to negotiations. Accordingly, the proposal is not rendered nonnegotiable by section 12(b)(5) of the Order.

The Council takes a similar view of the agency's contention that this proposal is nonnegotiable since it would require the agency to alter its staffing patterns. Such a contention relates to the provisions of section 11(b) of the Order which except "matters with respect to . . . the numbers, types, and grades of positions or employees assigned to an organizational unit, work project or tour of duty" from an agency's basic obligation to negotiate under section 11(a). However, on-call time, which need not be compensated under applicable law as discussed above, is not such a "matter with respect to" an agency's staffing patterns. That is, since employees in on-call status legally are considered to pursue activities predominantly in their own, and not in the agency's interest, they are not, when in that status, "assigned to an organizational unit, work project, or tour of duty" within the meaning of section 11(b) of the Order.[221]

Compensation

Because the compensation of federal employees is controlled primarily by the General Schedule and wage grades established by Congress and by other statutes and rulings—such as for overtime, premium pay, night differential—very few federal sector labor cases have addressed this topic.

------

221. *Id.* 6-7.

In the federal sector, unlike the private sector, the amount of pay or compensation for regular or overtime work is clearly nonnegotiable. *Memphis Naval Air Station* concerned the question of the negotiability of a union proposal regarding overtime compensation.[222] The FLRC deferred the decision to the Civil Service Commission for a ruling on whether the proposal violated congressional statute and CSC regulations on the federal wage system. The CSC answered that the bargaining proposal was inconsistent with CSC regulations, and hence the FLRC declared it to be nonnegotiable.

Certain of the standards used in determining the rate of monetary compensation are negotiable, but they must be consistent with statute and OPM regulations. In *U.S. Marshals Service* the union had proposed with respect to overtime that

[a]ll hours of work performed in excess of eight hours in any one day and all hours of work performed in excess of forty hours in one administrative work-week by an employee shall be overtime. All overtime shall be paid at the appropriate rate of pay.

a. Employees will be compensated under the provisions of 5 USC 5545(c) where the hours of work in excess of eight hours per day or 40 hours per week cannot be controlled administratively. This may include courtroom duty, prisoner pickups and return and special assignment where overtime for these assignments cannot be anticipated. To qualify for AUO, overtime work would not be predictable in terms of when it would occur and how long it would last and is administratively uncontrollable.

b. Employees will be compensated under the provisions of 5 USC 5542 for overtime work that can be controlled administratively. This includes serving of papers, prisoner coordination trips and all other overtime including those duties described in Section a. where the overtime work is predictable in terms of when it would occur and how long it would last and is administratively controllable. All overtime under paragraph b. shall be defined regularly scheduled overtime regardless of its duration in accordance with Title 5 U.S.C. 5542.

Premium compensation for AUO defined in Section a. and for regularly scheduled overtime defined in Section b. relate to independent mutually exclusive methods for compensating two distinct forms of overtime work. Employees are not precluded from receiving regular (hourly) overtime pay in addition to AUO premium pay. However, employees cannot claim both for the same hours worked.[223]

---

222. NAGE Local 5-65 and Memphis Naval Air Station, Millington, Tennessee, FLRC No. 74A-104 (1975).

223. Department of Justice, U.S. Marshals Service and International Council of USMS Locals AFGE, FLRC No. 78A-105 (1978).

The council referred the proposal to the comptroller general, who replied,

Two fundamental defects render the proposal inconsistent with existing law governing entitlement to premium pay. First, contrary to the explicit language set forth in law and regulations, the union proposal fails to specify that in order to qualify for AUO premium pay, an employee must occupy a position which has been determined to require substantial amounts of irregular, unscheduled, overtime duty with the employee generally being responsible for recognizing, without supervision, circumstances which require him to remain on duty, within the meaning of 5 USC 5545(c)(2) and 5 CRF 550.153-550.161.

Second, contrary to explicit statutory and regulatory prohibition, the union proposal would require paying employees for uncontrollable overtime work under the annual premium pay provision of 5 USC 5545(c)(2) in addition to overtime pay for controllable overtime work under 5 USC 5542. The statute and related CSC regulations provide that employees shall be paid annual premium pay (AUO) for "irregular, unscheduled overtime" duty, and only as an exception may they be paid for additional "regularly scheduled overtime" work under 5 USC 5542.

The phrases used in the proposal, "cannot be controlled administratively" and "can be controlled administratively" are not synonymous with the statutory phrases "irregular, unscheduled overtime" duty and "regularly scheduled overtime" work used for determining entitlement to premium pay under title 5.

Two types of "irregular, unscheduled overtime" duty are compensable as administratively uncontrollable overtime (AUO) under 5 USC 5545(c)(2): one is that generally at the recognition of the employee, the other is at the direction of the agency. In contrast, the union proposal would effectively redefine all overtime which "can be controlled administratively" to mean "regularly scheduled overtime." Such a redefinition could include some "irregular, unscheduled overtime" worked by an employee at his own recognition and, no doubt, a considerable amount of work which is directed by the agency but not assigned on a regularly scheduled basis.

It is our opinion that the proposal is barred from negotiation on the basis that the provisions of 5 USC 5545(c)(2) and CSC regulations would be violated if "irregular, unscheduled overtime" duty would be considered "controllable" by the negotiated agreement, and therefore require compensation as "regularly scheduled overtime" work under 5 USC 5542.[224]

Based on the comptroller general's opinion, the council held the proposal nonnegotiable.

In *Wright-Patterson Air Force Base* the union had submitted a proposal calling for compensation of employees on the basis of the highest level of duties assigned for a substantial portion of continuous

---

224. *Id.* 4-5.

work assignment for a representative period of time.[225] The FLRC determined that the proposal did not conflict with statute or the *Federal Personnel Manual* and then declared the proposal negotiable. The FLRC specifically pointed out, however, that such a contract provision would not be subject to a negotiated grievance procedure because, as a classification appeal, it would be subject to a statutory appeals procedure.

Also, in *Merchant Marine Academy* the FLRC declared negotiable a proposal calling for a reduction in the number of steps from entry level to top of grade in the academy's faculty salary schedule.[226] This decision, however, may be limited to the particularities in the case since payment under the General Schedule was not involved. Similarly, in *McGuire Air Force Base* the FLRC issued decisions regarding nonappropriated fund employees,[227] and in *Office of Dependent Schools*[228] the FLRC issued decisions regarding teachers paid under the Overseas Teachers Pay and Personnel Practices Act of 1959, as amended.[229] These decisions, too, are of limited applicability since they did not address compensation of General Schedule and wage grade employees.

Leave

Statutes and regulations govern the accrual and availability of most leave and holidays. Regulations control the employee's right to and accrual of annual leave (vacation time),[230] sick leave[231] and maternity leave,[232] and although the parties may negotiate about such, their proposals are nonnegotiable if inconsistent with what corresponding regulations authorize. Within the same limitations, the parties may also negotiate leaves of absence and administrative leave.[233]

---

225. Local Lodge 2333, International Association of Machinists and Aerospace Workers and Wright-Patterson Air Force Base, Ohio, FLRC No. 74A-2 (1974).

226. United Federation of College Teachers Local 1460 and U.S. Merchant Marine Academy, FLRC No. 71A-15 (1972).

227. FLRC No. 77A-18 (1978) and No. 77A-21 (1978).

228. FLRC No. 76A-142 (1978).

229. 20 U.S.C. § 901 *et seq.*

230. 5 U.S.C., § 6301, *et seq.* See also *FPM* chapters 630 and 550.

231. *Id.*

232. *FPM* chapter 630.

233. NAGE Local R3-84 and Washington, D.C., Air National Guard, FLRC No. 72A-23 (1973).

As to annual, sick, or maternity leave, the parties are obligated to negotiate the procedures and conditions for use of such leave. For example, the amount of leave that may be used on consecutive workdays, the conditions and criteria for approval or disapproval of leave requests, guaranteed availability of leave under certain conditions, and the standards for resolving competing leave requests are all negotiable. If to ensure a competent decision on leave requests, however, a proposal requires approval of a leave request by a particular agency manager, that person must be within the agency's jurisdiction. For example, in *Hill Air Force Base* the negotiability of the last sentence of the following proposal was at issue:

All requests for advanced sick leave will be processed through the employee's immediate supervisor. Approval/Disapproval will be accomplished by the medical authorities and the Civilian Personnel Office.[234]

The agency was the exchange service, and the exchange service was vested with no authority over the Air Force medical office or the Air Force Civilian Personnel Office (the agency construed "medical authorities" as meaning the Air Force medical office, and the union failed to contest the contention). As a result, the council determined that the proposal was outside "the scope of mandatory bargaining."

Adverse Actions and Other Discipline

The greatest changes introduced by the CSRA of 1978 were in its revamping of the adverse action and disciplinary procedures operating in the federal sector. There are now four recognizable categories of punitive actions in the federal sector. First, pursuant to Title 5, U.S.C., section 7501 et seq., an employee may be suspended fourteen days or less for conduct-related matters, as distinguished from inefficient performance. This is classified as an adverse action. Second, pursuant to section 7511, and also based on conduct-related matters, an employee may be suspended for more than fourteen days, reduced in grade or pay, or removed. This is classified as an adverse action. Third, pursuant to section 4303 et seq. and based on unacceptable performance, an employee may be reduced in grade or removed. This is no longer classified as an adverse action. Fourth, an employee may be reprimanded in writing, admonished orally, or reassigned to an undesirable

---

234. FLRC No. 77A-123 (1978).

location or position. This last category is not addressed by the CSRA of 1978.

Under Executive Order 11,491, as amended, the FLRC held nonnegotiable several proposals providing that imposition of proposed discipline would be delayed pending binding arbitration. In *Alcohol, Tobacco and Firearms*, the union had submitted a proposal that, in effect, would have required that when the agency had decided to suspend an employee for thirty days or less and the union had invoked arbitration under an expedited arbitration procedure contained in the negotiated agreement, the suspension would be held in abeyance pending the outcome of the arbitration procedure.[235] The proposal gave the parties only five days to select an arbitrator, required that the arbitration hearing be set on the first available date, and required the arbitrator to issue an award within seven days of hearing. It did not, however, stipulate an exact date or time limit beyond which the arbitration procedure could not extend and the discipline could not be held in abeyance. Grasping at this, the FLRC interpreted the proposal as allowing all disciplinary actions to continue for indefinite periods of time before reaching arbitration, and the council then made the factual assumption that such could be reasonably expected to occur under the proposal. From this point, the FLRC decided that the proposal would "unreasonably delay" management's reserved right to discipline and that the proposal would completely negate management's reserved right to discipline.

Subsequently, the FLRC held nonnegotiable another proposal dealing with the staying of disciplinary action. In *U.S. Customs Service* the union had submitted a proposal providing that suspensions of four to thirty days would be stayed if the union invoked arbitration within three days.[236] The arbitration hearing was required to be held within thirty days, and the arbitrator was required to issue a decision three days after completion of the hearing. The proposal further provided that, if arbitration was not held within thirty days of invocation, the suspension would be implemented. In holding this proposal nonnegotiable, the FLRC engaged in some rather unfortunate reasoning. Specifically, although the proposal explicitly provided that the arbi-

---

235. National Treasury Employees Union and Bureau of Alcohol, Tobacco and Firearms, FLRC No. 77A-58 (1978).

236. National Treasury Employees Union and United States Customs Service, FLRC No. 78A-88 (1978).

tration "shall be held within thirty days of the employer's receipt of the union's notice of appeal," the FLRC incorrectly claimed that the proposal's language only required that the arbitration be "scheduled." Next, the FLRC correctly observed that the proposal did not require that the hearing be completed within a specified, definite time. Finally, and based upon the unsubstantiated assumption that the arbitration hearing would commence but not finish within a reasonable period of time, the FLRC concluded that the length of the artibration hearing (usually four to six hours) would "unreasonably delay" management's right to discipline and therefore negate management's reserved right to discipline.

The decisions in *Alcohol, Tobacco and Firearms* and *U.S. Customs Service* are no longer controlling. The legislative history reflects that the Committee on Conference considered different House and Senate versions of what was to become later section 7106(b). Senate section 7218(b) provided that negotiations on procedures governing the exercise of reserved management rights could not "unreasonably delay the exercise by management of its authority to act on such matters," nor could impact and implementation negotiations otherwise negate reserved management authority.[237] In contrast, the House version contained no comparable language. The conferees rejected the Senate language:

The conference report deletes these provisions. However, the conferees wish to emphasize that negotiations on such procedures should not be conducted in a way that prevents the agency from acting at all, or in a way that prevents the exclusive representative from negotiating fully on procedures. Similarly, the parties may indirectly do what the section prohibits them from doing directly.[238]

Based on this legislative history, the Federal Labor Relations Authority has rejected the holdings of the Federal Labor Relations Council in *Alcohol, Tobacco and Firearms* and in *U.S. Customs Service*. In *Dix-McGuire Exchange* the union had proposed,

In the event of a disciplinary suspension or removal, the grievant will exhaust the review provisions contained in this Agreement before the suspension or removal is effectuated, and the employee will remain in a pay status until a final determination is rendered.[239]

---

237. *Supra* note 69 in Chapter 2.
238. Rep. No. 95-1717, 95th Cong., 2d Sess. 158 (1978).
239. 2 FLRA 16 (1979). The FLRA reached the same result in 2 FLRA 15 (1979).

The agency declared the proposal nonnegotiable, and the union petitioned the FLRA. Relying upon the language from the conference report quoted earlier, the FLRA rejected the FLRC precedent and declared the proposal negotiable.

This result is consistent with and implements the intent of Congress as to the significance of the provisions of Title VII with respect to the Civil Service Reform Act as a whole. Congress enacted the Civil Service Reform Act in order to provide increased management authority, among other things, to hire and to discipline employees. However, Congress also recognized the need to provide protections for employees to balance this increased management prerogative. The grievance and arbitration provisions of Title VII, as well as the provision permitting agencies and labor organizations to negotiate fully on procedures, are among the means Congress utilized to provide such protection for employees. By its decision herein the Authority gives full effect to this Congressional intent.[240]

Punishment Not Addressed by the CSRA of 1978

The only type of punishment not addressed by statute is the most insignificant. It is best defined as discipline other than those statutorily defined as adverse actions, i.e., removals, demotions, and suspensions. This would include letters of reprimand, oral admonishments, and disciplinary relocations. These disciplinary actions may be appealed under negotiated grievance and arbitration procedures and may be held in abeyance pending completion of any negotiated appellate procedures. From a union's standpoint, one of the most effective proposals in this area is one providing that a letter of reprimand or written confirmation of an oral admonishment will be removed from all files after a few months and never again used.

Removal or Demotion Based on Unacceptable Performance

Under Title 5, U.S.C., section 4303, an agency may reduce in grade or remove an employee for unacceptable performance. This section also provides a network of due process procedures that serve as the bases for much potential negotiation. First, section 4303(b)(1)(A) provides that an employee is entitled to a notice period consisting of thirty days advance written notice of the proposed action and that the written notice must identify both specific instances of unacceptable performance serving as the basis for the proposed action and the "critical elements" of the employee's position involved in each in-

---

240. 2 FLRA 16 (1979) 4–5.

stance of the employee's unacceptable performance. These requirements provide room for extensive negotiation. Negotiable proposals could probably provide that

> critical elements will be defined in objective terms of observable, measurable performance, and the employee will be appraised of such;

> critical elements will be defined in mutually exclusive terms;

> supervisors will inform employees as soon as any element of performance starts to slip and before it slips to the unacceptable level;

> the line between unacceptable and minimally acceptable performance will be identified and defined to the greatest extent practicable;

> throughout the year the employee will be advised in writing of every performance deficiency, and failure to advise the employee of such is prima facie evidence of no performance deficiency;

> when the employer is contemplating issuing a thirty-day letter, sixty days before the letter's due date the employer will so advise the employee; during the sixty-day period the employee will be afforded extra, special counseling to provide ample opportunity for performance improvement; and the employer will provide the employee with a status report at the end of each week;

> the thirty-day letter will particularize what the employee must do within the thirty-day period to bring his or. her performance to an acceptable level;

> attached to the thirty-day letter will be all evidence or documentation relied upon by the employer in arriving at the decision to issue the letter;

> any proposal to demote or discharge will be based upon the employee's performance during the preceding twelve months.[241]

---

241. Section 4303(c)(2)(A) provides that the decision to reduce in grade or remove "may be based only on those instances of unacceptable performance by the employee which occurred during the one year period ending the date of the notice."

In addition to these proposals, the parties may potentially negotiate that pursuant to section 4304(a)(b)(2) the thirty-day notice will be extended to sixty days.[242]

Second, section 4303(b)(1)(B) provides that an employee is entitled to "be represented by an attorney or other representative." In all likelihood, unions will want to negotiate proposals providing that the exclusive representative will be presumed to be the employee's representative unless the employee indicates to the contrary. Such proposals would circumvent FLRC decisions holding that an exclusive representative represents an employee in an adverse action only when the employee has affirmatively designated the exclusive representative as his or her personal representative.[243]

Third, under section 4303(b)(1)(C) an employee is entitled to "a reasonable time to answer orally and in writing." Reasonable time may be defined in a proposal as presumed to consist of a specified minimum number of hours to investigate and prepare the answer, and a proposal may state that the employee will not be discriminated against for utilizing however many hours the employee actually requires. Proposals concerning the presentation of the oral and written answer could probably provide that the oral answer will be before a qualified official at a level higher than the official who proposed the demotion or discharge; that the oral response will be transcribed and a free copy of the transcript provided to the employee; that in making the oral answer the employee will be entitled to request on his or her behalf the production and testimony of other employees; that the employee will be permitted to question the proposing official; that the hearing official will answer pertinent questions posed by the employee at the oral answer; and that lack of training or inadequate counseling may be raised as a defense to the proposed action.

---

242. Section 4303(b)(2) provides that "an agency may, under regulations prescribed by the head of such agency, extend the notice period under subsection (b)(1)(A) of this section for not more than 30 days. An agency may extend the notice period for more than 30 days only in accordance with regulations issued by the Office of Personnel Management."

243. One of the fundamental purposes of unions, especially in the federal sector, is to defend employees against discharge and suspensions. Nevertheless, in *Louisville Ordinance Station*, the FLRC held that in an adverse action an exclusive representative is presumed not to represent an employee unless the employee affirmatively designates, as his or her personal representative, the exclusive representative. United States Department of the Navy, Naval Ordinance Station, Louisville, Kentucky and International Association of Machinists and Aerospace Workers, AFL-CIO, Local Lodge 830, FLRC No. 74A-54 (1975).

Fourth, section 4303(b)(1)(D) provides that the employer must provide the employee with a written decision that, "(i) . . . specifies the instances of unacceptable performance by the employee on which the reduction in grade or removal is based, and (ii) unless proposed by the head of the agency, has been concurred in by an employee who is in a higher position than the employee who proposed the action." To be of benefit, proposals in this area will want to address the contents of the written decision. Written decisions usually report only conclusions, not reasoning. Written decisions almost never address contentions raised in the employee's answer. Bargaining proposals might therefore require that

the written decision will, with particularity and detailed analysis, address the substance of every argument raised by employee's written and oral answers;

the written decision will provide detailed reasoning supporting every conclusion;

the written decision will list all information reviewed and all persons spoken to by the deciding official;

before reaching an adverse decision, the deciding official will make efforts to determine whether the employee might be laterally reassigned to a different position in which he or she could reasonably be expected to perform acceptably, and the deciding official will report the results of all such efforts in the written decision;

the decision will be based only upon instances particularized in the original notice letters.[244]

Fifth, section 4304(d) provides:

If, because of performance improvement by the employee during the notice period, the employee is not reduced in grade or removed, and the employee's performance continues to be acceptable for one year from the date of the advance written notice provided under subsection (b)(1)(A) of this section, any entry or other notation of the unacceptable performance for which the action was proposed under this section shall be removed from any agency record relating to the employee.

---

244. Section 4303(c)(2)(B) provides, in effect, that the final decision may be based only upon those instances of unacceptable performance of which the employee was provided notice.

This or similar language may be rolled over into a negotiated agreement. Proposals could also require the final decision to document all improvement and, for each type of instance of unacceptable performance, to cite, as proof that unacceptable performance continued within the thirty-day period, an instance of the same type from within the thirty-day notice period.

Sixth, section 4303(e) provides that an employee discharged or demoted for unacceptable performance may appeal, pursuant to section 7701, to the Merit Systems Protection Board (MSPB); and section 7121(e)(1) provides that, as an alternative, the employee may elect to appeal the matter to binding arbitration under a negotiated grievance procedure. Although the agency's final decision may be appealed under the negotiated grievance procedure, appeal may well be a futile waste of time because the officials hearing the grievances in at least the early steps would probably be lower in the organizational hierarchy than the deciding official on the removal or downgrade. Given the nature of bureaucratic hierarchies and internal power politics, it would be all but unheard of for a lower level official to reverse the decision of a higher level official. For this reason, it is suggested that the parties commence directly to arbitration without going through the grievance procedure; alternatively, the parties might commence with the last one or two steps of the grievance procedure preceding arbitration.

Section 7121(e)(1) also provides that an employee may not appeal through both a negotiated procedure and the MSPB. Section 7701(c)(1)(A) provides that the MSPB is to affirm the agency's decision if it is supported by substantial evidence, and section 7121(e)(2) provides that an arbitrator, too, must apply the substantial evidence standard contained in section 7701(c)(1)(A). As a result, a negotiated grievance procedure may not provide that an arbitrator may apply any standard other than substantial evidence when passing upon an action based on unacceptable performance. Whereas the MSPB will rarely if ever mitigate a penalty, arbitrators are seldom reluctant to mitigate where the circumstances warrant such. Moreover, while the MSPB's predecessor the FEAA, tended to rubber-stamp agency actions, an arbitrator is more likely to render an independent decision.

Conduct-related Suspensions

Suspensions of fourteen or fewer days are classified as adverse actions and are addressed in subchapter I, chapter 75, Title 5, U.S.C., at section 7501 et seq. Section 7503(a) provides that, to promote the efficiency of the service, an employee may be suspended for fourteen or fewer days:

Under regulations prescribed by the Office of Personnel Management, an employee may be suspended for 14 days or less for such cause as will promote the efficiency of the service (including discourteous conduct to the public confirmed by an immediate supervisor's report of four such instances within any one-year period or any other pattern of discourteous conduct).

The parenthetical clause has weighty implications for any federal employee having contact with the general public, particularly enforcement officers who encounter members of the general public who frequently may equate enforcement of the law with discourteous conduct. It is anticipated that negotiable proposals such as the following will in all likelihood appear:

Whenever an agency receives a complaint alleging discourteous conduct, a copy of the complaint will be forwarded to the employee without delay.

Whenever a complaint has been lodged, the employee will be afforded time and opportunity to gather rebuttal evidence.

Whenever agents of the agency interview the complaining party or witnesses, the affected employee will immediately receive a copy of all reports; the employee will be permitted to file a rebuttal statement, with evidence, in respect to any complaint of discourtesy.

Within five days of receipt, the supervisor will reveal all information possessed or known about a complaint to the affected employee; any information or evidence not revealed may not later be used against the employee.

A supervisor's report will be subject to the negotiated grievance procedure. It will include, as an attachment, all evidence on which the report is based and will reflect all investigations conducted by the supervisor or other agency employees: dates when conducted, what was reported by whom, and the supervisor's conclusions, if any.

Any questions posed to the employee by the supervisor will constitute an examination, at which the employee is entitled to be assisted by a union representative.

Section 7503(b) establishes procedures for suspension that serve as starting points for negotiations: "An employee against whom a suspension for 14 days or less is proposed is entitled to—(1) an advance written notice stating the specific reasons for the proposed action; (2) a reasonable time to answer orally and in writing and to furnish affidavits and other documentary evidence in support of the answer; (3) be represented by an attorney or other representative; and (4) a written decision and the specific reasons therefore at the earliest practicable date."

First, it provides that an employee is entitled to advance written notice stating specific reasons for the proposed disciplinary action. This leaves negotiable the length of the notice period; for example, the parties may negotiate a thirty-day notice period. In addition, the following suggested proposals should be negotiable:

upon the employee's request the length of the notice period will be extended;

the notice will advise the employee of his or her appeal rights and the time limits for them;

the notice letter will include all reasons and evidence that is or may be used to support the proposed suspension;

the notice letter will specify the rule of conduct, if any, alleged to have been violated;

the notice letter will clearly specify the precise conduct on which the proposed discipline is predicated;

if one or more reasons or charge is listed, the notice letter will state the priority of relative seriousness;

the notice letter will state the period during which the employee was investigated and the names of all persons or organizations contacted;

the notice letter will include, as attachments, all information collected during the investigation of the employee;

it will articulate with particularity the nexus between the proposed discipline and the efficiency of the service;

it will particularize and quantify the actual harm or actual damage, if any, that the employee's conduct has caused;

it will include, as attachments, all recommendations or requests that discipline, in any form, be or not be imposed; and

it will explain how the quantum of proposed punishment was decided.

Second, section 7503(b) provides that an employee is entitled to a reasonable time to answer orally and in writing and to furnish affidavits and other documentary evidence in support of the answer. The parties are free to negotiate "reasonable time," defining it as thirty days or any other reasonable period. The following suggested proposal ideas should also be negotiable:

upon request the employee will be granted additional time to answer;

the employee may investigate, gather evidence, and construct a response while on official time;

the employee will be permitted to interview during duty hours persons over whom the agency has control;

upon request, the agency will answer inquiries or questions posed by the employee in attempting to construct an answer;

the employee may use agency typing and copying facilities and services;

the answer will be presented to an official higher than the proposing official;

if the official hearing the oral answer or receiving the written answer is only a recommending official, a copy of the recommendation will be provided to the employee;

the manager to whom the answer is presented will respond with specificity to the substance of pertinent questions posed by the employee;

the oral answer will be transcribed verbatim and a free copy provided to the employee; and if subsequent to the answer the agency should conduct a supplemental investigation, copies of everything collected or summaries of statements reported will be provided to the employee for comment.

Third, section 7503(b) provides that the employee is entitled to a written decision and the specific reasons therefore at the earliest practicable date. In regard to the written decision, the following ideas for proposals should be negotiable:

the written decision will address the issue of whether, in line with the concept of progressive discipline, a lesser penalty might be appropriate;

it will make complete factual conclusions, separate and apart from legal conclusions;

it will address, with particularity and detailed analysis, each procedural, substantive, and other argument raised by the employee;

the decision will make legal conclusions with respect to the merits of each reason that was stated in the notice letter and each legal conclusion will also recite the facts and reasoning on which it is predicated; and

if the making of the written decision requires any credibility resolutions or rejection of any of the employee's allegations, the written decision will specify analytical, objective reasons for the credibility resolution or rejection of the allegation.

The CSRA of 1978 contains no provision for appealing agency decisions on suspensions of fourteen or fewer days to the Merit Systems Protection Board. Such agency decisions may be appealed, however, under the negotiated grievance procedure and to binding arbitration.

Conduct-related Suspensions for More than Fourteen Days, Removals, Reductions in Grade or Pay, and Furlough

Under section 7513(a) an agency may, for cause that will "promote the efficiency of the service," take any of the following actions against an employee: removal, suspension for more than fourteen days, reduction in grade, reduction in pay, or furlough for thirty or fewer days. These are considered adverse actions.[245]

Sections 7513(b)(c) and (d) establish adverse action procedures that serve as starting points for extensive negotiations:

(b) An employee against whom an action is proposed is entitled to—(1) at least 30 days, advance written notice, unless there is reasonable cause to believe the employee has committed a crime for which a sentence of imprisonment may be imposed, stating the specific reasons for the proposed action; (2) a reasonable time, but not less than 7 days, to answer orally and in writing and to furnish affidavits and other documentary evidence in support of the answer; (3) be represented by an attorney or other representative; and (4) a written decision and the specific reasons therefor at the earliest practicable date. (c) An agency may provide, by regulation, for a hearing which may be in lieu of or in addition to the opportunity to answer provided under subsection (b)(2) of this section. (d) An employee against whom an action is taken under this section is entitled to appeal to the Merit Systems Protection Board under section 7701 of this title. (e) Copies of the notice of proposed action, the answer of the employee when written, a summary thereof when made orally, the notice of decision and reasons therefor, and any order effecting an action covered by this subchapter, together with any supporting material, shall be maintained by the agency and shall be furnished to the Board upon its request and to the employee affected upon the employee's request.

An employee against whom section 7513 action is proposed is entitled to at least thirty days notice stating the specific reasons for the proposed action; the only exception is when there is reasonable cause to believe the employee has committed a crime for which a sentence of imprisonment may be imposed. This means that a notice may not be less than thirty days or fail to state the specific reasons, but beyond this, everything else is negotiable.

The following are examples of what would in all likelihood be negotiable proposals:

the notice period will, upon the employee's request, be extended to sixty days;[246]

the notice will advise the employee of his or her appeal rights and time limits for them;

---

245. Section 7511 *et seq.*, constitute subchapter II of chapter 75 of Title 5, U.S.C., the chapter titled "Adverse Actions."

246. The only limitation on the length of the notice period should be that it could not be contrary to any regulations promulgated in the *Federal Personnel Manual*.

the notice letter will state the period during which the employee was investigated and state the places, dates, and the names of all persons or organizations contacted;[247]

the notice letter will include, as attachments, all information collected during the investigation of the employee;[248]

the notice will articulate with particularity the nexus between the proposed discipline and the efficiency of the service;

the notice will particularize and quantify the actual harm or actual damage, if any, that the employee's conduct has caused;

the notice letter will include, as attachments, all recommendations or requests that discipline, in any form, be or not be imposed;

it will explain how the quantum of proposed punishment was decided and include all reasons and evidence that is or may be used to support the proposed action; and

the notice letter will specify the rule of conduct, if any, alleged to have been violated and that if more than one reason or charge is listed, it will state the priority of relative seriousness.

Second, section 7513(b)(2) provides that an employee against whom action has been proposed is entitled to a reasonable time— never less than seven days—to answer orally and in writing and to furnish affidavits and other documentary evidence in support. Section 7513(c) provides that, either in lieu of or in addition to the 7513(b)(2) answer, a hearing may be held. Thus, it provides the basis for a pretermination hearing. With respect to the "reasonable time" before which the employee must respond, the following suggested proposals should be negotiable:

---

247. There would no doubt be objections raised under the Privacy Act of 1974 to such a proposal. These objections should usually be dismissed out of hand. Title 5, U.S.C., section 552a, indicates that names of providers of information should be withheld only when an express promise of confidentiality has been provided and that such promises should be kept to a minimum.

248. The propensity in the federal sector is to provide only the information that the agency "relied upon" in proposing an adverse action. Usually such information is completely inadequate to defend the employee. At a minimum, the information needed to defend an employee consists of all information reviewed by the proposing official and all information reviewed by anyone who submitted a recommendation or report to the proposing official.

the employee will be granted thirty days before responding, and upon request and reasonable showing of need, additional time;

the employee will be on official time while investigating and gathering evidence;

the employee will be provided opportunity to interview during official hours persons over whom the agency has control;

upon request, the agency will answer inquiries or questions posed by the employee in attempting to construct an answer;

the employee will be permitted to use agency typing and copying facilities and services.

With respect to the section 7513(b)(2) answer, the following proposals should be negotiable:

the answer will be presented to an official higher than the proposing official;

if the official hearing or receiving the answer is only a recommending official, a copy of the recommendation will be provided to the employee;

the manager to whom the answer is presented will respond with specificity to the substance of pertinent questions posed by the employee;

the oral answer will be transcribed verbatim and a free copy provided to the employee;

the agency will provide its decision within ten or some other reasonable number of days; and

if subsequent to the employee's answer the agency should conduct a supplemental investigation, copies of everything collected or reported will be provided to the employee for comment.

With respect to the potential pretermination hearing under section 7513(c), the following proposals should be negotiable:

the hearing official must be qualified, and if the union objects to the designated hearing official, then the agency will appoint another one;

the agency is to have the burden of proof;

either the employee or his or her representative or both will be entitled to cross-examine witnesses and to call witnesses in his or her defense;

the employee will not be required to testify against himself or herself;

the agency will produce all called witnesses over whom it can exert control; and

the hearing will be transcribed verbatim and a free copy provided to the employee.

Third, section 7513(b)(4) provides that the employee is entitled to a decision and the specific reasons for it at the earliest possible date. In regard to a decision, the following suggested proposals should be negotiable:

the written decision will address the issue of whether, in line with the concept of progressive discipline, a lesser penalty might be appropriate;

the written decision will make complete factual conclusions, separate and apart from the legal conclusions;

the written decision, with particularity and detailed analysis, will address each procedural, substantive, and other argument raised by the employee; and

the decision will make legal conclusions with respect to the merits of each reason stated in the notice letter, and each legal conclusion will also recite the facts and reasoning on which it is predicated.

Fourth, section 7513(d) provides that an employee may, pursuant to section 7701, appeal a final agency decision to the Merit Systems Protection Board, and section 7121 provides that, as an alternative, the employee may appeal the matter to arbitration under a negotiated grievance procedure. Section 7121 also provides that an employee may not appeal through both a negotiated grievance procedure and to the MSPB. Section 7701(c)(1)(B) provides that the MSPB is to affirm the agency's decision if it is supported by a preponderance of the evidence, and section 7121(e)(2) provides that an arbitrator must apply the preponderance of evidence standard contained in section

7701(c)(1)(B). As a result, a negotiated grievance procedure may not provide that an arbitrator may apply any standard other than a preponderance of the evidence when passing upon an adverse action under sections 7512 and 7513. With respect to electing between the MSPB and an arbitrator, two observations deserve reemphasis. First, whereas the MSPB will rarely if ever mitigate a penalty, arbitrators are seldom reluctant to mitigate where the circumstances warrant it. Second, whereas the MSPB's predecessor, the FEAA, tended to rubber stamp agency actions, an arbitrator is more likely to render an independent decision.

Discipline and EEO Discrimination as a Defense

When an employee raises an EEO allegation in connection with a disciplinary action, the EEO issue need not be divorced from the issue of the merits of the disciplinary action.[249] When the grievance-arbitration clause of the negotiated grievance procedure is of the maximum scope, the EEO issue may be processed thereunder. Where EEO discrimination is alleged in connection with either type of adverse action under chapter 75 or with a removal or demotion for unacceptable performance under chapter 43, then the EEO issue may be processed under the negotiated grievance-arbitration agreement; thereafter the disposition of the EEO issue may be appealed for review to the MSPB or EEOC. Where EEO discrimination is alleged in connection with any other type of disciplinary matter—which is not to be appealed to the MSPB—then the EEO issue may be heard under the grievance-arbitration provision and an appeal made to the EEOC.

---

249. Section 7121(d) provides: "An aggrieved employee affected by a prohibited personnel practice under section 2302(b)(1) of this title which also falls under the coverage of the negotiated grievance procedure may raise the matter under a statutory procedure or the negotiated procedure, but not both. An employee shall be deemed to have exercised his option under this subsection to raise the matter under either a statutory procedure or the negotiated procedure at such time as the employee timely initiates an action under the applicable statutory procedure or timely files a grievance in writing, in accordance with the provisions of the parties' negotiated procedure, whichever event occurs first. Selection of the negotiated procedure in no manner prejudices the right of an aggrieved employee to request the Merit Systems Protection Board to review the final decision pursuant to section 7702 of this title in the case of any personnel action that could have been appealed to the Board, or, where applicable, to request the Equal Employment Opportunity Commission to review a final decision in any other matter involving a complaint of discrimination of the type prohibited by any law administered by the Equal Employment Opportunity Commission."

Reductions in Force

Under section 7106(a)(2)(A) the agency retains the right to lay off employees. This means that the agency may unilaterally decide whether or not the work force will be reduced. Although the agency makes the basic decision—that there will or will not be a reduction in force (RIF)—the parties are obligated to negotiate the procedures to be used in the implementation of the decision and the impact upon employees laid off and retained. For example, in *Great Lakes Naval Hospital* the assistant secretary held that an agency is required to negotiate the procedures used in determining which employees will be subject to a RIF.

Thus, while the decision to effectuate a RIF action is, in my view, a matter upon which there is no obligation under the Executive Order to meet and confer, there is no basis in the Order to conclude 'that such reservation of decision making and action authority is intended to bar negotiations of procedures, to the extent consonant with law and regulations, which management will observe in reaching the decision or taking the action involved, provided that such procedures do not have the effect of negating the authority reserved.[250]

A similar decision was reached in 1976 in the decision in *Office of Federal Highway Projects*.[251]

A proposal must not have the effect of requiring an agency to fill existing vacant positions in order to avoid laying off an employee or of requiring an agency, when filling positions not within the type and series being laid off, to give preference to employees from other types and series being laid off. In *McGuire Air Force Base* the question of the negotiability of the last sentence of the following proposal was before the council:

The Civilian Personnel Office will notify the Union as soon as possible, but not less than 30 days, if one or more unit employees are being separated due to a RIF action. The notice shall contain the number of spaces and/or positions to be affected, the projected date of the action and the reasons. In order to minimize the impact of a RIF, vacant positions in any base NAFI will be used for placement of employees otherwise to be separated, if qualified.[252]

---

250. United States Department of Navy, Bureau of Medicine and Surgery, Great Lakes Naval Hospital, Illinois, A/SLMR No. 289 (1973) 5.

251. U.S. Department of Transportation, Federal Highway Administration, Office of Federal Highway Projects, Vancouver, Washington, A/SLMR No. 612 (1976).

252. FLRC No. 77A-18 (1978) and FLRC No. 77A-21 (1978).

The FLRC noted that management retained the right to fill or not fill particular positions and then held the proposal nonnegotiable due to its conflict with this reserved right:

The provision in question in the present case expressly states that management *will* fill existing vacancies in nonappropriated fund installations with unit employees adversely affected by reduction-in-force actions. Thus, the agency is plainly constricted, by the literal language of the disputed provision, in its reserved authority under section 12(b)(2) to decide *not* to fill existing positions, as well as its right to *change* such decision once made.

For the foregoing reasons, we find that . . . [the proposal] . . . is violative of section 12(b)(2) of the Order. Therefore, the agency's determination of nonnegotiability was proper and must be sustained.[253]

In making this decision, however, the FLRC provided advice in a footnote that should assist somewhat in the construction of a narrow range of RIF proposals that should prove to be negotiable:

We do not, of course, here decide that provisions which, for example, would accord priority consideration in the filling of vacant positions to employees adversely impacted by reductions-in-force, would be nonnegotiable. For comparison, *see*, FPM, chapter 351, subchapter 10; FPM, chapter 330, subchapter 2-1 through 5, which apply to employees who, unlike the employees here involved, are in the competitive service.[254]

Another RIF proposal was at issue in *McGuire Air Force Base*. It read, in part: "Recall and position offers shall be in reverse order." In analyzing the proposal, the FLRC first observed that management possessed the reserved right to hire or not to hire in order to fill positions within the agency. The council construed this as the right to fill or not fill positions. The council interpreted this right as entailing also the right to select an individual once management had decided to fill a position. The council then construed this right as precluding negotiation of any proposal requiring the agency, when filling a position, to give preference to any individual. Finally, based on this reasoning, the council decided the proposal

which would require preference in recalls and position offers to the most senior employee adversely impacted by RIF action, would interfere with management's reserved authority to fill positions within the unit and would thereby violate section 12(b)(2) of the Order.[255]

The applicability of this decision may be limited, however, as the council stated in a footnote:

---

253. *Id.* at 18.
254. *Id.* at note 27.
255. *Id.* at 20.

As indicated in n. 27, *supra*, we do not decide in the present case that provisions which, for instance, would grant priority or special consideration in the filling of vacant positions to employees adversely affected in a RIF action, would be violative of section 12(b)(2) of the Order. See also, for comparison, FPM chapter 335, subchapter 4-3(c)(2) which applies to employees in the competitive service.[256]

Ostensibly, a proposal, which for layoff and recall purposes grants priority consideration based on seniority, might well be negotiable with respect to employees in the competitive service.

Overall, although the FLRC ruled upon the negotiability of many RIF proposals, no clear body of case law emerged to serve to guide the parties at the bargaining table. This may be attributed to two major causes. First, many of the FLRC's decisions concerning RIF were decided on a compelling need basis.[257] In effect, many decisions turned on the language of regulations unique to only one agency. For this reason, these particular decisions are of limited applicability. Second, a number of the FLRC decisions concerning RIF involved National Guard bargaining units, and this fact alone serves to limit the applicability of the decisions.[258] The reason is that RIF for National Guard and similar employees is unique in that membership in the National Guard is prerequisite to National Guard employment; cessation of National Guard membership inevitably means cessation of employment within the National Guard. This duality leads to a unique problem: the bargaining relationship extends only to National Guard employment; it does not extend to National Guard membership. For RIF purposes, however, the National Guard practice is to total one performance rating from National Guard employment and another performance rating from National Guard military membership. Obviously, for RIF purposes, both the civilian employment rating and the military membership ratings are of critical importance. Therefore, in the series of National Guard cases, the

---

256. *Id.* at note 30.

257. For example, *see* NAGE Local R5-100 and Adjutant General, State of Kentucky, and NAGE Local R14-76 and Adjutant General, State of Wyoming, FLRC No. 76A-109 (1977); AFGE Local 2953, AFL-CIO and Nebraska National Guard, FLRC No. 77A-106 (1978); and FLRC No. 77A-18 (1978) and FLRC No. 77A-21, part of proposal VII therein (1978).

258. For example, *see* NAGE and Adjutant General of North Carolina and Tennessee, FLRC No. 78A-37 (1978); Association of Civilian Technicians and Michigan National Guard, FLRC No. 78A-32 (1978); NAGE Local R8-22 and Michigan National Guard, FLRC No. 78A-11; NAGE Local R7-60 and Illinois National Guard, FLRC No. 78A-64 (1978).

union had submitted a proposal providing a procedure whereby an employee could appeal his or her military membership rating, and giving equal weights to the civilian employment point value and the military membership point rating for RIF purposes. The FLRC held the proposal nonnegotiable on the ground that the bargaining relationship extended only to the civilian employment half of the dual relationship.

Although . . . National Guard technicians are required by law to maintain military status in the National Guard as a condition of their civilian technician employment relationship (which relationship is, of course, subject to the Order), the military relationship itself is not covered by the Order but is totally mandated by statute. Consequently, since the union's proposal concerns a matter in connection with the military aspects of technician employment for members of the bargaining unit, it concerns a subject which is not a working condition arising under or controlled by the Order. Accordingly, it is outside the obligation to bargain under section 11(a) of the Order and, in nonnegotiable.[259]

Health and Safety

Labor organizations have a legitimate interest in the health and safety of employees. Health and safety surely constitute "working conditions." Thus a health and safety proposal is normally negotiable unless it extends into matters made nonnegotiable by section 7106. The landmark health and safety case is *Yuma*.[260] There the union had proposed that drag roads (unpaved roads paralleling the United States–Mexico border) be free of excessive dust and maintained at reasonable levels so as to minimize back injuries and kidney damage to employees riding over the roads. The FLRC rejected the agency's first argument that the proposal was excepted from the obligation to negotiate by the technology of work language and held the proposal negotiable.

---

259. FLRC No. 78A-11 (1978) 3. Using more refined reasoning, the council could have logically found the proposal negotiable on the ground that, while the bargaining relationship does not extend to military matters, when those military matters are removed from the exclusive military province and brought into the civilian employment province to affect a negotiable matter such as a RIF, then the proposal is negotiable to the extent that it is used in making the civilian employment decision. The FLRA, however, has taken the identical position that the FLRC took. Association of Civilian Technicians, Pennsylvania State Council and the Adjutant General, Department of Military Affairs, Commonwealth of Pennsylvania, Case No. 0-NG-50, 3 FLRA 8 (1980).

260. FLRC No. 70A-10 (1971).

Contrary to the agency's contentions, such provisions do not require bargaining on the 'technology' of drag roads which require a smooth surface of dust in order to detect the footprints of illegal entrants. Rather, the proposal would merely require that this 'technology,' as adopted by the agency, be *implemented* in a manner consistent with the health and safety of the Border Patrol Officers.[261]

Then the FLRC rejected the agency's second argument, that the proposal encroached upon reserved rights under section 12 (b) of the executive order.

Likewise, the union's proposal specifies only *what* health and safety standards shall be operative, i.e., 'regular' maintenance of the drag roads, so that they are 'reasonably' level and free of 'excessive' airborne particles. This proposal does not specify in any manner *how* these standards are to be achieved by the agency and, therefore, does not conflict with the agency's right to order its employees and to determine the methods and means by which its operations are to be conducted, as reserved to management under section 12(b)(1) and (5) of the Order. Finally, the proposal seeks only to improve the health and safety of the Border Patrol Officers, and, contrary to the position of the agency, such objective, if accomplished would contribute to, and not conflict with the management right to maintain the efficiency of its operations under section 12(b)(4) of the Order.[262]

Overall, the council's reasoning in *Yuma*, as applied in subsequent cases, is perhaps best viewed as a two-part proposition. First, if a proposal purports to decide whether or not, or to what extent, a technology will be used, then the proposal is nonnegotiable. Second, if the proposal requires only that, should a technology be used, it be maintained by the agency according to a general health and safety standard, then it is negotiable.

The *Yuma* analysis was applied in *INS-1975*, in which the safety proposal provided that appropriate communications equipment would be installed in the vehicles of employees working in remote areas.[263] The FLRC determined this proposal to be nonnegotiable, due to the technology exception, because it required the agency to adopt a particular technology in the performance of the agency's work. In contrast, in *Food Safety and Quality Service*, the negotiability of the first sentence of the following proposal was in question:

The Employer agrees to furnish all necessary protective clothing such as gloves, frocks, and cooler coats, special tools and equipment such as bacon

261. *Id.* at 3.
262. *Id.* at 5.
263. FLRC No. 74A-13 (1975).

bombs, ham-triers, meat thermometers, and other such equipment, which the Employer determines is necessary for the employees of the unit to perform their duties.[264]

Despite the fact that this proposal directed precisely what technology was to be used, the FLRC held, in conflict with the *Yuma* decision, that the proposal was negotiable. The decisions in *Food Safety and Quality Service* and *Yuma* and *INS-1975* cannot be satisfactorily reconciled. At best, it can be said that the proposal in *Food Safety and Quality Service* had a much more direct bearing upon health and safety of the employees' performance of their jobs than did the proposal in *INS-1975*.

The agency argued in *General Services Administration, Baltimore* that the following safety proposal was nonnegotiable:

No employee shall be required to perform work on or about equipment without proper precaution, protective equipment and safety devices, nor shall any employee be required to work in areas where conditions are detrimental to health without proper protective equipment and safety devices.[265]

Observing that the proposal did not grant employees the right to refuse to work, the FLRC held that the proposal was negotiable. The council reasoned that since the proposal specified only what health and safety standards were to be operable and not how the standards were to be achieved, none of management's reserved rights were offended.

A proposal must not be determinative of the numbers, type, or grades of positions or employees assigned to a work unit, project, or tour of duty. A second safety proposal in *INS-1975*, provided that, for obvious safety purposes, an appropriate number of vehicles and agents would be assigned to checkpoints along the border where illegal aliens and smugglers might be crossing.[266] The portion of the proposal applying to vehicles was nonnegotiable because it encroached upon the technology language; as it applied to agents, the proposal was nonnegotiable because it violated the staffing patterns language pertaining to the assignment of numbers of employees to a work project. The council explained that requiring an appropriate or sufficient number is equivalent to requiring a number. The same reasoning was applied to hold nonnegotiable a third safety proposal in *INS-1975*,

---

264. FLRC No. 77A-63 (1978).
265. FLRC No. 74A-48 (1975).
266. FLRC No. 74A-13 (1975).

which provided that employees working in law enforcement activities would be assigned in pairs.[267] Similarly, in *Internal Revenue Service* the union had submitted a proposal providing that a health facility would be maintained by a full-time nurse.[268] Since this proposal would have required the agency to establish a particular type of position and to assign a particular type of employee to that position, the council ruled that the staffing patterns exception made the proposal nonnegotiable.

Negotiable proposals may provide that, when dangerous conditions exist, employees will be removed from the area or may remove themselves. The union had submitted the following proposal in *U.S. Customs Service:*

Whenever a designated health and safety official determines, based on inspection, that conditions or practices exist in any place of employment which could reasonably be expected to cause death or physical harm immediately, or before the imminence of such danger can be eliminated through normal abatement procedures, he shall inform the employees and the official in charge of the establishment or the person authorized to act for him in his absence shall take immediate abatement procedures and the withdrawal of employees not necessary for abatement of dangerous conditions.[269]

Citing *General Services Administration, Baltimore,* the FLRC held that this proposal did not violate section 12(b) of the executive order and therefore was negotiable. Subsequently, in *VA, Atlanta Regional Office,* the last sentence of the following proposal was at issue:

If any reasonable doubt regarding the safety of existing conditions is raised by either the supervisor or steward, the supervisor and steward will jointly inspect the work area to insure it is safe. If the Union believes that work is being required under conditions which are unsafe or unhealthy beyond the normal hazards inherent in the operations in question, it may request a ruling from the Safety Committee and/or have the right to file a grievance. When a short-term exposure requires immediate solution and it is not possible to obtain employer concurrence beforehand, then the employee may at his discretion terminate his/her on duty action and so notify the employer.[270]

Citing *U.S. Customs Service,* the FLRC ruled that the proposal was negotiable.

In *Food Safety and Quality Service,* the union had, for safety purposes, proposed that where employees worked in front of conveyor chains

---

267. *Id.*
268. FLRC No. 74A-93 (1976).
269. FLRC No. 76A-28 (1977).
270. FLRC No. 77A-94 (1978).

while grading beef carcasses, the chain would be limited to a maximum speed of 180 carcasses an hour. But a private sector enterprise, not agency management, controlled the chain speed. The proposal was held nonnegotiable, as being outside the agency's obligation to negotiate.[271]

Energy Research and Development Administration involved a dispute over the negotiability of a proposal obligating the agency to comply with "prescribed and mandatory operational safety standards set forth in AEC Manual Chapter 0550 and AEC Appendix 0550, and any other safety standards prescribed by the Director, Division of Operational Safety, Headquarters."[272] Curiously, the agency raised no nonnegotiability arguments under section 11(a), 11(b), or 12(b) of the order, but rather, alleged that the proposal was not targeted at any specific personnel policy, practice, or working condition. The FLRC resoundingly rejected this argument and held the proposal to be negotiable, stating that "nothing demands that the subject standards themselves be expressly stated in the parties' agreement: They may be identified by reference."[273]

On February 26, 1980, President Carter signed Executive Order 12,196, which is titled "Occupational Safety and Health Programs for Federal Employees."[274] Executive Order 12,196 requires heads of agencies to comply with standards issued under section 6 of the Occupational Safety and Health Act. In addition, this order creates several matters that will probably stimulate bargaining between union and management. First, agencies are required to furnish working areas free of recognized hazards likely to cause serious physical harm. Unsafe or unhealthy working conditions must be promptly abated. Employee reports of imminent dangerous conditions must be responded to within twenty-four hours, reports of potentially serious conditions must be acted upon within three workdays, and all other reports must be responded to within twenty workdays. Second, employees who report unsafe or unhealthy working conditions are entitled to anonymity. Agencies may not take reprisal against, coerce, or otherwise interfere with employees who file reports of unsafe or unhealthy working conditions. Third, agency heads are required to es-

271. FLRC No. 77A-63 (1978).

272. AFGE Local 2118 and Los Alamos Area Office, ERDA, FLRC No. 74A-30 (1975).

273. *Id.*

274. 45 Fed. Register 12769-72 (Feb. 27, 1980).

tablish an occupational safety and health program. Periodic inspections by trained employees must be conducted, and employee representatives are entitled to accompany the inspections. Fourth, agencies may establish occupational safety and health committees. Section 1-301 of Executive Order 12,196 provides that

[i]f committees are established, they shall be established at both the national level and, for agencies with field or regional offices, other appropriate levels. The committees shall be composed of representatives of management and an equal number of nonmanagement employees or their representatives. Where there are exclusive bargaining representatives for employees at the national or other level in an agency, such representatives shall select the appropriate nonmanagement members of the committee.

Fifth, agencies must authorize official time to employees to participate in activities conducted pursuant to Executive Order 12,196.

Grooming, Uniforms, and Courtesy Requirements

In a 1974 opinion the assistant secretary held that grooming standards are equivalent to a part of the uniform, and, although the subject of uniform wearing is nonnegotiable, an agency must negotiate regarding its impact and implementation.[275] But this legal reasoning and conclusion no longer govern in the federal sector.

A proposal regarding the wearing of a uniform is negotiable if the uniform itself does not constitute one of the means by which the agency accomplishes its work. Critical elements to examine include the extent to which the employee has contact with the general public; the necessity of the general public easily recognizing that the employee is an employee of a particular agency; and other factors such as safety.

In *INS-1977* the agency, the Immigration and Naturalization Service (INS) had ordered employees to wear on the right shoulder of their uniform a bicentennial logotype.[276] Thereupon, the union, mindful that removal of the patch at the end of the bicentennial year would lead to an unsightly dark area on the uniform shoulder, proposed that at the end of the bicentennial year employees should be able to substitute the AFGE emblem on the uniform's right shoulder in place of the bicentennial patch. The employer declared that the

---

275. New Mexico Air National Guard, Department of Military Affairs, Office of the Adjutant General, Santa Fe, New Mexico, A/SLMR No. 362 (February 28, 1974).

276. Department of Justice, Immigration and Naturalization Service and American Federation of Government Employees, I & NS Council, FLRC No. 76A-26 (1977).

proposal was nonnegotiable under the language "means by which operations are conducted." The council agreed with the agency and held the proposal nonnegotiable, deeming it essential that the public be able to recognize quickly uniformed employees who are law enforcement officers. The FLRC decided that the AFGE emblem on the right shoulder might confuse the public into thinking that the employee was an AFGE representative rather than an INS law enforcement officer. Thus, the FLRC reasoned, the purpose of the uniform would be rendered ambiguous, and this would interfere with the means with which the agency had chosen to conduct its operations. In the text of the decision, the FLRC emphasized that the opinion in *INS-1977* should not be construed to mean that no bargaining over uniforms is permissible: "Proposals concerning, e.g., comfort and maintainability or the wearing of inconspicuous uniform buttons or other indicia of union affiliation, *which do not* negate the purpose for which such uniforms are required, would not be violative of section 12(b)(5)."[277]

Consistent with the dictum in *INS-1977*, the FLRC held negotiable some proposals providing that employees did not have to wear uniforms. In *Kansas National Guard*, the FLRC issued an opinion on a host of consolidated negotiability petitions concerning, among other things, the wearing of uniforms and hair grooming standards.[278] The council held negotiable one proposal providing that National Guard technicians could wear civilian attire while performing daily functions as civilian technicians for the guard—the wearing of uniforms had no functional relationship to the performance of the work—and another proposal providing that National Guard technicians, when performing work as civilian technicians for the guard, did not have to wear a hair style conforming with National Guard regulations. The council determined that no compelling need existed for guard regulations allegedly barring negotiations of the proposals. Subsequently, the respondent agencies in *Kansas National Guard* requested that the FLRC reconsider its decision in light of the means of performing operations language then found in section 12(b)(5) of Executive Order 11,491, as amended; this request for reconsideration had been instigated by the council's opinion in *INS-1977* issued the same day as the opinion in *Kansas National Guard*. The council dismissed the request, saying that

---

277. *Id.*
278. National Association of Government Employees, Local R 14-87 and Kansas National Guard, FLRC No. 76A-16, and other cases consolidated therewith (1977).

the means language did not bar negotiation. The agency's request for reconsideration asked whether employees could be required to wear uniforms on special days. But, as the FLRC observed, the proposal before the council addressed day-to-day attire; it did not address special attire on special days.

In *State of Ohio National Guard,* the National Guard management managed to have submitted to the FLRC the type of proposal that the guard management had asked the FLRC to rule upon in the request for reconsideration in *Kansas National Guard.*[279] The union had submitted a proposal providing that civilian technicians would not have to wear military uniforms, even during the periods when the agency conducted an organizational readiness inspection, ORI. The agency argued that the proposal would be determinative of the means by which agency operations are conducted: an ORI consists of a two- to five-day inspection to determine the unit's military effectiveness and readiness, and to make this determination, agency management attempts to inspect the unit in the condition that best approximates the wartime operational mode. The FLRC accepted the agency argument and held the proposal nonnegotiable.

The opinion in *New Mexico National Guard* addressed also a host of consolidated negotiability petitions.[280] The union had submitted proposals that would have exempted civilian technicians from having to wear military uniforms, from having to comply with military grooming standards, and from having to observe military courtesy requirements (saluting military officers) while on the job. The agency argued that the proposals were excepted from the obligation to negotiate and hence nonnegotiable because they conflicted with National Guard regulations making mandatory the wearing of the uniform and the observance of military grooming and courtesy requirements. The FLRC held that the proposals were negotiable because the agency had failed to prove a compelling need for the regulations, that is, to show that they are essential to mission accomplishment. The agency was unable to show why mission accomplishment would be impaired simply because a civilian technician dressed in civilian clothes instead

---

279. AFGE, AFL-CIO, Council 27, and State of Ohio National Guard, FLRC No. 77A-114 (1978).

280. NFFE Local 1636 and State of New Mexico National Guard, FLRC No. 76A-75; Association of Civilian Technicians, Montana Army and Air Chapter and State of Montana National Guard, FLRC No. 76A-76; and Association of Civilian Technicians, Michigan State Council and Adjutant General, State of Michigan, FLRC No. 76A-84 (1977).

of a military uniform. Likewise, mission accomplishment should not be harmed or made impossible merely because the hair of civilian technicians is a bit longer than before or because military officers are no longer saluted.

Facilities and Services

Labor organizations have long sought to negotiate union use of employer facilities and services. These efforts have logically resulted from the need to communicate effectively and quickly with bargaining unit employees, the need for union stewards to be able to advise and assist employees at the work site, the need for a secure file system where documents may be maintained and used as needed, and the need for a convenient office from which to conduct operations.

Negotiability of proposals dealing with facilities and services under the CSRA of 1978 can be best analyzed against the background of Executive Order 11,491, as amended. Section 23 of Executive Order 11,491, as amended, required agencies to issue policies and regulations, consistent with the order, "with respect to the use of agency facilities by labor organizations."[281] Logically, any policy or regulation that precluded a labor organization from meeting its section 10(e) responsibility and constraining an employee's section 1(a) rights was inconsistent with the order. In addition, section 19(b)(3) of the executive order contained a reference to facilities and services that an agency furnishes to a labor organization.[282]

The CSRA of 1978 does not contain a provision similar to section

---

281. For example, the *Treasury Personnel Manual*, chapter 711, paragraph 7-3, permits use of bulletin boards by labor organizations.

282. Section 10(e) of Executive Order 11,491, as amended, provided in part, that a labor organization accorded exclusive recognition "is the exclusive representative of employees in the unit and is entitled to act for and negotiate agreements covering all employees in the unit. It is responsible for representing the interests of all employees in the unit."

Section 1(a) read: "Each employee of the executive branch of the Federal Government has the right, freely and without fear of penalty or reprisal, to form, join, and assist a labor organization. . . . The head of each agency shall take the action required to assure that . . . .no interference, restraint, coercion or discrimination is practiced within his agency to encourage or discourage membership in a labor organization."

Section 19(b): "Agency management shall not. . . (3) sponsor, control, or otherwise assist a labor organization, except that an agency may furnish customary and routine services and facilities under section 23 of this Order when consistent with the best interests of the agency, its employees, and the organization, and when the services and facilities are furnished, if requested, on an impartial basis to organizations having equivalent status."

23 of Executive Order 11,491, as amended. This, however, does not mean that union use of agency facilities and services is no longer negotiable. Section 7114 of the CSRA is comparable to section 10(e) of the executive order, section 7102 comparable to section 1(a) of the order, and section 7116(a)(3) comparable to section 19(b)(3) of the order. The latter clearly contemplates the furnishing of agency facilities and services to an exclusive representative.

> For the purpose of this chapter, it shall be an unfair labor practice for an agency. . .to sponsor, control or otherwise assist any labor organization, other than to furnish, upon request, customary and routine services and facilities if the services and facilities are also furnished on an impartial basis to other labor organizations having equivalent status.

More important, any absolute restraint on union use of an agency facility would probably be inconsistent with section 7114(a) in that the exclusive representative would be substantially impeded from assisting and representing employees in grievance proceedings, the making of statutory appeals, and so forth. These activities entail more than mere union business. They are integral to the labor-management relationship. Of course, this reasoning would not apply to the conduct of internal union business, such as the conduct of union elections or the planning of union parties and dances.

There is no real question that reasonable union use of bulletin boards, agency rooms, the federal telephone system, and other agency facilities is negotiable.[283] These facilities and services are necessary for a labor organization to function as an exclusive representative and to discharge the section 7114(a) obligation to act for and represent the interests of employees in the bargaining unit.

The use of agency facilities and receipt of agency services are privileges, not rights, and as such may be reasonably conditioned.[284] When negotiated and included in a collective bargaining agreement, however, such are elevated to the level of rights. Equally, if not more important, once employees and a labor organization make use of certain agency facilities or receive agency services so that a past practice is established, thereafter such facilities and services are elevated to the level of rights and may not be unilaterally changed.[285]

---

283. 2 FLRA 77 (1980) proposal II.

284. Los Angeles Air Route Traffic Control Center, Federal Aviation Administration, A/SLMR No. 283, June 30, 1973.

285. Id. See also Internal Revenue Service, Office of the Regional Commissioner, Western Region, A/SLMR No. 473 (January 16, 1975); Veterans Administration,

The compelling need concept has had, and will continue to have, the effect of expanding the scope of negotiations over facilities and services. Before the 1975 amendment to Executive Order 11,491, as amended, agencies had promulgated many regulations that had significantly restricted the scope of negotiations over union use of agency facilities and services. For example, in *General Services Administration, Region 3* the union had proposed that the employer would furnish to the union a small amount of office space in the agency office building and furniture.[286] The agency argued that an agency regulation barred the furnishing of office space and furniture to labor organizations, and the FLRC upheld this argument, citing the higher level agency regulation. The 1975 amendment to Executive Order 11,491, as amended, added the compelling need language, and it is carried over in section 7117(a)(2) of the CSRA of 1978. As a result, agency regulations cannot bar the negotiation of reasonable office space in the agency building for the union unless the agency can prove, under FLRA standards, a compelling need for the regulation and also demonstrate that the regulation was issued at the national headquarters or the level of a primary national subdivision. This conclusion is confirmed by the FLRC's decision in *GSA, Region 5*, in which the union had proposed that management would, on a continuing basis, assign office space to the union.[287] Agency management argued that the proposal conflicted with an internal regulation for which a compelling need existed, but was unable to substantiate the compelling need for the regulation; and the FLRC held the proposal negotiable.

One case particularly highlights the influence of the compelling need concept as it applies to proposals regarding facilities and services. In *Coast Guard Base, Miami* a bargaining proposal would have given the union access to the agency's public address system for the purpose of announcing meetings.[288] The employer argued that a higher level regulation barred negotiations on the proposal. The union argued that there existed no compelling need for the regulation. The FLRC took notice of the fact that the 1975 amendments were not

---

Veterans Administration Regional Office, New York Region, A/SLMR No. 694 (August 6, 1976).

286. AFGE Local 2151 and General Services Administration, Region 3, FLRC No. 75A-28 (1975).

287. AFGE Local 1626 and General Services Administration, Region 5, FLRC No. 76A-121 (1977).

288. FLRC No. 75A-77 (1976).

retroactive and for this reason held that the proposal was nonnegotiable. To deter subsequent disputes, however, the council admonished affirmatively that its decision in *Coast Guard Base, Miami* should not be construed as deterring future negotiations on the subject.

Parking spaces were involved in one FLRC negotiability determination. In *GSA, Region 5* the union had submitted a proposal providing that parking space, for a union official, would be reserved at one of the agency's facilities.[289] The agency contended that this proposal was nonnegotiable because it was not consistent with priorities, established in interagency regulations issued by GSA, governing the distribution of parking spaces for all executive agencies. Casting a blind eye to the conflict of interest, the FLRC referred the proposal to GSA, the respondent in the negotiability appeal, and asked whether the proposal was negotiable. As might have been expected, the GSA reiterated its position and reported that the proposal was nonnegotiable on the ground that it conflicted with GSA regulations. Based on this, the FLRC held the proposal nonnegotiable. However, a proposal not in conflict with the GSA-established priorities for assignment of parking spaces should be negotiable. Moreover, it is entirely possible that the FLRA may hold negotiable a proposal providing that an agency would request to lease additional parking spaces.

The Office of Management and Budget has issued requirements affecting negotiations over parking.[290] Among other things, these requirements direct that available parking spaces be assigned in the following priority order: official vehicles used during the day, handicapped employees, van pools, car pools with four or more participants, other car pools, and single occupant cars. In addition, charges for use of parking spaces must, under certain circumstances, be imposed.

In *Wright-Patterson Air Force Base*, the FLRA set aside an agency's declaration of nonnegotiability of a proposal requiring the employer to provide adequate space and facilities for a day care center to be operated by the union.[291] The agency had argued that day care centers were not a subject coming within the scope of the duty to bargain and that if they did come within the scope, the proposal was nonnegotiable

---

289. FLRC No. 76A-121 (1977).
290. OMB Circular No. A-118 (Aug. 13, 1977).
291. 2 FLRA 77 (1980).

because it infringed upon the budget language of section 7106(a)(1). The authority found that the proposal came within the scope of the duty to bargain.

On the contrary, the availability of day care facilities affects the work situation and employment relationship in a variety of significant ways. For example, the existence and availability of such facilities can be determinative of whether an individual will be able to accept a job with an employer and of whether an employee will be able to continue employment with an employer. Thus, in addition to being an asset to management in recruiting and keeping a stable workforce, such facilities can be a decisive factor in the maintenance by unit employees of an employment relationship. Furthermore, problems with child care arrangements can result in employee tardiness and absenteeism. Thus, they have a detrimental effect on employee use of leave and on employee productivity, resulting in lowered morale and lessened ability to perform satisfactorily in relation to established expectations. It is also noted that, because of the increased number of families in which both parents work, as well as the necessity for single parents to work, the significance of day care facilities to the employment relationship has increased over recent years.[292]

Then the authority dismissed the agency's "budget" contention as lacking merit.

The underlying assumption of this position appears to be that a proposal is inconsistent with the authority of the agency to determine its budget within the meaning of section 7106(a)(1) if it imposes a cost upon the agency which requires the expenditure of appropriated agency funds. Such a construction of the Statute, however, could preclude negotiation on virtually all otherwise negotiable proposals — an agency's authority to determine its budget extends to the determination of the programs and operations which will be included in the estimate of proposed expenditures and the determination of the amounts required to fund them. . .a union proposal attempting to prescribe the particular programs or operations the agency would include in its budget or to prescribe the amount to be allocated in the budget for them would infringe upon the agency's right to determine its budget. . . .

Moreover, where a proposal which does not by its terms prescribe the particular programs or amounts to be included in an agency's budget, nevertheless is alleged to violate the agency's right to determine its budget because of increased cost, consideration must be given to all the factors involved. That is, rather than basing a determination as to the negotiability of the proposal on increased cost alone, that one factor must be weighed against such factors as the potential for improved employee performance, increased productivity, reduced turnover, fewer grievances, and the like. Only where an agency makes a substantial demonstration that an increase in costs is signif-

---

292. *Id.* at 3.

icant and unavoidable and is not offset by compensating benefits can an otherwise negotiable proposal be found to violate the agency's right to determine its budget under section 7106(a) of the Statute.[293]

Grievance and Arbitration Procedures

A brief history of the scope of grievance and arbitration procedures in the federal sector is prerequisite to appreciation of their current effect on negotiability determinations. Gradually, severe restrictions have been lifted. Executive Order 10,988 permitted but did not obligate the parties to negotiate procedures for the consideration of grievances. This permission, however, was only conditional; first, a grievance procedure could be negotiated only insofar as it conformed to existing Civil Service Commission standards; second, the grievance procedure could not include binding arbitration but could include advisory arbitration, i.e., the award would be merely advisory in nature and subject to the agency head's approval or rejection; third, this advisory abitration could be invoked only upon a grant of approval by the employee concerned.

Several changes came with Executive Order 11,491. The requirement that the grievance procedure conform to CSC standards was retained. Binding arbitration, however, could be invoked. Unfortunately, an artificial distinction was created between employee grievances and "labor arbitration disputes." Arbitration of employee grievances could be invoked only with the approval of the employee involved, and only the labor organization could invoke arbitration of disputes over interpretation and application of the contract. Also, the negotiated procedure could cover only disputes over the interpretation and application of the collective bargaining agreement.

Subsequently Executive Order 11,491 was amended to rid it of the artificial distinction between employee grievances and labor organization disputes. The word grievance was substituted as encompassing both. In addition, the requirement that the negotiated grievance procedure conform to the CSC standards was deleted. The order continued to provide that a negotiated grievance procedure could not cover matters other than interpretation and application of the contract.

The 1975 amendments to Executive Order 11,491 authorized the

---

293. *Id.* 4–5.

parties to negotiate grievance and arbitration procedures encompassing all matters except those for which statutory appeals existed:

The Council has carefully considered whether the Order should contain any specific limitations upon the scope and coverage of the negotiated grievance procedures other than the exclusion of matters covered by statutory appeal procedures. It has concluded that the Order should not contain any other specific limitations. Instead, the coverage and scope of the negotiated grievance procedure should be negotiated by the parties, so long as it does not otherwise conflict with statute or the Order, and matters for which statutory appeal procedures exist should be the sole mandatory exclusion prescribed by the Order. This will give the parties greater flexibility at the negotiating table to fashion a negotiated grievance procedure which suits their particular needs. For example, it will permit them to include grievances over agency regulations and policies, whether or not the regulations and policies are contained in the agreement, provided the grievances are not over matters otherwise excluded from the negotiations by sections 11(b) and 12(b) of the Order or subject to statutory appeal procedures.[294]

Thus an agency regulation could not restrict negotiations on the scope and coverage of the grievance procedure, and the negotiated procedure could encompass agency regulations and policies.

As of 1978, Executive Order 11,491, as amended, provided that every collective bargaining agreement was required to contain a grievance procedure that would be the exclusive procedure for resolving matters within the scope of its coverage. The parties could negotiate the scope and coverage of the grievance procedures, and it could cover any matter, including agency regulations and policies, except those matters for which a statutory appeal procedure existed, so long as it did not otherwise conflict with statute or the order. The negotiated procedure could provide for binding arbitration of grievances, but only the agency or labor organization could invoke arbitration. Furthermore, questions of grievability and arbitrability could by agreement be submitted to the arbitrator along with the merits of the grievance.

The Civil Service Reform Act of 1978 requires that a negotiated agreement contain a grievance procedure.[295] This means, among other things, that the parties must negotiate the steps and procedures of the

---

294. "Report and Recommendations of the Federal Labor Relations Council on the Amendment of Executive Order 11491, as amended" (Jan. 1975), in *Labor-Management Relations in the Federal Service* (Washington, D.C.: GPO, 1975), p. 43.

295. Section 7121(a)(1) provides, in part, that ". . .any collective bargaining agreement shall provide procedures for the settlement of grievances, including questions of arbitrability."

grievance procedure, including time limits and the persons who will and may attend grievance meetings.[296] The procedures must be fair, simple, and expeditious.[297] They must provide that the union may, in its own behalf or on behalf of employees, present and process grievances.[298] Unless a provision to the contrary is negotiated, a unit employee has the right to be represented by an attorney or personal representative other than the exclusive representative.[299] The exclusive representative, however, must always be given the right to be present at any proceeding under a negotiated grievance procedure.[300]

The Civil Service Reform Act of 1978 has clarified and somewhat expanded the scope and coverage of grievance and arbitration procedures. First, the CSRA provides a statutory definition of grievance that, in effect, serves to define the scope of a negotiated grievance procedure and those eligible to file grievances. Section 7103(a)(9) provides that

"grievance" means any complaint—
(A) by any employee concerning any matter relating to the employment of the employee;
(B) by any labor organization concerning any matter relating to the employment of any employee; or
(C) by any employee, labor organization, or agency concerning—

---

296. AFGE Local 2154 and Department of the Army, Headquarters Fort Sam Houston, Camp Stanley Storage Facility, Texas, FLRC No. 78A-34 (1978).

297. Section 7121(b) provides, in part, that, "any negotiated grievance procedure referred to in subsection (a) of this section shall: (1) be fair and simple; (2) provide for expeditious processing. . . ."

298. Section 7121(b)(3) provides, in part, that, "any negotiated procedure . . . shall . . . (a) assure an exclusive representative the right, in its own behalf or on behalf of any employee in the unit represented by the exclusive representatives, to present and process grievances. . . ." Hence, while an agency may forgo or waive its right to present and process grievances, an exclusive representative may not forgo or waive its right to present and process grievances.

299. Section 7114(a)(5) provides, in part, that, "the rights of an exclusive representative under the provisions of this subsection shall not be construed to preclude an employee from—(A) being represented by an attorney or other representative, other than the exclusive representative, of the employee's own choosing in any grievance or appeal action . . . except in the case of grievance or appeal provisions negotiated by this chapter."

300. Section 7121(b)(3) provides, in part, that, "any negotiated grievance procedure . . . shall. . . (B) assure such an employee the right to present a grievance on the employee's own behalf, and assure the exclusive representative the right to be present during the grievance proceeding." A proceeding under a negotiated grievance procedure would also constitute a "formal discussion" within the meaning of section 7114(a)(2)(A), and this section would thus vest the exclusive representative with an independent right to be present at the proceeding.

(i) the effect or interpretation, or a claim of breach, of a collective bargaining agreement; or

(ii) any claimed violation, misinterpretation, or misapplication of any law, rule, or regulation affecting conditions of employment.

The statutory definition of grievance encompasses alleged violations of the collective bargaining contract, agency regulations and policies, interagency and governmentwide rules and regulations, statutes, or any other matter concerning employment. A matter coming within the scope of the negotiated grievance procedure may not be raised under the agency grievance procedure.[301] Also, it is noteworthy that a grievance may be filed by an employee, a labor organization, or an agency; this will probably mean that collective bargaining agreements will contain one procedure for grievances that employees or the labor organization file and a separate procedure for grievances that the agency files.

The extent and fashion to which the parties are required to negotiate the scope and coverage of a negotiated grievance procedure presents an intriguing issue. When the Committee on Conference convened to consider the different House and Senate versions of the CSRA of 1978, it was faced with two bills that prescribed opposite approaches to the grievance procedure. The Senate bill required the

---

301. Rep. 95-1717, 95 Cong., 2d Sess. 157 (1978). The joint explanatory statement of the Committee on Conference states that, "Senate Section 7221(a) provides that, except for certain specified exceptions, an employee covered by a collective bargaining agreement must follow the negotiated grievance procedures rather than the agency procedures available to other employees not covered by an agreement. House Section 7121(a) does not limit the employee to the negotiated procedures in the case of any type of grievance. The House recedes." Accordingly, section 7121(a)(1) provides that, "except as provided in subsections (d) and (e) of this section, the procedures [in the collective bargaining agreement] shall be the exclusive procedures for resolving grievances which fall within its coverage." The referenced subsection (d) pertains to prohibited personnel practices alleging a variety of types of discrimination (race, color, religion, sex, national origin, age, handicapped status, or marital status) and provides that they may be raised under the statutory procedure or the negotiated grievance procedure, but not both, although an employee may ask the Merit Systems Protection Board, or, where applicable, the Equal Employment Opportunity Commission, to review a final decision rendered under the negotiated grievance procedure. The referenced subsection (e) pertains to conduct- and performance-related discipline and provides that matters covered under Title 5, U.S.C., sections 4303 and 7512, may be appealed under either the statutory procedures or the negotiated grievance procedures, but not both. Additionally, it should be noted that section 7121(f) provides that, as to arbitration awards rendered on matters within the purview of section 4303 or section 7512 or matters "similar" to those within the purview of those sections, judicial review may be had, under section 7702, in the same manner and under the same conditions as if the Merit Systems Protection Board had rendered the decision.

parties to negotiate the scope and coverage of the grievance procedure; in contrast, the House bill did not permit the parties to negotiate scope and coverage, but rather, by prescribing a statutory definition of grievance, set forth the matters required to be submitted to the negotiated grievance procedure.[302] In other words, the Senate bill provided that scope and coverage were mandatory bargaining matters, and the House bill provided that scope and coverage were prohibited bargaining matters. The Committee on Conference basically followed the House approach but with a compromise. The committee drafted language providing that all matters within the scope of the statutory definition of a grievance must be within the scope of any negotiated grievance procedure, but that, if the parties agreed to exclude certain matters, then such matters would not be covered by the negotiated grievance procedure.[303] Hence, section 7121(a)(2) provides that the parties may agree to exclude any matter from the application of the negotiated grievance procedure.

Any collective bargaining agreement may exclude any matter from the application of the grievance procedures which are provided for in the agreement.

The intriguing issue is whether the scope of the grievance procedure is permissive bargaining matter that may be—but is not required to be—negotiated, or whether the scope is mandatory matter that the parties must negotiate. On the one hand, the FLRA staff is accustomed to permissive bargaining matter being defined not as matter about which the union is not required to negotiate, but rather, as matter about which management is not required to negotiate. The FLRA may be unreceptive to the idea that permissive bargaining matter may include matters about which a union may, but is not required to, negotiate. While section 7121(a)(2) uses a permissive rather than a directive verb, it would not be unreasonable to construe the language as implying that the parties must negotiate scope. Such a construction, however, would be tantamount to adoption of section

---

302. *Id.* "The Senate provides that the coverage and scope of the grievance procedures shall be negotiated by the parties (section 7221(a)). House section 7121(a) does not authorize the parties to negotiate over the coverage and scope of the grievances that fall within the bill's provisions but prescribes those matters which would have to be submitted, as a matter of law, to the grievance procedures."

303. *Id.* "The conference report follows the House approach with an amendment. All matters that under the provisions of law could be submitted to the grievance procedures shall in fact be within the scope of any grievance procedure negotiated by the parties unless the parties agree as part of the collective bargaining process that certain matters shall not be covered by the grievance procedures."

7221(a) of the Senate bill that was before the Committee on Conference, and the conference committee clearly rejected the Senate approach and explicitly adopted basically the House approach. On the
other hand, if scope is permissive bargaining matter, for whom is it
permissive? Is the consent of both parties required before scope can
be negotiated? If one party requests to negotiate scope, then is the
other party required to do so? If this is the case, which party is vested
with sole authority to insist that scope be negotiated or to decline to
negotiate scope?

The actual language of 7121(a)(2) provides no definitive answers.
Whatever construction is ultimately rendered, unjust results should
be avoided. Except for a few matters that may be appealed under
either a negotiated grievance procedure or a statutory procedure, the
grievance procedure is the sole forum for resolution of all matters
within its scope. Inasmuch as union membership is voluntary and
unions are obligated to represent members as well as nonmembers
within the bargaining unit, a union might well find itself in the
position of being financially unable to present meritorious grievances
to an arbitrator. Yet the employee would be barred from seeking
relief in other forums. Such a lack of adequate recourse would be
unjust.

The only possible compromise approach would be for the FLRA
to rule that parties may no longer negotiate about how *grievance* will
and will not be defined, and instead, must start with the statutory
definition of grievance. Then a party must submit for negotiation
specific items proposed to be excluded from the scope of the grievance
procedure. The difficulty with this theoretical middle ground, however, is that in actual practice it is likely to prove to be unworkable.
It assumes not only that the parties will in fact start with the statutory
definition but also that afterward the parties will propose to exclude
specific matters. There is no guarantee that the parties will actually
abide by the former assumption, and the latter one can easily be
subverted by proposals providing that "everything will be excluded
except. . . ." Such a compromise approach is likely to produce a result
requiring the parties to negotiate the actual scope of the grievance
procedure, a result that the Committee on Conference rejected and a
result that the CSRA of 1978 was intended to avert.

Overall, agencies would most prefer for the FLRA to declare,
directly or indirectly, that the scope and coverage of the grievance
procedure is a matter the parties are required to bargain, and unions

would most prefer for the FLRA to declare that scope is negotiable but only at the union's election.[304] How the FLRA will ultimately rule is a most uncertain but serious question.[305] The position that the FLRA ultimately adopts will exert a profound effect on how the FSIP—in light of the CSRA's legislative history—will want to handle impassed proposals on the scope of negotiated grievance procedures.

In addition to matters that may by mutual agreement be excluded from the scope of the negotiated grievance procedure, the language of the CSRA lists certain statutory appeals that may not come within the scope or coverage of a negotiated grievance procedure. In contrast to Executive Order 11,491, which excluded from the scope of a grievance procedure all matters for which statutory appeals existed, section 7212(c) of the CSRA is more definite.

The preceding subsections of this section shall not apply with respect to any grievance concerning—(1) any claimed violation of subchapter III of chapter 73 of this title (relating to prohibited political activities); (2) retirement, life insurance, or health insurance; (3) a suspension or removal under section 7532 of this title; (4) any examination, certification, or appointment; or (5) the classification of any position which does not result in the reduction in grade or pay of an employee.

The following matters find their genesis in statute or regulation but nonetheless may probably be appealed under a negotiated grievance procedure of maximum scope and coverage:

---

304. On October 14, 1978, the day after the president had signed the CSRA of 1978, Congressman William D. Ford (D-Mich.), who had been a major participant in fashioning the language of the House bill and who then had served with the Committee on Conference as one of the managers on the part of the House, discussed the newly enacted legislation on the House floor. Among other things, he stated that, "The labor organization is required to meet a duty of fair representation for all employees . . .who use the negotiated grievance procedure. The costs involved . . .are high. Although the basic House approach of stating in the statute the scope of the procedure was followed, the conferees also adopted a provision aimed solely at allowing the exclusive representative, at its option, to propose and agree to a reduced coverage for the negotiated grievance procedure—perhaps for financial reasons. . . . We can analogize this situation to management's 'permissible' areas of bargaining under section 7106(b)(1) . . . the union is free to propose a narrowed scope of grievances, is free to withdraw that proposal at any time, and is free to insist to impasse on the narrowed scope if the agency does not agree. An agency, however, may not insist to impasse that the union agree to a reduced scope of grievances under the negotiated procedure." 124 Cong. Rec. H13609 (daily ed., Oct. 14, 1978).

305. See AFGE, AFL-CIO, Local 3669 and Veterans Administration Medical Center, Minneapolis, Minnesota, Case No. 0-NG-32, 3 FLRA 48 (1980); AFGE, AFL-CIO, Local 3354 and U. S. Department of Agriculture, Farmers Home Administration, St. Louis, Missouri, Case No. 0-NG-37, 3 FLRA 50 (1980).

1. Adverse actions (5 U.S.C. §§ 7512, 7543(d))

   Removal or demotion for performance reasons (5 U.S.C. § 4303)

   Termination of retained grade or pay benefits because of refusal to accept a reasonable offer (5 U.S.C. § 5366)

   Adverse action based on adverse suitability rating (5 C.F.R. Part 754)

   Retention of salary of employees demoted without personal cause to General Schedule positions (5 U.S.C. § 5337; 5 C.F.R. Part 531.517)

2. Withholding of within-grade (step) increase (5 U.S.C. § 5335)

3. Fair Labor Standards Act (P.L. 93-259)

4. Reduction in Force (5 C.F.R. 351.901)

5. Employment practice administered or required by the Office of Personnel Management (5 C.F.R. 300.104(a))

6. Violation of reemployment rights (5 C.F.R. 330.202)
   Restoration to duty following military service (38 U.S.C. § 2023)

   Restoration to duty following recovery or partial recovery from a compensable injury (5 C.F.R. 353.401)

   Reemployment rights based on movement between executive agencies during emergencies (5 C.F.R. 352.209)

   Reemployment rights following details or transfers to international agencies (5 C.F.R. 352.313)

   Reinstatement rights after service under the Foreign Assistance Act of 1961 (5 C.F.R. 352.508)

   Reemployment rights after service in the Economic Stabilizing Program (5 C.F.R. 352.607)

   Reemployment rights after service under the Indian Self-Determination Act (5 C.F.R. 352.707)

7. EEO discrimination complaint involving no other appealable action such as, for example an adverse action (i.e., a case that is not "mixed")

EEO discrimination in connection with adverse action under chapter 75 of Title 5, U.S.C., or removal or reduction in grade for unacceptable performance under chapter 43

EEO discrimination in connection with any other action or employment practice that would be within jurisdiction of MSPB (except discrimination in connection with Hatch Act case or decisions concerning retirement or life or health insurance).[306]

The following matters find their genesis in statute or regulation and probably may *not* be appealed under a negotiated grievance procedure of maximum scope and coverage:

1. Classification/job grade: appealable to the Office of Personnel Management (5 U.S.C. §§ 5112 and 5346)

2. Examination rating: appealable to the Office of Personnel Management (5 U.S.C. § 3301)

3. Political activities: appealable to the Merit Systems Protection Board (5 U.S.C. §§ 1504 to 1507; 5 U.S.C. § 7325)

4. Denial of health permit claim by an insurance carrier (5 C.F.R. 890.105)

   Final decision of Office of Personnel Management regarding employee coverage under life and health benefit programs (5 C.F.R. §§ 870.205(b) and 890.103(b))

5. Retirement applications and annuities: appealable to Merit Systems Protection Board (5 U.S.C. § 8347(d))

6. EEO discrimination in connection with Hatch Act case or decisions concerning retirement or life or health insurance under appellate jurisdiction of MSPB.[307]

Under Executive Order 11,491, as amended, a grievance procedure could, but was not required to, provide for arbitration of grievances. Unions had to buy binding arbitration at the bargaining table. The CSRA of 1978 removes this bargaining chip from the agency's arsenal: section 7121(b)(3)(C) requires that all negotiated grievance procedures culminate in binding arbitration.

---

306. *See* the OPM publication *Grievance and Appeal Options of Bargaining Unit and Non-Bargaining Unit Employees under Reorganization Plans No. 1 and 2 of 1978 and the Civil Service Reform Act* (Washington, D.C.: OPM, 1979), pp. 1–8, 11–12.

307. *Ibid.*, pp. 1-4, 8-9, 11.

Second, under Executive Order 11,491, as amended, grievability and arbitrability questions—except those centering on the issue of whether or not the matter of the grievance was subject to a statutory appeal—could, but were not required to be, submitted to an arbitrator. Unions had to buy at the bargaining table the right to have grievability and arbitrability disputes decided by an arbitrator. The CSRA also removes this bargaining chip from the agency's arsenal: section 7121(a)(1) requires that all negotiated grievance procedures must provide for submission of grievability and arbitrability disputes to the arbitrator.

Third, under Executive Order 11,491, as amended, attorney fees were rarely if ever provided to an employee against whom an unfavorable action had been imposed but who had prevailed in a grievance contesting the action. The CSRA of 1978 creates the concept of an "unjustified or unwarranted personnel action," which is defined as an action that is unjustified or unwarranted and has resulted in the withdrawal or reduction of all or a part of the pay, allowances, or differentials to the employee. The CSRA goes on to provide that an employee against whom such an action has been imposed, upon having prevailed in the grievance or arbitration procedure, is entitled to reasonable attorney fees, appropriate back pay, and restoration of annual leave.[308] Inasmuch as this is a statutory right, it need not be negotiated in order to be exercised.

Official Time

Section 7131 directly addresses the question of whether union activities may be conducted during official time. Distinctions must be made between official time spent in the conduct of negotiations, the conduct of internal union business, and the conduct of representational and other functions such as attendance of formal discussions.

Internal union business may not be conducted during official time. Section 7131(b) provides,

Any activities performed by any employee relating to the internal business of a labor organization (including the solicitation of membership, elections of labor organization officials, and collection of dues) shall be performed during the time the employee is in a non-duty status.

---

308. *See* 5 U.S.C. § 5596(b), as amended by the CSRA of 1978.

Hence, if a proposal deals with performance of internal union business during duty hours, it is nonnegotiable unless it also provides that the employee will be in a nonduty (nonpay) status. The Federal Labor Relations Authority, however, has declared that it will give a narrow construction to the term internal union business. A matter constitutes internal union business only if it relates solely to the "institutional structure" of a labor organization: the activities listed in 7131(b)—membership solicitation, election of officers, and dues collection—epitomize matters that are internal union business.[309] Whatever time is negotiated must be reasonable, necessary, and in the public interest; a proposal is negotiable if it provides official time for union interface with either agency management or with the "public interest."[310] For example, a proposal providing official time to prepare reports required by the Department of Labor is negotiable, even though the reports may deal with election of union officers.[311] Submission of these reports serves the public interest by opening to public scrutiny the manner in which union business has been transacted.

The CSRA of 1978 does not grant employees official time to perform representational and other nonbargaining functions that do not constitute solely internal union business; however, the parties may negotiate official time for the conduct of such functions. Section 7131(c) provides,

Except as provided in the preceding subsections of this section, (1) any employee representing an exclusive representative, or (2) in connection with any other matter covered by this chapter, any employee in an appropriate unit represented by the exclusive representative, shall be granted official time in any amount the agency and the exclusive representative involved agree to be reasonable and in the public interest.

This means that official time may also be negotiated for union stewards and officers and other employees to

discuss potential grievances, investigate, prepare, and present employee-union grievances;

investigate, hear, and prepare responses to grievances filed by management;

---

309. AFGE Local 2823 and Veterans Administration, Regional Office, Cleveland, Case No. 0-NG-8, 2 FLRA 1 (1979).
310. *Id.*
311. *Id.*

discuss, prepare for, and present statutory appeals and discrimination complaints;

attend meetings with management officials;

consider and prepare responses to proposed employer directives;

prepare for negotiations and receive training in the labor-management relationship;[312] and

attend formal discussions within the meaning of section
7114(a)(2)(A) and attend investigative examinations of employees
within the meaning of section 7114(a)(2)(B).

All these activities either are of mutual interest to the agency and
the labor organization, relate to contract administration, or go to the
heart of the labor-management relationship, and are not matters of
internal union business. Incidentally, there is no maximum number
of hours that may be negotiated for these purposes.[313]

The only significant change concerning official time ushered in
by the CSRA involves the conduct of negotiations. Under Executive
Order 11,491, as amended, the parties could agree that, when negotiating a contract, employees representing the exclusive representative
would be on official time for either forty hours or up to one-half the
time spent in negotiations.[314] The FLRC ruled that the forty hours or

312. AFGE, AFL-CIO, Local 1692 and Headquarters, 323rd Flying Training
Wing (ATC), Mather Air Force Base, California, Case No. 0-NG-183, 3 FLRA 47
(1980); Federal Uniformed Firefighters and U. S. Army Armament Research & Development Command, Dover, New Jersey, Case No. 0-NG-73, 3 FLRA 49 (1980).

313. On February 23, 1976, the comptroller general issued a ruling limiting the
amount of time an employee may spend on labor relations activities to 160 hours per
year (B-156287). On September 15, 1976, the comptroller general retreated from this
position and reversed himself. *See* 675 GERR A-6. The *Federal Personnel Manual* was then
amended to provide that employees may spend a reasonable amount of time (*FPM*
letter 711-120). With enactment of the CSRA, section 7131 would now take precedence
over either comptroller general decisions or *FPM* provisions and contains no cap on the
number of hours that may be negotiated.

314. Section 20 of Executive Order 11,491, as amended, provided, "Solicitation of
membership or dues, and other internal business of a labor organization, shall be
conducted during non-duty hours of employees concerned. Employees who represent
a recognized labor organization shall not be on official time when negotiating an
agreement with agency management, except to the extent that the negotiating parties
agree to other arrangements which may provide that the agency will either authorize
official time up to 40 hours or authorize up to one-half the time spent in negotiations
during regular working hours, for a reasonable number of employees, which number
normally shall not exceed the number of management representatives."

one-half time provision of the executive order applied only to the negotiation of the master agreement; if the union wished to negotiate midterm (mid-contract) changes during the life of the master contract, then any official time for such was required to be provided by a mid-contract negotiation provision contained in the master contract or by a reopener clause whereby official time could be negotiated for negotiation of a midterm change.[315] Unfortunately, the FLRC's holding was not consistent with basic labor relations theory. One of the primary reasons for the existence of collective bargaining is to resolve problems and cope with exigencies as they arise in the workplace, and this purpose can be maximized only if the duty to bargain is continuous. The obligation to negotiate continues throughout the life of a master agreement. Any midterm negotiations constitute an extension of the master agreement negotiations; in other words, a midterm agreement ordinarily complements or supplements the master agreement—as distinguished from a midterm agreement that modifies the terms of the master agreement or that constitutes a separate and independent agreement. The FLRC's construction erroneously assumed not only that midterm bargaining is not an extension or a continuation of the bargaining duty that served to produce the master agreement, but also that any midterm agreement is separable from the master agreement.

Section 7131(a) of the CSRA of 1978 addresses official time for negotiations.

Any employee representing an exclusive representative in the negotiation of a collective bargaining agreement under this chapter shall be authorized official time for such purposes, including attendance at impasse proceeding, during the time the employee otherwise would be in a duty status. The number of employees for whom official time is authorized under this subsection shall not exceed the number of individuals designated as representing the agency for such purposes.[316]

Thus, by virtue of the CSRA, employees negotiating for a union are on official time for the entire time, and the number of employees on the union bargaining team enjoying such official time can equal but

---

315. *See* FLRC No. 76A-106 (1977).

316. In conjunction with this section, the FLRA has ruled that employees are on official time when traveling to and from negotiations and also that employees are entitled to per diem and travel expenses paid by the agency. 2 FLRA 31 (1979).

not exceed the number of individuals on the agency bargaining team.[317]

After the CSRA had first become effective, the burning issue with respect to official time for the conduct of negotiations was whether section 7131(a) provides time only for the negotiation of a master agreement or whether it also provides time for the conduct of midterm negotiations during the life of the master agreement. On the one hand, agencies argued that the FLRA should limit section 7131(a) to the negotiation of a master agreement so that unions would have to negotiate for any official time for midterm bargaining. The agencies favored this interpretation because it could have deterred union exercise of the right to engage in midterm bargaining. On the other hand, the unions favored the interpretation authorizing official time for midterm as well as master contract negotiations because it would enable them to avert the disadvantageous situation that existed under the executive order, wherein an agency could prolong the bargaining, causing union officials to expend all negotiated official time for bargaining and thereafter to have to use annual leave (vacation time) for bargaining. This pressure tactic had generally worked to cause unions to surrender to agency bargaining demands.

A traditional, fundamental rule of statutory construction is that like language must be afforded like construction and interpretation. The section 7114(a) duty to bargain requires the parties to negotiate a "collective bargaining agreement," and it was and is beyond doubt that this language imposed the duty to negotiate a master agreement as well as midterm changes occurring during the life of a master agreement. Section 7131(a) provides official time for negotiation of the identical entity—a "collective bargaining agreement." As used in section 7131(a), the term collective bargaining agreement should ordinarily be afforded the same meaning as when the term is used in section 7114(a)(4). Any other construction of section 7131(a) would violate one of the most fundamental rules of statutory construction.

Using this reasoning, on December 19, 1979, in an interpretation and guidance decision, the FLRA determined that section 7131(a)

---

317. NFFE Local 1451 and Naval Training Center, Orlando, Florida, Case No. 0-NG-75, 3 FLRA 14 (1980). The authority's decision in this case has been appealed to the Circuit Court of Appeals for the District of Columbia. National Federation of Federal Employees Local 1451 v. FLRA, Case No. 80-1708.

provides official time to union negotiators engaged in midterm bargaining as well as those engaged in the negotiation of a master agreement.[318]

The most significant result of this decision, however, stems from an additional determination contained therein. The authority also addressed the question of whether employees on official time under section 7131 are entitled to have travel and per diem paid by their agency. The authority first observed that

it is well established that such expenses are authorized when an employee "is engaged on official business for the Government" (Chapter 57, Subchapter I — *Travel and Subsistence Expenses; Mileage Allowances*, 5 U.S.C. § 5701, *et seq.*).[319]

The authority then reasoned that when using official time under section 7131, an employee is, in effect, engaged in official business for the government. The employee is engaging in collective bargaining while on official time—as opposed to being in a leave status—and

Congress, in adopting the Statute, specifically found in section 7101(a) that collective bargaining "contributes to the effective conduct of public business" and that "collective bargaining in the civil service [is] in the public interest."[320]

From this point, the authority concluded that a unit employee using time under section 7131 is entitled to travel expenses and per diem paid by the employee's agency. In support of this conclusion, the authority also gleaned from the CSRA's legislative history an intent that management and union negotiators should enjoy equal status when using time under section 7131. Based on this, the authority reasoned that its decision would foster the legislative intent.

The payment of travel and per diem expenses would not only more nearly equate the status of union and management negotiators as contemplated by Congress, but would also facilitate more effective union representation at the bargaining table, thereby implementing the purpose of the Statute, as reflected in section 7101(a), to encourage collective bargaining in the Federal sector.[321]

The import of the authority's decision is twofold. First, the federal sector enjoys voluntary unionism; an agency or union shop is

---

318. Interpretation and Guidance [statement on major policy issue], 2 FLRA 31 (1979).

319. *Id.* at 5.

320. *Id.* at 5.

321. *Id.* at 6.

illegal. Because of this, federal sector unions can normally derive less dues income than unions in sectors where an agency or union shop is legal. In the private sector where the agency or union shop is legal, the practice calls frequently for unions to reimburse its negotiators for lost pay. But the same practice cannot reasonably be expected to prevail on the same scale in a sector in which unions have less money because of voluntary unionism. From this perspective, the authority's decision may be viewed as constituting implicit recognition that the trade-off for voluntary unionism is the requirement that an agency share an increased proportion of the union's collective bargaining expenses.

Second, under the executive order, agencies and unions normally conducted national negotiations in Washington, D.C., and unions bore the travel and per diem costs incurred by unit employees on the union's team. With this knowledge, agencies frequently employed the pressure tactic of delaying and prolonging negotiations; when stretched to their financial limit, unions would frequently surrender to agency demands. The authority's interpretation of section 7131 can be expected to preclude future use of this bargaining tactic by agencies. The fact that agencies must pay official time, travel expenses, and per diem to members of both bargaining teams should serve as impetus motivating agencies to reach agreement as quickly as possible. This is significant because in the federal sector there is no threat of the strike or lockout that in the private sector can induce the crisis bargaining that serves as impetus motivating parties to reach agreement.

Voluntary Dues Withholding and Involuntary Security Fees

Under section 21(a) of Executive Order 11,491, as amended, an agency was obligated to negotiate a dues withholding agreement, but the agency could impose a charge for the service.[322] Unions had to buy

---

322. Section 21(a) provided that "when a labor organization holds exclusive recognition, and the agency and the organization agree in writing to this course of action, an agency may deduct the regular and periodic dues of the organization from the pay of members of the organization in the unit of recognition who make a voluntary allotment for that purpose."

cost-free dues withholding at the bargaining table.[323] This is another bargaining chip that the CSRA of 1978 removes from the agency's arsenal. Under section 7115(a), dues withholding is assured, and agencies may impose no charge or service fee. Dues revocation may ordinarily be effectuated on only one date during a year.[324]

The CSRA adds an anomaly in federal sector dues withholding. Section 7115(c) provides that, when an appropriate unit has no exclusive representative but a labor organization has obtained signatures of 10 percent of the bargaining unit employees, then the labor organization is entitled to negotiate a dues withholding arrangement with the agency.[325] The question of whether the agency may charge a fee for making this type of deduction is a negotiable item.

Section 12(c) of Executive Order 11,491, as amended, provided that

nothing in the negotiated agreement shall require an employee to become or to remain a member of a labor organization, or to pay money to the labor organization except pursuant to a voluntary, written authorization by a member for the payment of dues through payroll deductions.

While the CSRA provides that an employee may not be required to become a member of a labor organization,[326] it does not explicitly

---

323. National Federation of Federal Employees Local 476 and Joint Tactical Communications Office, Fort Monmouth, New Jersey, FLRC No. 72A-42 (1973).

324. Section 7115(a) provides, "If an agency has received from an employee in an appropriate unit a written assignment which authorizes the agency to deduct from the pay of the employee amounts for the payment of regular and periodic dues of the exclusive representative of the unit, the agency shall honor the assignment and make an appropriate allotment pursuant to the assignment. Any such allotment shall be made at no cost to the exclusive representative or the employee. Except as provided under subsection (b) of this section, any such assignment may not be revoked for a period of 1 year."

325. Section 7115(c) provides, "(1) Subject to paragraph (2) of this subsection, if a petition has been filed with the Authority by a labor organization alleging that 10 per cent of the employees in an appropriate unit in an agency have membership in the labor organization, the Authority shall investigate the petition to determine its validity. Upon certification by the Authority of the validity of the petition, the agency shall have a duty to negotiate with the labor organization solely concerning the deduction of dues of the labor organization from the pay of the members of the labor organization who are employees in the unit and who make a voluntary allotment for such purpose. (2)(A) The provisions of paragraph (1) of this subsection shall not apply in the case of any appropriate unit for which there is an exclusive representative. (B) Any agreement under paragraph (1) of this subsection between a labor organization and an agency with respect to an appropriate unit shall be null and void upon the certification of an exclusive representative of the unit."

326. Section 7102 provides, in part, that "each employee shall have the right to form, join or assist a labor organization, or to refrain from such activity. . . ."

provide that union and management are prohibited from negotiating a provision requiring nonunion members within the bargaining unit to pay a security fee or charge to a labor organization.[327] The legislative history of the CSRA, however, is dispositive of the question of whether nonunion members within their bargaining unit may be involuntarily required to contribute the fair share toward the costs the exclusive representative incurs in obtaining benefits for, and rendering services to, the bargaining unit as a whole. The Committee on Conference was faced with a House bill that was silent with respect to both required payment of membership dues (union shop) and other required payments to a labor organization (ordinarily, agency shop arrangements). In contrast, the Senate bill provided that a negotiated agreement could not require an employee to pay money to a labor organization, except pursuant to a voluntary, written authorization for dues withholding. The Committee on Conference adopted the House wording. In doing so, however, the committee emphasized that section 7102 was not intended to authorize the negotiation of union or agency shop arrangements.

House section 7102 guarantees each employee the right to form, join, or assist any labor organization, or to refrain from any such activity. The Senate in addition provides that "no employee shall be required by an agreement to become or to remain a member of a labor organization or to pay money to an organization." The conferees adopt the House wording. The conferees wish to emphasize, however, that nothing in the conference report authorizes, or is intended to authorize, the negotiation of an agency shop or union shop provision.[328]

Based on this legislative history, in *Fort Shafter* the authority held that union or agency shop arrangements may not be negotiated in the federal sector.[329]

---

327. A security fee or charge is ordinarily imposed via an agency shop arrangement. The fee or charge may be equal to or less than regular dues. *See* generally *Basic Patterns in Union Contracts,* 9th ed. (Washington, D.C.: BNA, 1979), p. 84. As used in the federal sector, however, the word dues is defined as including dues, fees, and assessments. *See* section 7106(a)(5) of the CSRA of 1978.

328. Rep. No. 95-1717, 95th Cong., 2d Sess. 159 (1978).

329. Service Employees International Union AFL-CIO, Local 556 and Department of the Army Headquarters, U. S. Army Support Command, Fort Shafter, Hawaii, Case No. 0-NG-2, 1 FLRA 64 (1979). While in *Abood* v. *Detroit Board of Education,* the Supreme Court upheld as constitutional a portion of the Michigan Public Employment Relations Act authorizing public employers and unions to negotiate agency shop arrangements requiring nonunion members of the bargaining unit to pay a security fee, in contrast, the federal sector prohibits an agency shop arrangement. 97 Sup. Ct. 1782 (1977).

Contracting Out and Work Preservation

As with the private sector, federal sector unions have sought to negotiate contract provisions restraining the employer's contracting out
of work traditionally performed by bargaining unit employees and to
restrain the employer's assigning to non-bargaining-unit employees
work normally performed by bargaining unit employees. The substance of both is nonnegotiable. Section 7106(a)(2)(B) explicitly reserves to agency management the right to contract out, and section
7106(a)(2)(B) the right "to determine the personnel by which agency
operations will be conducted," to decide whether bargaining unit or
other agency personnel will perform agency work. Of course, impact
and implementation is negotiable.[330]

In *Philadelphia Naval Shipyard* the union had submitted, among
others, a proposal providing that, in reaching a decision on whether
to contract out work, management's consideration would be limited
to the factors of cost, capacity of unit employees to perform the work,
and technological considerations.[331] The proposal was found to be
nonnegotiable because, by limiting consideration to certain specified
factors, it limited management's discretion in making the decision to
contract out or not to contract out. The council's language suggested
that this proposal would have been negotiable had its language merely
obligated management to consider the specified factors, among any
others management might wish to consider, in reaching the decision
whether to contract out. This speculation is consistent with the decision in *Veterans Administration Research Hospital* where the council found
negotiable a proposal establishing procedures management would
observe in reaching a decision to contract out.[332]

Moreover, the council held negotiable a proposal in *Philadelphia
Naval Shipyard* calling for the employer, when contracting out or assigning bargaining unit work to non-bargaining-unit employees, to
minimize displacement action through realignment, return, and re-

---

330. FLRC No. 71A-56 (1973); AFGE Local 916 and Tinker Air Force Base,
Oklahoma City, Oklahoma, FLRC No. 76A-96 (1977); AFGE Local 3124 and Department of Transportation, U.S. Coast Guard Supply Center, Brooklyn, New York,
FLRC No. 77A-25 (1977). *See* OMB Circular A-76 as it may have impact on the
grievability of negotiated language concerning contracting out.
331. FLRC No. 72A-40 (1973).
332. Veterans Administration Independent Service Employees Union and Veterans
Administration Research Hospital, Chicago, Illinois, FLRC No. 71A-31 (1972).

stricting in-hires and to exert other action necessary to retain career employees. This proposal merely provided arrangements for employees adversely affected by the reserved management decision.[333]

Miscellaneous

Travel and Per Diem

In *Food Safety and Quality Service* the FLRC held nonnegotiable a proposal providing that "employees using their private vehicles in the performance of their work will be paid mileage portal to portal when work is performed at one or more duty points."[334] The proposal conflicted with statute and comptroller general decisions. In contrast, in *FAA*, the following proposal was held to be negotiable:

All in-agency training shall be construed to be advantageous to the government. When such training requires the employee to be away from his duty station for two weeks or more, the employee may choose to travel by privately owned vehicle. Such travel by P.O.V. shall be advantageous to the government, and adequate travel time for such travel shall be authorized. Per diem and mileage monies shall be paid for travel accomplished under this section to the full amount authorized by law.[335]

In *National Labor Relations Board* the FLRA held negotiable the following proposal:

Consistent with operating needs, employees detailed (to temporary duty stations away from their permanent duty stations) pursuant to the terms of this supplemental agreement, will not be obliged to incur or suffer dual lodging expenses which would cause their total travel expenses for any particular day to exceed the maximum $50 per diem rate.

The authority explained that

[t]he proposal would require that the agency not make assignments which would oblige an employee to incur or suffer dual lodging expenses in excess of $50 per day unless there is an operating need to do so. . . .

Accordingly, this proposal merely establishes a general requirement that when management assigns detailees in circumstances which would result in dual lodging situations, the assignment must be consistent with operating needs. Thus, since the agency retains the discretion to determine its operating

---

333. FLRC No. 72A-40 (1973).
334. FLRC No. 77A-63 (1978).
335. Federal Aviation Science and Technological Association, NAGE, and FAA, Department of Transportation, FLRC No. 78A-26 (1978).

needs and, subsequently, to assign employees, the proposal here constitutes a procedure which is within the duty to bargain. . . .[336]

Eating at Desks

In *National Archives and Records Service*, the FLRC held nonnegotiable, as inconsistent with the technology of work language, a proposal providing that "the employees will not eat or drink at their desks in their offices if and when there are archives on their desks."[337]

Retirement Plans

Most employees in the competitive service enjoy the Civil Service Retirement System.[338] With respect to nonappropriated fund (NAF) employees, in *McGuire Air Force Base* the following proposal was held nonnegotiable:

Section 1. The UNION and MANAGEMENT agree to formulate a Committee within 10 days of the signing of the contract for the purpose of procuring an employees retirement plan.

Section 2. The committee shall consist of nine members, six (6) appointed by the Union and three (3) appointed by management. The committee shall be tasked with completion of an agreement no later than sixty (60) days after the formulation of the committee.

Section 3. The cost of the plan will be on a contributory basis with ninety (90) percent of the cost borne by the employer and ten (10) percent by the employee. All NAF employees shall be eligible to participate.[339]

The FLRC determined that the proposal violated agency regulations for which a compelling need existed—a central retirement program already existed for most NAF employees.

Union Participation on Agency Committees

In *U.S. Customs Service, Region VII*, the union proposed that a union representative could sit with the agency's budget committee and that the union representative's role would be "limited to presentation of the union's viewpoint and the making of non-binding recommenda-

---

336. National Labor Relations Board Union and National Labor Relations Board, Washington, D.C., Case No. 0-NG-147, 3 FLRA 81 (1980) 3.
337. AFGE Local 2578 and National Archives and Records Service, General Services Administration, FLRC No. 78A-44 (1978).
338. 5 U.S.C. § 8301, *et seq.*
339. FLRC No. 77A-18 (1978) and FLRC No. 77A-21 (1978).

tion."[340] The FLRC held the proposal nonnegotiable on the ground that it did not come within the obligation to negotiate. This decision is compatible with the decision in *VA Hospital, Danville*, where the council held nonnegotiable a proposal providing that a bargaining unit member would sit in an advisory capacity on the clinical advisory committee, the professional equipment commission, the health standards review commission, and the administrative accreditation commission.[341]

The decisions in *U. S. Customs Service, Region VII* and in *VA Hospital, Danville* may not serve as controlling law today. The Federal Labor Relations Authority has signaled that it will recognize that at least some agency committees may indeed exert a pronounced effect upon personnel policies and practices and matters affecting working conditions and hence union participation is a negotiable subject. In *Marine Corps Development and Education Command* the agency had established management teams to conduct local wage surveys in order to collect data that would be used in establishing hourly pay rates for certain NAF employees. The union had proposed that these teams would become joint union-management teams.[342] The authority, noting that the proposal applied only to existing teams and did not require the establishment of new teams or committees, held the proposal negotiable.

Union Support of Charity Campaigns and Employee Programs

In *Laughlin Air Force Base* the FLRC held nonnegotiable, as outside the scope of the obligation to negotiate, a proposal providing that the union and employer would support voluntary charity drives, such as the Combined Federal Campaign, and that the union and employer would encourage employees to participate in savings bond programs and blood donation drives.[343] In the same opinion, the FLRC held negotiable a proposal providing that the union would support and encourage members to participate voluntarily in the civilian personnel drug and alcohol abuse program.

---

340. NTEU and U.S. Customs Service, Region VII, FLRC No. 76A-111 (1977).

341. AFGE Local 1963 and Veterans Administration Hospital, Danville, Illinois, FLRC No. 78A-56 (1978).

342. AFGE Local 1786 and Marine Corps Development and Education Command, Quantico, Va., Case No. O-NG-4, 2 FLRA 58 (1980).

343. FLRC No. 77A-86 (1978).

Punishment of Supervisors

In *INS-1977* the union had proposed that

[a]ny official found to have improperly discriminated on the basis of an employee's color, race, religion, national origin, politics, marital status, non-disqualifying physical handicap, sex, age, membership or non-membership in an employee organization, or on the basis of any other non-merit factor including personal favoritism or patronage, in the rating of an employee for promotion or in making a selection for promotion shall be subject to disciplinary action.[344]

The FLRC determined this proposal to be nonnegotiable on the ground that it infringed upon management's right to decide when discipline will and will not be imposed.

Release of Information to Union

In *National Personnel Records Center,* the FLRC held negotiable a proposal providing that

[i]nformation pertaining to any employee will be released to or discussed with the Union representative in accordance with Civil Service Commission regulations and upon request by the Union.[345]

Also on this issue, section 7114(b)(4) of the CSRA provides,

The duty of an agency and an exclusive representative to negotiate in good faith . . . shall include the obligation . . . in the case of an agency, to furnish to the exclusive representative involved, or its authorized representative, upon request and, to the extent not prohibited by law, data—

  (A) which is normally maintained by the agency in the regular course of business;

  (B) which is reasonably available and necessary for full and proper discussion, understanding, and negotiation of subjects within the scope of collective bargaining; and

  (C) which does not constitute guidance, advice, counsel, or training provided for management officials or supervisors, relating to collective bargaining. . . .

Equal Employment Opportunity

In *Wright-Patterson Air Force Base* the FLRA held that the subject matter of discrimination in employment constitutes a condition of employment coming within the scope of the duty to bargain.[346] The

---

344. FLRC No. 76A-68 (1977).

345. AFGE Local 2928 and General Services Administration, National Personnel Records Center, FLRC No. 78A-7 (1978).

346. 2 FLRA 77 (1980).

authority held negotiable proposals that required the agency to establish equal employment opportunity plans and that specified the content of the plans.

In *National Personnel Records Center,* the FLRC held negotiable the following proposal:

When a new part-time Equal Employment Opportunity Counselor is to be selected from among employees of the unit, the Union will be asked to nominate employees of the unit to serve as EEO Counselors. The Director, NPRC will consider the nominations along with nominations obtained from other sources, and will appoint EEO Counselors. The regular term of appointment for EEO Counselors will be two years.[347]

The council decided that, contrary to the agency's argument, the proposal did not violate the *Federal Personnel Manual.*

In contrast to the council's decision in *National Personnel Records Center,* in *Wright-Patterson Air Force Base,* the authority held nonnegotiable a proposal requiring that half of all EEO counselors be selected from a list provided by the union.[348] The authority held the *Wright-Patterson* proposal nonnegotiable on the ground that it prescribed assignment of EEO counselor duties to only those employees whose names appeared on the list to be submitted by the union and precluded assignment of those duties to other employees, whether within the bargaining unit or not. This is distinguishable from the proposal in *National Personnel Records Center,* wherein the proposal included the language, "along with nominations obtained from other sources," and therefore did not preclude assignment of counselor duties to those employees whose names did not appear on the list provided by the union.

Waiver of Overpayment

When an employee has received pay in excess of that to which he or she is entitled, he or she may be required to repay the amount of the overpayment. Under certain conditions prescribed in regulations promulgated by the comptroller general, an agency is vested with discretion to waive all or any part of the overpayment.[349] Unions have an interest in ensuring that in exercising discretion to waive or not to waive overpayment, agencies will decide to waive overpayment when-

---

347. FLRC No. 78A-7 (1978).
348. 2 FLRA 77 (1980).
349. *See* 4 C.F.R. § 91.1, *et seq.*

ever possible. In *U.S. Customs Service, Region IX*, the following proposal was declared nonnegotiable:

The Employer agrees that where, through administrative error or oversight, an employee receives a monetary payment above that to which he or she would otherwise be entitled, said overpayment shall be waived upon a showing that:

1. The amount involved is not more than five hundred dollars ($500.00) or the equivalent;

2. The employee was not responsible for the error; and

3. Collection action under the claim would be against equity and good conscience and not in the best interests of the U. S. Government, that is, notice of the mistaken overpayment was not brought to the employee's attention by the Employer within five (5) calendar days of the payment.[350]

The proposal was declared nonnegotiable on the grounds that the comptroller general's regulations provide, among other things, that waiver not be granted when a reasonable person should have detected the overpayment and caused correction to be made. Since the proposal omitted this criterion, the proposal was inconsistent with the comptroller general's regulations and therefore nonnegotiable. Presumably, the proposal would have been declared negotiable if it had also included the criterion that the employee be free from fault.

Reestablishment of Abolished Positions

In *U.S. Customs Service, Region IX*, the following proposals were found to be negotiable:

A. The employer agrees that when an employee has been reassigned due to the abolishment of his/her position, he/she will be considered first if that position is reestablished within one (1) year and he/she applies for the position within fifteen (15) days after written notification is given to the employee of its reestablishment.

B. If an abolished position is reestablished within one (1) year, it is in the interest of the U. S. Customs Service to reassign an employee who applies to his/her former position and he/she will be reimbursed for relocation expenses to the extent authorized under Federal Travel Regulations.

C. If there are two (2) or more displaced applicants for any reestablished position, the applicant with the greater amount of Customs service will be given first consideration.[351]

---

350. NTEU and U.S. Customs Service, Region IX, FLRC No. 78A-29, 2 FLRA 8 (1979).

351. *Id.*

Bargaining Ground Rules and Impasse Resolution

Section 7114(a) of the CSRA addresses the subject of ground rules. It provides in part that

the agency and the exclusive representative may determine appropriate techniques, consistent with the provisions of section 7119 of this title, to assist in any negotiation.

The referenced section 7119 is titled "Negotiation Impasses; Federal Service Impasses Panel."[352] If the parties to bargaining reach an impasse, they must initially seek the services of the Federal Mediation and Conciliation Service or some other third-party mediator.[353] Next, section 7119(b) provides that

[i]f voluntary arrangements, including the services of the Federal Mediation and Conciliation Service or any other third party mediation, fail to resolve a negotiation impasse—
  (1) either party may request the Federal Service Impasses Panel to consider the matter, or
  (2) the parties may agree to adopt a procedure for binding arbitration of the negotiation impasse, but only if the procedure is approved by the Panel.

If the parties reach impasse and mediation has failed to produce agreement, it is permissive—but not mandatory—for the parties to negotiate an agreement to submit the impasse to binding arbitration; the type of binding arbitration and the particular forum would be negotiable matters.[354] Even if, however, the parties reach final agree-

---

352. Title 5, U.S.C., section 7119(c)(1) provides that, "the Federal Service Impasses Panel is an entity within the Authority, the function of which is to provide assistance in resolving negotiation impasses between agencies and exclusive representatives."

353. Title 5, U.S.C., section 7119(a) provides, in part, that, "the Federal Mediation and Conciliation Service shall provide services and assistance to agencies and exclusive representatives in the resolution of negotiation impasses."

354. There are various forms of binding arbitration. One is final offer arbitration, in which the final proposals submitted by the agency and the union are examined and the one that is more reasonable is selected. Another alternative would be to use final offer arbitration but to base selection not on which is more reasonable but rather upon other agreed criteria. Still another alternative would be arbitration in which the arbitrator is empowered to amend, modify, reject, or consolidate impasse proposals. The forum could be a single arbitrator or a panel of arbitrators, and the parties might actually name the arbitrators. The identification of the arbitrators is important because at present only a few arbitrators are sufficiently versed in the federal sector so as to be able to realize and appreciate the significant differences between it and the other sectors. This problem becomes even more acute when the matter being arbitrated is not a grievance, but rather, a negotiation impasse in which the arbitrator must thoroughly understand the limits and unique constraints on bargaining in the federal sector.

ment to submit the impasse to binding arbitration, the agreement is not effective unless approved by the Federal Service Impasses Panel (FSIP). If the panel disapproves a request to submit an impasse to binding arbitration, or if the parties have not agreed to submit the impasse to binding arbitration, then the only recourse is to submit the impasse to the FSIP.[355]

In actual practice, the Federal Service Impasses Panel processes virtually all federal sector impasses. Title 5, U.S.C., section 7119(a), provides that the panel determines "in what manner it shall provide services and assistance." Section 7119(c)(5)(A)(ii) provides that, to resolve an impasse, the panel may assist the parties "through whatever methods and procedures, including factfinding and recommendations, it may consider appropriate. . . ." If such nonbinding means do not resolve the impasse, then under section 7119(c)(5)(B) the panel may hold hearings and take whatever action is necessary to resolve the impasse. This includes the rendering of binding decisions.

In *Wright-Patterson Air Force Base,* the authority addressed the negotiability of a proposal, intended to establish a ground rule applicable to midterm bargaining, addressing the issue of whether the employer could implement the change in working conditions even though bargaining proposals about the change were being processed before the Federal Service Impasses Panel.[356] The proposal provided that, barring overriding exigency or unreasonable delay, the change would not be implemented, and that if because of the exigency or unreasonable delay the change was implemented, then the decision of the FSIP would be applied retroactively to the date of implementation. The authority held the proposal negotiable.

---

355. Title 5, U.S.C., section 7119(c)(5) generally describes the procedures that the FSIP may apply in resolving a negotiation impasse.
356. 2 FLRA 77 (1980).

4.
Negotiability Appeals

One of the FLRA's functions is to render opinions in response to petitions requesting negotiability determinations. Section 7117 of the CSRA of 1978 provides two procedures for submission of negotiability disputes to the FLRA. The first, section 7117(b), prescribes a procedure for resolution of disputes over whether a compelling need exists for an agency regulation that would render a proposal nonnegotiable.[1] The procedures contained in section 7117(b) are very general and contain no definite time limits. Second, section 7117(c) contains procedures governing the resolution of all negotiability disputes where compelling need is not at issue.[2] The procedures of section 7117(c) are specific, and definite time limits are prescribed.

---

1. Section 7117(b) provides, "(1) In any case of collective bargaining in which an exclusive representative alleges that no compelling need exists for any rule or regulation referred to in subsection (a)(3) of this section which is then in effect and which governs any matters at issue in such collective bargaining, the Authority shall determine under paragraph (2) of this subsection, in accordance with regulations prescribed by the Authority, whether such a compelling need exists. (2) For the purpose of this section, a compelling need shall be determined not to exist for any rule or regulation, only if — (A) the agency, or primary national subdivision, as the case may be, which issued the rule or regulation informs the Authority in writing that a compelling need for the rule or regulation does not exist; or (B) the Authority determines that a compelling need for a rule or regulation does not exist. (3) A hearing may be held, in the discretion of the Authority, before a determination is made under this subsection. If a hearing is held, it shall be expedited to the extent practicable and shall not include the General Counsel as a party. (4) The agency, or primary national subdivisions, as the case may be, which issued the rule or regulation shall be a necessary party at any hearing under this subsection."

2. Section 7117(c) provides, "(1) Except in any case to which subsection (b) of this section applies, if an agency involved in collective bargaining with an exclusive representative alleges that the duty to bargain in good faith does not extend to any matter, the exclusive representative may appeal the allegation to the Authority, in accordance with the provisions of this subsection. (2) The exclusive representative may, on or before the 15th day after the date on which the agency first makes the allegation referred to in paragraph (1) of this subsection, institute an appeal under this subsection by—(A) filing a petition with the Authority; and (B) furnishing a copy of the petition to the head of the agency. (3) On or before the 30th day after the date of the receipt by the head of the agency of the copy of the petition under paragraph (2) (B) of this subsection, the agency shall—(A) file with the Authority a statement—(i) withdrawing

Both the section 7117(b) and (c) negotiability procedures are supposed to be expedited. This should mean, at the least, that the FLRA is not supposed to procrastinate for one to two years before issuing a negotiability determination in response to a petition as the FLRC did.[3]

It is certain that, in the future, some negotiability petitions will involve compelling need issues as well as section 7106 issues. In such mixed petitions it would make no sense for a single proposal to be processed simultaneously under a compelling need negotiability procedure and under another negotiability procedure. For this reason, the FLRA regulations provide that all petitions (requests) for negotiability determinations be processed under a single procedure. This procedure contains four steps that mirror the procedure contained in section 7117(c).[4]

First, when during negotiations an agency has declared a union proposal nonnegotiable,[5] the union must file, in the FLRA's office in Washington, D.C., and by no later than fifteen days after the agency first alleged the proposal to be nonnegotiable, a petition requesting a negotiability determination; a copy of the petition must be served upon the head of the agency.[6] The petition should contain a copy of

---

the allegation; or (ii) setting forth in full its reasons supporting the allegation; and (B) furnish a copy of such statement to the exclusive representative. (4) On or before the 15th day after the date of the receipt by the exclusive representative of a copy of statement under paragraph (3) (B) of this subsection, the exclusive representative shall file with the Authority its response to the statement. (5) A hearing may be held, in the discretion of the Authority, before a determination is made under this subsection. If a hearing is held, it shall not include the General Counsel as a party. (6) The Authority shall expedite proceedings under this subsection to the extent practicable and shall issue to the exclusive representative and to the agency a written decision on the allegation and specific reasons therefor at the earliest practicable date."

3. Time may be of the essence in circumstances where a change will be only temporary because, if the change is no longer in existence, the FLRA may dismiss the petition on grounds of mootness. Federal Union of Scientists and Engineers, NAGE Local R1-144 and Naval Underwater Systems Center, Newport Naval Base, Newport, Rhode Island, Case No. 0-NG-140, 3 FLRA 24 (1980).

4. 5 C.F.R. § 2424.

5. An agency may not file a negotiability petition. When during negotiations a union has alleged that an agency's proposal is nonnegotiable and refuses to negotiate, the agency's recourse is to file an unfair labor practice charge. AFGE Local 1738 and Veterans Administration, Veterans Administration Medical Center, Salisbury, N.C., Case No. 0-NG-179, 2 FLRA 54 (1980).

6. When an agency orally alleges that a proposal is nonnegotiable, the labor organization may request, in writing, that the agency put the allegation in writing. The fifteen-day filing period commences the day after the labor organization has received the written allegation. If within ten days of the labor organization's request the agency

the proposal,[7] a statement that the agency declared the proposal nonnegotiable or a copy of the agency's position to such effect, a statement that the proposal is or is not involved in a current unfair labor practice,[8] a statement that the petition and its attachments have been served on the agency head, and a request that the FLRA determine whether the proposal is negotiable.[9]

Second, the agency must, within thirty days of its receipt of the labor organization's petition, file in the FLRA's office in Washington, D.C., a statement either withdrawing the allegation of nonnegotiability or setting forth the agency's position and arguments in support thereof. A copy must be be served upon the union.[10]

Third, the union must, within fifteen days of its receipt of the agency's statement, file in the FLRA's office in Washington, D.C., a response setting forth the union's position, arguments in support thereof, and the union's rebuttal to the agency's arguments. A copy must be served both on the agency head and on the agency's representative of record.[11]

No other submissions may be made unless the authority formally grants a request to make such.[12]

Fourth, pursuant to section 7117(c)(5), the authority may issue a negotiability decision[13] or may hold a hearing and then issue the decision.[14] The FLRA's written decision must state the reasons in support thereof. There is no time limit within which the FLRA must

---

has not reduced to writing the allegation that the proposal is nonnegotiable, the labor organization may then file the negotiability petition. 5 C.F.R. § 2424.3.

7. The language of the proposal submitted to the FLRA normally may not deviate from the language that the agency declared nonnegotiable. AFGE, AFL-CIO, Local 2578 and General Services Administration, National Archives and Records Service, Case No. 0-NG-163, 3 FLRA 16 (1980).

8. The FLRA will not simultaneously process a negotiability petition and an unfair labor practice charge containing the same negotiability issue. At the time the second procedure is invoked, the labor organization must select in writing the procedure under which the issue is to be processed. Action under the other procedure will then be suspended. 5 C.F.R. §§ 2423.5 and 2424.5.

9. 5 C.F.R. § 2424.4.

10. 5 C.F.R. § 2424.6.

11. 5 C.F.R. § 2424.7.

12. 5 C.F.R. § 2424.8. For example, see AFGE Local 695 and Department of the Treasury, U.S. Mint, Denver, Colorado, Case No. 0-NG-114, 3 FLRA 7 (1980).

13. See 5 C.F.R. § 2424.10.

14. See 5 C.F.R. § 2424.9. In actual practice, a hearing is seldom, if ever, held. In fact, the authority's rules do not even address how a negotiability hearing is to be conducted.

issue a written decision, although the entire negotiability procedure is supposed to be expedited.[15]

After the FLRA has issued a determination upon a negotiability petition, a dissatisfied party may, within sixty days, file a petition requesting judicial review in an appropriate United States court of appeals.[16] The court of appeals may review the FLRA's interpretation, application, and conclusions of law, as well as questions of fact. The authority's findings on questions of fact will be sustained if supported by substantial evidence considered on the record as a whole.[17] This should eventually mean that, when a negotiability petition pending before the authority is going to turn on questions of fact, the respective parties may no longer rely exclusively upon unsworn representations made in briefs submitted by each party's respective attorney or other representative. Rather, where issues of fact are relevant and material, both parties will find it necessary to submit affidavits and other documentary evidence, and where there exists dispute over allegations contained in affidavits, the authority should find it necessary either to conduct an investigation or to hold a hearing so as to form a rational basis on which to make a credibility determination.

---

15. In actual practice, the FLRA is taking from three months to more than a year before issuing negotiability decisions. This creates the difficulty of negotiations at the bargaining table being held in limbo until the FLRA issues the negotiability decision. This will create considerable delay, for example, if an agency may not implement a midterm change until the negotiation process has been completed.

16. 5 U.S.C. § 7123 (a).

17. *Id.* § 7123 (c).

5.
Negotiability
in Perspective

Contrasted with the private sector, the scope of negotiability in the federal sector is very narrow. The duty to negotiate applies only to personnel policies and practices and matters affecting working conditions, except for several specific statutory exclusions. This does not, however, serve to make federal sector negotiability a relatively simple subject. To the contrary, negotiability in the federal sector is unique and complex. First, there exists a hierarchical relationship among collective bargaining agreements or proposals and federal statutes, agencywide rules and regulations, and interagency rules and regulations. Negotiable proposals must not be inconsistent with these statutes, rules, and regulations but may mirror or supplement them. For this reason, it is impossible to understand fully and interpret a bargaining proposal or actual contract language without first knowing and appreciating the statutory and regulatory environment in which the proposal or language interacts.

Second, there exists the unusual compelling need concept. Depending upon the level of recognition and the existence of a compelling need, a proposal conflicting with departmental, agency, or bureau rules and regulations may or may not be negotiable. A proposal or contract language can be properly interpreted only when viewed in conjunction with the environment of relevant departmental, agency, and bureau rules and regulations.

Third, there exists in section 7106(a) a set of broad, ill-defined rights reserved to agency management on which substantive bargaining is illegal; however, impact and implementation bargaining on the exercise of these reserved rights is mandatory. The difficulty emerges when impact and implementation proposals move into the gray area where they become virtually indistinguishable from the exercise of the reserved management right. The meaning of each of the section 7106(a) rights must be understood in order to determine whether a

189

proposal is negotiable, and subsequent contract language dealing with procedures for the exercise of reserved management rights must not be interpreted and applied in a manner that negates the 7106(a) rights. A proposal may be negotiable to the extent that it can be interpreted as not negating the reserved management right while simultaneously being nonnegotiable to the extent that it can be interpreted as negating the reserved right.

Fourth, for the permissive bargaining matter described within section 7106(b)(1) and several other provisions of the CSRA of 1978, the language must be analyzed to determine whether an agency may decline to negotiate a proposal. But if the agency does negotiate the proposal and agreement is struck, the language is binding notwithstanding a section 7114(c) review. Contract language may be interpreted and applied in a manner that negates section 7106(b)(1) reserved rights.

Despite the complexity and intricacy of negotiability, it is clearly possible to develop a systematic approach for analyzing the negotiability of proposals dealing with the major subjects of bargaining in the federal sector. By applying the analysis described in the preceding pages, one may arrive at a reasonably accurate conclusion as to the negotiability of any particular proposal or agreed contract language. The significance of being able to do this is that, more so perhaps than in any other sector, in the federal sector negotiability law casts a pervasive, influential shadow across the entire spectrum of labor-management relations. It is crucial that all involved persons—union, management, and neutrals— develop an analytical approach toward negotiability.

Those most obviously requiring an understanding and knowledge of negotiability are those who engage in bargaining. Parties may write intelligent proposals and responsive counterproposals and otherwise engage in effective bargaining only if they are aware of what is and is not negotiable and why. To bargain effectively, negotiators must recognize and give direction to the controlling, preexisting environment of statutes, regulations, and reserved management rights. This can be accomplished only by carefully drafting language that fits snugly in juxtaposition with, but does not overstep, those statutes, regulations, and reserved management rights.

Ignorance of negotiability decisions may result in the commission of an unfair labor practice. For example, in *ATF, Midwest Region* the union had submitted a proposal containing language from another proposal that had been declared negotiable in another case.¹ The agency committed an unfair labor practice by declaring the proposal nonnegotiable.

Arbitrators, too, require an understanding of negotiability. The CSRA of 1978 mandates that grievability-arbitrability disputes be submitted to an arbitrator. There will be many cases in which the issue cannot be resolved without examining negotiability decisions. An arbitrator must understand negotiability in order to know the rules governing which interpretations may be given to contract language and how the language may be applied. Moreover, arbitrators new to the federal sector frequently voice dismay when, in the arbitration of a mere contract grievance, union and management offer into evidence, in addition to the contract, chapters from the *Federal Personnel Manual*, statutes, interagency regulations, and chapters from department- or agency-level personnel manuals. When this happens, the parties are not burdening the record or wasting time. Rather, these documents, placed in their proper hierarchy describe the legal environment to which the disputed contract provision is inherently related. Without this information, an arbitrator cannot intelligently interpret and apply the contract language or render a just and workable award.

FMCS, FSIP, and FLRA personnel also require an appreciation of negotiability. Before proposals at impasse can be intelligently assessed and compared, mediators as well as FSIP personnel must quickly gain an understanding of pertinent statutes, regulations, rules, and reserved management rights. It is counterproductive for mediators to tell union or management that "we just have to spend more time at the table because the federal sector requires an enormous amount of patience," and then to suggest alternative proposals that are clearly nonnegotiable. Mediators need to be able to distinguish between serious nonnegotiability allegations and shams intended to distract their attention.

Since the scope of bargaining is greatly limited, the subjects that are important to union and management differ from those that are important in the private sector.² FLRA personnel need to appreciate

---

1. NTEU Chapter 94 and Department of the Treasury, Bureau of Alcohol, Tobacco and Firearms, Midwest Region, Chicago, Illinois, Assistant Secretary Case No. 50-17024(CA), 2 FLRA 74 (1980).

2. It is widely recognized that a limited scope of bargaining affects the way in which a mediator can operate. *See* William Simikin, *Mediation* (Washington, D.C.: BNA, 1971), pp. 340–42.

the fact that, in a sector in which the scope of bargaining is narrow, an exclusive representative must guard its right to negotiate more jealously and exercise it with respect to less significant changes in working conditions than might an exclusive representative in a sector in which the scope of bargaining is broad. The limited scope of bargaining cannot be ignored when passing upon the merits or desirability of many proposals at impasse. FSIP personnel must recognize and deal fairly with the circumstance wherein controlling statutes, rules, and regulations are so constricting that compromise is impossible and a proffered proposal is at the this-or-nothing point.

FLRA personnel processing and prosecuting unfair labor practice charges alleging a refusal or failure to bargain over midterm changes have a special need for knowledge of negotiability decisions. Initial examination must ascertain whether a change affected personnel policies, practices, or matters affecting working conditions and hence came within the scope of the duty to bargain. If the change was thus negotiable, advance notification provided to the union, and a timely request to bargain submitted, then investigation must determine whether substance or only impact and implementation was negotiable. In many cases, the merits of the unfair labor practice allegation will turn on whether the change's substance or only impact and implementation was negotiable. If in the latter case the union either requested to negotiate only substance or submitted proposals addressing only substance, then either of these reasons may potentially be used as a basis for determining that no unfair labor practice was committed. If only impact and implementation was negotiable and the union requested to negotiate impact and implementation, or if substance was negotiable, then an unfair labor practice may have been committed.[3]

---

3. *See* General Services Administration, Region 2 and AFGE, District 2, Council of General Services Administration Locals, A/SLMR No. 916 (1977). *See also* 5 C.F.R. § 2324.5.

Appendix

NLRC Decisions by Docket, Report and Volume Number

FLRC *Docket Number*	FLRC *Report Number*	FLRC Bound *Volume Citation*
70A-4	1	1 FLRC 51
70A-5	1,7	1 FLRC 78
70A-6	2	1 FLRC 53
70A-9	1,5	1 FLRC 61
70A-10	3,6	1 FLRC 71
70A-11	2,5	1 FLRC 65
70A-12	4	1 FLRC 59
71A-6	5	1 FLRC 55
71A-11	7,11	1 FLRC 100
71A-15	12,30	1 FLRC 210
71A-20	11	1 FLRC 121
71A-22	12,39	1 FLRC 390
71A-28	12, 18	1 FLRC 152
71A-30	12,36	1 FLRC 322
71A-31	14,31	1 FLRC 227
71A-41	17	1 FLRC 129
71A-46	20,30	1 FLRC 219
71A-48	18,41	1 FLRC 423
71A-49	18,49	1 FLRC 427
71A-50	18	1 FLRC 155
71A-51	18	1 FLRC 158
71A-52	20,31	1 FLRC 235
71A-56	18,41	1 FLRC 431
71A-57	21,37	1 FLRC 349
71A-60	22, 36	1 FLRC 276
72A-7	24	1 FLRC 182
72A-10	24,38	1 FLRC 361
72A-16	26,36	1 FLRC 287
72A-18	26,44	1 FLRC 525
72A-23	26,37,39	1 FLRC 335
72A-25	24,38	1 FLRC 361

72A-27	27,40	1 FLRC 415
72A-29	24	1 FLRC 188
72A-33	28,41	1 FLRC 444
72A-35	28,41	1 FLRC 450
72A-37	39	1 FLRC 381
72A-39	38	1 FLRC 372
72A-40	41	1 FLRC 456
72A-41	46	1 FLRC 584
72A-42	43	1 FLRC 499
72A-46	47	1 FLRC 610
72A-47	43,47	1 FLRC 513
72A-50	42,52	2 FLRC 106
72A-51	42	1 FLRC 468
73A-1	48	2 FLRC 48
73A-5	43	1 FLRC 509
73A-6	53	2 FLRC 137
73A-7	39	1 FLRC 398
73A-10	39	1 FLRC 402
73A-12	42	1 FLRC 465
73A-13	44	1 FLRC 549
73A-14	39	1 FLRC 387
73A-16	55	2 FLRC 157
73A-21	48	2 FLRC 55
73A-22	48	2 FLRC 65
73A-23	45	1 FLRC 567
73A-24	45	1 FLRC 571
73A-25	57	2 FLRC 207
73A-28	43	1 FLRC 516
73A-36 (1973)	47	1 FLRC 616
73A-36 (1975)	73	3 FLRC 324
73A-47	46	1 FLRC 607
73A-48	49	2 FLRC 88
74A-2	60	2 FLRC 280
74A-13	75	3 FLRC 380
74A-20	62	3 FLRC 91
74A-24	74	3 FLRC 352
74A-30	71	3 FLRC 296
74A-31	69	3 FLRC 247
74A-32	64	3 FLRC 138
74A-33	61	3 FLRC 75
74A-36	62	3 FLRC 100
74A-48	75	3 FLRC 396
74A-55	59	2 FLRC 259
74A-63	77	3 FLRC 439
74A-66	89	3 FLRC 735
74A-67	92	3 FLRC 767
74A-69	64	3 FLRC 143
74A-71	100	4 FLRC 153

74A-93	98	4 FLRC 125
74A-101	67	3 FLRC 198
74A-104	79	3 FLRC 483
75A-6	85	3 FLRC 665
75A-13	85	3 FLRC 635
75A-27	93	3 FLRC 810
75A-28	86	3 FLRC 668
75A-40	82	3 FLRC 587
75A-58	74	3 FLRC 377
75A-77	110	4 FLRC 420
75A-81	107	4 FLRC 353
75A-85	103	4 FLRC 230
75A-90	114	4 FLRC 523
75A-97	93	3 FLRC 839
75A-103	107	4 FLRC 376
75A-111	93	3 FLRC 817
75A-113	124	5 FLRC 297
75A-118	118	4 FLRC 597
76A-16	120,125	5 FLRC 124
		5 FLRC 336
76A-17	120	5 FLRC 124
76A-19	122	5 FLRC 198
76A-26	120	5 FLRC 104
76A-28	123	5 FLRC 249
76A-29	98,128	4 FLRC 139
		5 FLRC 461
76A-38	129	5 FLRC 516
76A-40	120	5 FLRC 124
76A-43	120	5 FLRC 124
76A-47	114	4 FLRC 500
76A-54	120	5 FLRC 124
76A-58	127	5 FLRC 427
76A-60	105	4 FLRC 307
76A-65	132	5 FLRC 665
76A-68	136	5 FLRC 808
76A-75	120,125	5 FLRC 146
		5 FLRC 336
76A-76	120	5 FLRC 146
76A-79	128	5 FLRC 497
76A-81	130	5 FLRC 597
76A-84	120	5 FLRC 146
76A-88	144	6 FLRC 208
76A-92	130	5 FLRC 569
76A-96	131	5 FLRC 604
76A-102	123	5 FLRC 263
76A-106	125	5 FLRC 372
76A-109	132	5 FLRC 645
76A-111	131	5 FLRC 609

76A-121	131	5 FLRC 614
76A-128	137,144	5 FLRC 828
76A-132	133	5 FLRC 721
76A-139	127	5 FLRC 440
76A-142	143	6 FLRC 230
76A-157	137	5 FLRC 838
77A-1	135	5 FLRC 783
77A-9	137	5 FLRC 841
77A-12	137	5 FLRC 848
77A-18	142	6 FLRC 135
77A-21	142	6 FLRC 135
77A-25	138	5 FLRC 881
77A-28	145	6 FLRC 253
77A-33	141	5 FLRC 423
77A-38	129	5 FLRC 507
77A-58	142	6 FLRC 464
77A-63	150	5 FLRC 964
77A-70	139	5 FLRC 964
77A-74	137	5 FLRC 878
77A-86	151	6 FLRC 524
77A-89	151	6 FLRC 487
77A-90	141	6 FLRC 132
77A-94	159	6 FLRC 828
77A-105	138	5 FLRC 115
77A-106	143	6 FLRC 182
77A-109	149	6 FLRC 391
77A-110	151	6 FLRC 497
77A-114	156	6 FLRC 704
77A-120	139	5 FLRC 947
77A-123	153	6 FLRC 612
77A-125	152	6 FLRC 540
77A-126	159	6 FLRC 845
77A-130	152	6 FLRC 584
77A-140	165	6 FLRC 1071
77A-144	150	6 FLRC 440
77A-148	166	6 FLRC 1113
78A-4	152	6 FLRC 546
78A-6	149	6 FLRC 432
78A-7	168	6 FLRC 1235
78A-11	151	6 FLRC 501
78A-26	156	6 FLRC 722
78A-33	155	6 FLRC 670
78A-34	157	6 FLRC 745
78A-37	155	6 FLRC 655
78A-44	157	6 FLRC 756
78A-49	160	6 FLRC 858
78A-56	158	6 FLRC 766
78A-62	162	6 FLRC 1031

Index to
Cases Cited

General Index

213